WHETHER YOU'RE A PRO OR A NOVICE, YOU WANT TO KNOW WHICH MAGAZINES WILL CONSIDER YOUR STORY

You may be just starting out, and wondering what your first move should be.

You may have been writing for years, but are still looking to expand your markets.

Whatever your status, this information-packed handbook will put you on the inside track to the most receptive magazine audience for your work.

THE WRITER'S GUIDE TO MAGAZINE MARKETS: FICTION

KAREN KRIEGER and HELEN ROSENGREN FREEDMAN have worked for numerous magazines as editors, and have been published in national magazines. They are also the authors of THE WRITER'S GUIDE TO MAGAZINE MARKETS: NON-FICTION, available in a Plume edition.

THE WRITER'S GUIDE TO MAGAZINE MARKETS: FICTION

Karen Krieger
and Helen Rosengren Freedman

A PLUME BOOK
NEW AMERICAN LIBRARY
TIMES MIRROR
NEW YORK AND SCARBOROUGH, ONTARIO

NAL BOOKS ARE AVAILABLE AT QUANTITY DISCOUNTS WHEN USED TO
PROMOTE PRODUCTS OR SERVICES. FOR INFORMATION PLEASE WRITE TO
PREMIUM MARKETING DIVISION, THE NEW AMERICAN LIBRARY, INC., 1633
BROADWAY, NEW YORK, NEW YORK 10019.

 PLUME TRADEMARK REG. U.S. PAT. OFF. AND FOREIGN COUNTRIES
REGISTERED TRADEMARK-MARCA REGISTRADA HECHO EN FORGE
VILLAGE, MASS., U.S.A.

SIGNET, SIGNET CLASSIC, MENTOR, PLUME, MERIDIAN and
NAL BOOKS are published *in the United States* by the New
American Library, Inc., 1633 Broadway, New York, New York
10019, *in Canada* by the New American Library of Canada
Limited, 81 Mack Avenue, Scarborough, Ontario M1L 1M8

Library of Congress Cataloging in Publication Data:

Krieger, Karen.
The writer's guide to magazine markets.

1. Fiction—Marketing.   2. American periodicals—Directories.
I. Freedman, Helen Rosengren.   II. Title.
PN3355.K74   1983   070.5   83-13162
ISBN 0-452-25451-5

In acknowledgment:

The authors would like to thank all the magazine editors who gave so freely of their time to make this book possible.

We would also like to thank the Coordinating Council of Literary Magazines (CCLM—a national nonprofit literary grant and service organization located at 2 Park Avenue, New York, NY 10016) for the use of their research facilities.

Contents

Appendix A: The Annual Short-Story Collections   301

Appendix B: Some Useful Information   307

Introduction

Publication of a short story in a major magazine or literary journal can seem an impossible dream. Given the small number of magazines that publish fiction and the large number of aspiring writers, pessimism is not out of place. But the difficulty is increased by writers who consistently submit their work to the wrong publications.

Most of the short stories received by the magazines are so far off-base they are not even read all the way through. A writer with any real hope of a career has to give serious attention to placing his stories.

This book is designed to help. It gives extensive, thoughtful information about the kind of fiction each listed magazine wants (and doesn't want), the statistical chances of a new or unknown writer's getting published (there are magazines that haven't bought an unsolicited manuscript in five years), the names of the magazines that are "break-in" markets, the "inside information" on what happens to your manuscript once it arrives at the magazine, and details as to the best way to submit your story to each publication.

A writer who acts without this kind of knowledge is courting a rejection slip. Used properly, this book can save a writer a lot of wasted effort.

Along the way, the writer will find some fascinating "backstage" views from the editors interviewed: how they think about their jobs, how they put magazines together, why one good story is published and another is returned to sender.

Information in the listings is based on in-person and phone interviews as well as questionnaires. It was up to the editors to talk as comprehensively as they chose. Research into back issues filled in gaps. The result is a compendium of information available in no other source.

How to use the guide

The over 100 listings in this book are organized into three alphabetical sections. The first group is "The Consumer Magazines." It includes all the well-known monthly or weekly newsstand publications that print short stories. It also includes several less well-known magazines that give general-interest short fiction a regular home, and explores the possibilities of fiction in newspapers.

The second group is "The Specialty Magazines." These are the publications—usually monthlies, sold on newsstands—that are interested in specific types of fiction. Among them are science fiction, mystery stories, Westerns, teen fiction, stories for military wives, stories for farm women.

The third group is "The Literary Magazines"—most often published quarterly, usually paying little or nothing, and generally printing a great deal of quality fiction.

Each of the consumer and specialty listings opens with the name of the person interviewed—who, unless otherwise indicated, is the person to whom manuscripts should be addressed.

Following—under the heading "In short"—is a capsulized picture of the magazine's accessibility to new, unknown, unagented writers. In every case, the editors agree that it is an accurate assessment of their openness to unsolicited material.

Listings are organized into sections. "About the magazine" tells how much fiction is used, then describes the magazine's editorial focus and target audience.

"Getting published" first lists the basic facts a writer needs to know about money, rights, reply time, and so on. This is followed by a realistic appraisal of the quality of attention paid to unsolicited submissions. How many unsolicited stories come in? How many will be published over the course of a year? Who is the first reader? How many stories make it past the first reader to a senior editor? How many editors have to agree on a story's publication? Who are they? Is a cover letter important? Does a list of credits change the handling of a story? Do the editors ask for rewrites on promising pieces? In essence: Is this magazine a reasonable break-in possibility for a new writer?

"The story" is a discussion of the kind of fiction the magazine is looking for and what it definitely does not want. Names of stories and authors are included, often with the editor's explanation of why that particular piece made it into the magazine.

Finally, "Rejection" is discussed. Does the magazine always use printed forms? Are the forms graded to offer different degrees of encouragement? How often does the editor respond with criticism or encouragement? There are magazines that use the rejection process to help the author learn to write. These are indicated.

Literary magazine listings are organized differently. They open with information about the magazine: publication frequency, distribution, size, price, affiliation. Then there is specific information concerning short stories: how much fiction is published, money, rights, reply time. The listings are then completed in essay form.

A note about the slush pile:

Editors regularly refer to unsolicited submissions as the "slush pile." The phrase may be denigrating, but common use has removed its sting. And the use of the term does not lessen the seriousness with which manuscripts are read. Writers do submit stories through the slush pile and find themselves published in magazines.

How to get a story published

Is it really possible to break into print with an unsolicited short story? The answer is: "Yes, if . . . " If the work is good (whether it's entertainment or literature), if you're persistent in sending stories out, and if you're sending them to the right places.

According to the editors, most of the material submitted is very bad—not even close to being publishable. All the marketing advice in the world will do nothing for the authors. But for the skilled writer producing quality work, who is clear-sighted about the kind of work he is doing, the answer is yes. It is possible to get published. Instances of writers breaking into print with an unsolicited first story, or of careers that began with an unsolicited submission, will be found throughout this book.

Unfortunately there is no magic plan or secret knowledge that automatically leads to publication. But if a writer gives some intelligent consideration to marketing, he will at least know he is not sabotaging his own work—that he is doing his best for himself. Therein lies the purpose of this book—to give the writer the information to make the most of his chances.

Suppose you have written a story you would like to see published in one of the women's magazines. Study the appropriate listings; you will see that while all the women's magazines want fiction with high reader identification, they have different readers. Some of the publications are interested in pure romantic entertainment, some want stories celebrating the joys of family life, some want stories that hint at the complexities and ambiguities of modern relationships.

Some of the magazines will clearly be wrong for your story. The question is, which of the possibilities should you try first? If one of the publications is your favorite magazine, by all means send it the story. But beyond that, look at the numbers. Consider how many unsolicited stories are submitted every year. Consider whether the first reader is an editorial assistant, a freelance reader, or the fiction editor. Look at the number of unsolicited stories bought every year. All this will tell you how seriously your unsolicited manuscript is likely to be read. It makes sense to go to the magazines where the odds are in your favor. It makes little sense to send a story to a magazine that has not bought an unsolicited piece from an unknown writer in five years.

The listings should be read seriously; if the editor says she does not want stories about divorce, believe it. Don't assume that your divorce story is good enough to change the rules. Chances are an assistant editor or freelance reader will reject the story before it even gets to the fiction editor.

Length is another subject it pays to take seriously. It is tempting to take the high road and ignore length limits—ideally a story should be as long as it takes to tell the tale. But fiction editors often have little say in this matter. They may have to fight for editorial inches. If an editor says up to 15 typed pages, it's not a matter of personal taste; it's the amount of room available. A long story may have to be "wonderful" to be accepted in a magazine where space is tight.

The writer whose sights are set on *The New Yorker, Harper's,* or *The Atlantic,* will note that standards are high and chances of getting published are slim. Still, in a way the writer producing serious, literate fiction is lucky. Though there are very few paying markets, there are a lot of places that are looking for quality fiction—that is, the literary magazines. Many widely published, well-known writers began their careers there.

This is not to suggest that the literary magazines covered in this book are writing schools offering a showcase to amateurs, or just a stepping-stone to the "big time." Many people consider them the premier publishers of top-quality fiction today. Writers who are household names or close to it continue to publish in their pages.

The two drawbacks are obvious: little or no money and a small audience. But because there are so many literary magazines, a determined writer with a story he believes in has a lot of chances to get his work into print, building craft and reputation, as well as a chance to be seen by other writers, editors, and agents who may give important feedback on his work.

Choosing which literary magazines to try can be difficult. These publications are not easy to capture in a guidebook. Read through the listings; look at the numbers of submissions; look at the way editors deal with rejected manuscripts; look at some of the things the editors say about fiction, and about their magazines. Some of the listings will feel right to you, and will capture your interest. Then look at some issues of those magazines and read the fiction; you will soon find out if the magazine is right for you. For further discussion of literary magazines, see the beginning of the section listing them.

There is another way to use this book. Read through the listings, and note which magazines are open to—are even looking for—new writers. Study the editors' descriptions of what they need and read a few issues of those magazines. You might be able to write a story to fit. As a tactic for getting published and earning some money, it sounds good, although writing to formula demands technical control and a great deal of skill.

What do the editors want?

Editors have a lot to say about what kinds of stories they do and do not want. Some of it is very straightforward. One of the men's magazines wants adventure stories that can be explicitly described; a science fiction magazine wants stories with certain specific qualities.

Very often, however, meanings are less clear. A teen magazine editor wants stories that don't "talk down to teens," but gets stories that are "too adult"; a literary magazine editor says simply he is open to all "quality fiction."

What is the definition of "too adult"? Where is the dividing line between "quality fiction" and "formula fiction"?

There are, of course, no single answers to these questions. But it is up to the writer to judge his own work accurately. Constant rejection might well mean a writer is misdefining the terms and entirely missing his proper market.

The best way to check on the appropriateness of a story is to read the magazine. Comparing what you have written to what has already been published can be a big help. It can tell a writer whether his definition of teen fiction is everyone else's definition of adult fiction, or whether his idea of quality fiction is what other writers and editors think of as formula fiction.

Coping with rejection

No matter what kind of writing you're doing—what kind of magazine you are approaching—persistence is important. The stock tale of the now famous writer who once papered his wall with rejection slips is not fantasy—it is a common experience to accumulate hundreds of rejections.

Persistence does not only mean resubmitting the same story over and over again. It also means doing a lot of writing. If you are sitting down at your typewriter four Saturdays a month, chances you will ever be published are slim. The writer who sends a story out and then spends the next ten weeks waiting instead of writing is not a professional. The real point of the story about the writer with rejection-slip wallpaper is not his persistent submissions in the face of rejection—the point is his persistent production of material to submit.

As a general rule, there is reason for congratulations if you receive anything other than a form rejection. With the number of submissions received, editors generally write only when very impressed with a piece. When an editor asks to see more work it means he thinks the writer has real promise. Editors do hope to find new writers; it is not uncommon for an editor to correspond with a promising author for years before actually taking a story.

The reply times in the listings are approximations. Seasons, workloads, and staff firings and hirings all make a difference in how long it takes to get to an unsolicited manuscript. No response within the stated time may mean a story is being considered, passed from one editor to another. Unfortunately, this is not always the case. Work could just be piled up. Try to hold off on telephone queries until the listed reply time is well past.

Many of the magazines have several categories of printed rejection form. Some are meant to discourage further submissions, others to give slight encouragement. Always check the listings to make sure you are reading your rejection slip properly.

Very often an editor will take a story on the condition that the author make certain changes. In most cases these changes will be minor and the authors are glad to have the critical input. Editors say it is rare (but not unheard-of) for a writer to refuse the changes and withdraw the story.

Editors might ask for a rewrite and resubmission on speculation. It is, of course, a compliment that the editor sees enough in the story to want to have another look, but the request for a rewrite does *not* often lead to a sale.

This is so often true that editors are sometimes hesitant even to suggest a rewrite; they say that stories often come back in worse shape than when they started. If an editor suggests a rewrite along specific lines and the suggestions make sense, it is certainly worth a try. But if the editor's suggestions do not seem helpful to you, forcing the story to fit someone else's conceptions might be a futile exercise.

After a story is sold

In-house editing and rewriting of accepted stories varies. Editing is to be expected. Many magazines will send a story back to the author for major changes, but make minor changes (for instance, cutting) themselves. Some magazines, as indicated in the listings, will check with authors; others do not. As a general rule, the more seriously a magazine takes fiction the less changing it is willing to do. At some magazines where stories are very formularized and considered purely entertainment, cutting and rewriting are extensive. A writer should always ask an editor interested in his story whether any changes are planned.

Agents and the short-story writer

All the problems of unsolicited submissions can be avoided by the writer who has an agent. A top agent will know where to send stories; he will go directly to the right editor, who will read the work with attention; he will get a fast response; he will cover all possible markets; he will make sure the writer is getting the right kind of exposure; he will take care of negotiations on money and rights; he might help with criticism and/or encouragement. Most of the stories published in major magazines are chosen from agents' submissions.

If a writer knows one of the top agents (an agent who does not know the business and is not committed to his work is not worth signing with) or knows a client of a top agent who will give him a recommendation, he should grab the opportunity. Whether or not a writer without those advantages should spend time trying to find an agent is another matter. Talking to several of the top literary agents makes it clear that agents decide whether to take on writers in very idiosyncratic ways. It depends, they say—on the writer, his work, his credits, his intentions. And agents are very frank in saying that where short stories are concerned they can promise little.

Agents who take on clients relatively freely are the ones who promise least. They are willing to take the chance but don't promise results. The agents who do promise results are only willing to take on writers who have proved themselves with prestigious credits and are ready to expand their markets. In any case, there is only so much an agent can do for a short-story writer. The agent can make sure the work gets the best possible exposure, but he cannot create more paying markets. Even when an agent wants to sell a collection of short stories to a publishing house, he might well have to offer it as part of a package with a novel or two.

There are areas in which agreement among agents is general. Agents are pessimistic about the commercial possibilities of short stories. This is true even for agents who personally like short stories a great deal. Agents say they can have trouble selling the work of their well-known writers simply because there are so few places to try. They agree that the prospects for making a living on short fiction are bleak.

In general, agents do not take on clients who are solely short-story writers. There is not enough money involved to make it worthwhile. If a writer makes four sales to a major magazine a year—making him a very successful writer—he earns around $5000 (of course, this varies). The agent gets $500 to $750 for his work. Not much incentive. Top literary agents usually will handle short fiction for their novelists, but these days not even that is always true. Reputable agents are actually refusing to handle short fiction even for regular clients.

To every rule there are exceptions. For instance, if the short-story writer happens to be selling to *The New Yorker*, a magazine that pays very high rates and confers great prestige, most agents would be receptive.

Agents generally agree that a writer does not need an agent to approach literary magazines. However, it does happen that agents find a writer whose work impresses them so much they will take him on despite the lack of immediate financial incentive. The agent might then place the stories in literary magazines just to get the work before the public and build the writer's reputation. But this is very much the exception.

Emilie Jacobson, at Curtis Brown, Ltd., summed up the general opinion. "By and large, very few agents will take on a writer for magazine material alone. I suppose if I got a letter from a writer saying he had published ten stories in *McCall's, Playboy, Redbook,* in the last two years, I'd look at his work. But even then, I'd be much more interested in the person if the letter went on to say 'and now I'm thinking about a novel.' "

Georges Borchardt, of Georges Borchardt, Inc., agrees that "a writer doing magazine work only will have a hard time finding someone good to represent him." He adds that it is true that a writer who has prestigious credits or has had stories chosen for awards or collections will be able to find an agent. But the writer has to be realistic about what the agent can do for him: The problem is not with the writer, it is with the lack of markets. Borchardt suggests that the time when a short-story writer should look for an agent is when he is ready to put together a collection of his work in book form.

At Virginia Barber Literary Agency, Inc., Mary Evans says, "We do handle short stories, unlike many other agencies. The commercial places for short stories are limited, but we are involved in a writer's whole career. Still, it is rare to have a client who writes stories only."

When should the writer start looking for an agent? "We don't want to hear from unpublished short-story writers," Evans says. "Getting published separates a writer from all the people who think they have a novel in them and indicates seriousness. An agent can enhance, not create, a writer's career."

At Brandt & Brandt Literary Agency, Inc., Charles Schlessinger agrees that for most agents novels are the point. But he adds that the writer has to look at his own career and ask what he intends for himself. He can't ask an agent to take on a client who is going to produce two stories a year. "If a writer, even a beginning writer, is determined to succeed and believes he has the 'stuff,' and intends to work full-time, why not try and find an agent? It can't harm him and might help." He adds, "Most agents take on short-story writers in the hope a novel is coming, but I'd like to think that if John Cheever showed up he wouldn't be turned away."

Hy Cohen of Hy Cohen Literary Agency, Ltd., also sees no reason a beginning writer shouldn't try to find an agent. "It's so hard to get published, a writer should cover all his bases. I'm very atypical in this. I don't believe in queries—they tell you nothing. When a writer sends a manuscript I look at it. I don't spend a lot of time. I can tell pretty fast if I'll be able to sell it, and usually I say no. But if the story is interesting I'll try to sell it. I'll tell the writer not to expect too much—that I might not, or probably can't, do anything with the piece, but I'll give it a try."

There are many writers who choose not to have an agent. This is partly because with the small amount of money given for stories, they don't want to pay a commission. It may also be because by the time a writer is in the position of interesting a top agent, he no longer needs one—he already has connections at the major magazines. Some writers, too, prefer to have control over their own work. Agents do not report every move to clients; it may be hard to find out how often the story was submitted and to what magazines.

For the writer who is convinced that he wants an agent and who has no connections or recommendations, a query is the best path. List some credits and send it off. Agents do want to find new writers.

"Writers should be warned," Georges Borchardt says. "They think that getting an agent will solve all their problems. The solution rests on their writing. When they are ready they will find an agent. Certainly luck and connections count. They may not find an agent quickly or easily, but if the writer is ready the problem will be solved."

How to submit a story

What follows are the simple, commonsense rules for submitting a story. They concern neatness, politeness, and efficiency. Meeting their requirements will not sell a story, but ignoring them provides an excuse for quick rejection from an editor facing the day's thirtieth unsolicited submission.

SASE: Self-addressed, stamped return envelopes are always necessary both when sending manuscripts and when requesting guidelines. The necessity for the SASE is not mentioned in individual listings simply because it is universal. Most editors will not return stories that come without stamped envelopes; some will not even read them. Editors further insist that the envelopes be large enough to accommodate the manuscript and the postage be enough to carry it to its destination.

GUIDELINES: Magazines that have guidelines for fiction are indicated. In most cases these guidelines are very sketchy and of little real use. Among the exceptions are those of *Redbook*, *Amazing*, and *Analog*. A legal-size return envelope is sufficient for most guidelines.

"TO THE EDITOR": It is at least good manners to address a manuscript to the right person and to spell his name correctly. Each listing gives the magazine's preference for directing stories. Writers are advised to check latest issues of the magazine for staff changes. It is always possible to send stories "To the Fiction Editors."

PHONE NUMBERS: Fiction editors are rarely open to telephone queries and usually will not discuss rejected work with writers. Phone numbers are listed so that writers can check on the status of a manuscript when the reply time has passed. When no number is listed it is by the editor's request.

COVER LETTERS: Cover letters are important as much for the harm they can do as for the good. There are editors (indicated in the listings) who want cover letters. For some it is a courtesy. Others want specific information: for instance, whether the story would be a first published piece, whether the writer has attended a well-known workshop, and other credits.

There are other editors (again, indicated in the listings) who think cover letters are a waste of time—that a story must speak entirely for itself. The necessary information of name, address, and telephone number should be included on the title page.

What everyone agrees on is that an ill-written cover letter can hurt a story. If a cover letter is full of misspellings, bad grammar, and malapropisms, an editor loses faith in the story to follow. Another mistake is straining for personal contact with an editor by including biographical tidbits about hobbies or trips abroad or odd experiences. Editors are interested in professional credits that might be included in a biographical section, but nothing else.

In general, cover letters should be short and professional and should *never* include a story synopsis.

CREDITS: If you have good credits, or have attended a well-known workshop, or have studied with a well-known author, by all means mention it. It may get your story out of the slush pile and onto an editor's desk; it may win a second reading for a marginal piece. It is not necessary to list every sale ever made (most editors find pages of credits annoying and pretentious); simply hit a few of the highlights. Also note in the listings that there are editors who prefer not to see credits.

MANUSCRIPT PREPARATION: Neatness and legibility are key words in preparing a manuscript for submission. It is mostly a matter of common sense. Whether a writer numbers pages in the center or the corner of the page makes little difference as long as they are numbered. It matters little if the margins are exact to the millimeter as long as they make for easy reading. What follows are the points to pay attention to:

- Manuscripts must be typed; no italic or fancy types should be used.
- Always double-space.
- Use only one side of the paper.
- Use black ink; typewriter ribbons should not be worn.
- Paper should be 8½ x 11 inches.
- Paper should be opaque, white, 20-pound weight, and should not be onionskin, erasable, or anything else that smudges.
- Margins are usually 2¼ inches on top and left sides, 1 inch on bottom and right.
- Do not include a separate cover page: Put your name, address, and phone number on the opening (title) page of the story.
- Number pages.
- Your last name should be included on the corner of every page.
- The final page of a story should be indicated.
- Avoid handwritten inserts, although some retyping over erasures is acceptable. Clearly marked strikeouts are acceptable, though not too many to a page.
- Do not send binders or file folders.

PHOTOCOPIES: Editors generally will read good-quality, clear photocopies. This is very useful to the writer who does not have time or cannot afford to pay for a retyping of a story after each mailing. The problem is that photocopies suggest simultaneous submissions. If you are sending a copy, add a note either to the cover letter or on the title page stating the story is not being submitted elsewhere.

SIMULTANEOUS SUBMISSIONS: There are editors who will read stories being submitted simultaneously to other magazines. "Simultaneous submissions: acceptable" will be found in the listings. In most cases the editors want to be informed that the story is being sent elsewhere.

Any magazine without that listing does not accept simultaneous submissions: literary magazines almost universally do not accept them.

This is one of those issues on which editors and writers both feel ill-used. Editors want first call on a piece of writing they have spent time considering and shepherding through the acceptance process. Writers want to make a living and a reputation and resent waiting two months or more for a decision. The only answer is: Considering how few places there are to publish stories, it is probably better not to alienate editors.

MAILING: Editors prefer that manuscripts are sent unfolded, unstapled, in flat envelopes.

First Class costs more but is fast and guarantees both forwarding and return if the manuscript cannot be delivered.

Special Fourth Class Mail: Manuscript is much cheaper. It can be used for original material only—no photocopies—and is good only in the U.S. Return is not automatic, so be sure to mark the envelope "Return Postage Guaranteed."

Finally, stories do get lost in the mail; always keep a copy.

Making a living: money and rights

Unfortunately, it is very difficult to make a full-time living as a short-story writer. A beginning writer often has to measure success more in terms of credits than money. Still, it is important for a writer to know what to expect financially and how to protect ownership of his work. Information on money and rights is included in each listing. Some background information follows:

RATES: Magazines have different payment scales depending on length, fame, frequency as contributor, and so on. Some magazines make it worthwhile to become a regular contributor by their sliding rate scales. There are magazines that prefer not to publish their payment scale. These listings usually read: "Pays competitive rates." This means the magazine matches other publications similar in type and circulation.

Literary magazine listings might read "some money" or "occasionally pays." This generally refers to an honorarium or payment subject to the availability of grant money.

PAYMENT: Payment on acceptance does not mean immediately on acceptance. It can take 30 days or more for a check to be processed.

Payment on publication becomes a problem if a story is held for a long period. At the literary magazines, where payment is small, the writer simply has to wait. At some of the consumer magazines, the editors will negotiate if the publication wait is stretching out past what is expected, perhaps paying half the money before publication.

If you have waited for payment beyond the expected time, a call to inquire is reasonable.

PUBLICATION TIME: This can be a grim figure; many beginning writers don't realize how long the wait between sale and print can be. An attempt was made to get a realistic figure, but at many magazines the listing is optimistic. The only consolation is that the publication lag pleases editors no more than it does writers.

Putting together a magazine can be a difficult process. In the consumer press, editorial pages are often determined by advertising pages in a strict ratio. The fiction editor is given a certain number of inches to fill and must juggle the inventory to fit stories in. Then there are the problems of matching a light story to a serious one, a known writer to an unknown, seasonal material, and so on.

Further, changes of staff (quite frequent in the magazine business) can bring in an editor who doesn't like the previous editor's selections. A story can be put on "indefinite" hold. Eventually (after two years or so), the magazine may release the story so the author can try to resell it (the author does not return payment).

Literary magazines have different problems—they do not have to contend with advertising. Their pages are determined by tight budgets, mailing costs (these have risen astronomically in recent years), and decisions about single or double issues. Much can depend on when the next issue is scheduled to appear and what kind of fiction/poetry/essay/etc. ratio is planned.

SELLING AND RETAINING RIGHTS: It is always to a writer's advantage to retain as many rights to a piece as possible. In each listing the magazine's policy concerning rights bought is stated. A writer in the early stages of a career (and even an experienced writer at major magazines) usually has to accept the magazine's policy. As it happens, this is generally not a problem: Most magazines only take one form or another of first rights—that is, the magazine has the right of first publication, and ownership of all remaining rights is held by the author.

Rights can be transferred from writer to magazine orally, by written contract, by letter or note of intent, or by check endorsement (cashing of check means acceptance of terms; negotiate before cashing). A writer can and should insist on something in writing—if you sell a story to a magazine without a written agreement you are authorizing continued reprints of the story in that magazine with no additional payment to you.

When a magazine expresses interest in your story, ask what rights it intends to buy. Make sure you understand what the terms mean. Check such points as exclusive versus nonexclusive (for instance, if the magazine retains anthology rights, they can be exclusive or nonexclusive; one means the magazine has the sole right to anthologize the story, the other means the magazine retains the right to anthologize but the author can also sell to another collection).

When you sell first rights, check how long the magazine holds them after publication. How do you get the rights back? Automatically or by written request? Is there a closeout period? For instance, if the magazine hasn't published your piece within two years, do you have the right to demand it back? When you resell a story, what percentage does the first publisher get? Half? None? Are you obligated to give the first publisher written credit on any reprint?

These are all legitimate questions for a writer to ask. Again, a beginning writer is not going to receive the best possible deal on all these issues, but he should still find out where he stands.

The Consumer Magazines

Listed in the following section are the major magazines that publish short stories. Included are the widely distributed, high-circulation, monthly (or weekly) women's, men's, and general-interest magazines that everyone knows about and sees regularly on newsstands, in supermarkets, in dentists' waiting rooms, and in beauty-parlor magazine racks.

These magazines pay top rates and regularly publish the work of very well-known or experienced writers. Unfortunately, most do not use a great deal of fiction and receive thousands of submissions every year.

Still, even among these magazines, there is variation in receptiveness to new writers. Some have not pulled a piece from the slush pile in years; others find writers there with some frequency. Be realistic in approaching these magazines; they often have a large group of regular writers, and they are often well covered by agents. There is little point in submitting to them unless you are sure that you are meeting their needs.

Also included in this section are many less well-known, in some cases limited-circulation, general-audience publications that publish fiction. Many of these magazines are excellent break-in markets. The writer should read the listings with special care: These magazines often have well-defined audiences and well-defined requirements for their fiction.

For news about fiction in newspapers, see the listing for the PEN Syndicated Fiction Project.

THE ATLANTIC

8 Arlington Street
Boston, MA 02116
(617) 536-9500

SOURCE: Maureen Foley, assistant to the editors

IN SHORT: Looks for quality "first" stories

ABOUT THE MAGAZINE: Monthly; one or two stories per issue. Magazine for an intelligent, general readership. Its intent is to give balanced, considered treatment to issues of national importance. Subjects include politics, art, culture, society. Readers: 60% male; median age 37; most have attended college, 59% are graduates; 52% of readers are professionals or managers. Circulation: 400,000.

GETTING PUBLISHED: Rates: $1500-$2000. Payment: on acceptance. Rights: first North American serial. Reply time: four to six weeks. Guidelines: available.

The Atlantic rarely commissions stories. Everything published comes from the approximately 235 fiction manuscripts submitted every week. Initially, these submissions are divided into piles identified as special and general. Specials, about 60 a week, include stories from agents and known writers. Generals are everything else.

The special pile receives faster consideration and provides most of the magazine's published fiction. But the editors emphasize that all submissions are read with attention. "We believe it is our job to be on the lookout for new writers," says Maureen Foley, assistant to the editors.

"An Atlantic First" is a regular feature. A "first" is not a contest winner—it is simply a writer's first major publication of fiction. Editors are eager to find "first" stories. Foley estimates that two to three a year are usually published. Writers whose work has appeared as a "first" include James Jones, Louis Auchincloss, Joseph Heller, Ann Beattie, and Peter Matthiessen.

Time between acceptance and publication can be a year. Recent editorial changes have, in some cases, made the time even longer.

THE STORY: *The Atlantic* can use stories between 2000 and 10,000 words. Beyond that, an *Atlantic* story is hard to pin down.

"We publish a wide range of fiction," Foley says. "Nothing is rejected by definition. We are interested in quality, and anything that is well done will be considered."

The editors' best advice is to read the magazine. "Fiction is chosen as part of a general concept of the publication," Foley says. "We think of ourselves as a considered magazine. We try to give balanced, intelligent treatment to issues. At the same time we are looking for pieces that say something surprising, that give you some new viewpoint."

Though Foley was speaking of the magazine's nonfiction, "considered" and "surprising" are good descriptions of the fiction. The magazine is open to stories that involve idiosyncratic characters and offbeat situations. There is a story about a female, teenage bankrobber. Another story is about a young woman who has an illegitimate child, and who has fallen in love with a priest.

Two recent "firsts" are "Shiny Objects," by Dianne Benedict (Feb. '82), and "In the Zoot Car," by Heidi Jon Schmidt (July '81). In the first, a reclusive country woman takes in a foster child who is deformed, terminally ill, and religiously obsessed. It sounds as if it might be grotesque. In fact, the story is full of believable feeling without sentimentality or pathos. In the second story, a teenage girl receives an outlandish, shiny, painted, eight-year-old gas-guzzling Lincoln Continental for her birthday. In one day's drive with her mother and sister, the teen sees her family in a new light. More importantly, she begins to make the kind of judgments that indicate she is growing up.

These stories are notable for their engagement; the characters feel strong emotions and the reader is intended to feel for the characters. These are not cool, distanced pieces. The stories are also notable for their sharply delineated sense of place. They are rooted in carefully observed detail.

REJECTION: *The Atlantic* has two kinds of rejection notes. The first, used for most submissions, simply says: "Thank you and no." The second, used for submissions that show any promise, says the editors would be "happy to read your work in the future." If a piece is considered to have real potential, someone will write to the author and say so. "We are very careful whom we encourage," Foley says. "We don't want a lot of material we would never publish. But we would never send a form letter to someone we think has potential."

AVENUE

30 East 60th Street
New York, NY 10022
(212) 758-9516

SOURCE: Gary Fisketjon, fiction editor

IN SHORT: Specialized and not very open

ABOUT THE MAGAZINE: Published nine times a year; one piece of fiction (may be a novel excerpt) per issue. Distributed free to selected households in New York City, Los Angeles, San Francisco, Chicago, Houston, and Dallas; also goes to several expensive New York hotels. Not available by subscription or on newsstands. Median yearly income of reader is $190,000. Articles cover subjects of interest to people with great amounts of money. Included are art, fashion, architecture, clubs, profiles of successful New Yorkers in interesting and, in many cases, unexpected professions. Circulation: 70,000. Sample copy $3.

GETTING PUBLISHED: Rates: $400. Payment: on publication. Rights: first North American serial. Reply time: up to two months.

Fiction in *Avenue* generally comes from agents' submissions, well-known writers' novels, or solicited short stories. Approximately 50 unsolicited stories are submitted every month. In the last two years, two have been purchased.

Unsolicited stories are read by an assistant editor who passes roughly ten a month to fiction editor Gary Fisketjon. "The work we have been getting simply has not been good enough," he says. "We still are looking for writers of high-quality stories."

This is less of an invitation than it sounds. Fisketjon is looking for work of Cheever, Updike, Beattie quality. When *Avenue* was written up in one of the writers' magazines, the number of submissions jumped. None of the unsolicited stories was bought, and the editors do not want to be deluged by manuscripts again.

Publication time: six-to-eight-week lead; story should follow soon after. No guidelines.

THE STORY: Five years after *Avenue* began publication, fiction was added as a regular feature. The editors wanted to provide another place for quality fiction and at the same time to make the magazine look good with excerpts from novels by known writers. *Avenue* does not pay top rates, but for the novelist it's extra money and the appearance may serve to introduce a book to an audience that can afford hardcover prices.

The short fiction in *Avenue* has to engage sophisticated, traveled, educated people. "Genteel, upper-class stories have a better chance than cowboy stuff or low-life pieces," Fisketjon says. That doesn't mean a story has to be about people on Park Avenue. It does mean that it must deal with experience on a sophisticated, literate level.

About 3000 words is maximum length.

REJECTION: Standard form used in most cases. Fisketjon has written to writers from the slush pile whose work he thought warranted encouragement. He adds, however, that in only one case has a further submission led to a sale.

COMMENTARY

165 East 56th Street
New York, NY 10022
(212) 751-4000

SOURCE: Marion Magid, managing editor

IN SHORT: Difficult, not very open market

ABOUT THE MAGAZINE: Monthly; would like to publish more fiction. An intellectual journal that publishes thought-provoking essays on political, cultural, and social subjects. Interested in general topics and those with a Jewish theme. Managing editor Marion Magid says that fiction in *Commentary* is scarce only because editors are not seeing stories of the high literary quality they want. One problem is that the magazine is not thought of primarily as a fiction market, so talented writers, whose work editors would like to see, tend to look elsewhere. Editors rarely solicit fiction. Circulation: approximately 45,000.

GETTING PUBLISHED: Rates: $500 and up; average payment $750. Payment: on publication. Rights: first North American serial. Reply time: tries for three to four weeks. Guidelines: very sketchy guidelines available.

Approximately 100 unsolicited stories are submitted every month. Magid is the first reader. If she finds anything promising in a story she will circulate it among three other editors. She estimates that maybe three stories a week are read by someone besides herself.

Everything that comes in is read whether a cover letter is included or not. A cover letter with an impressive list of previous credits may lead to a story's getting a faster reading, but all stories are read.

Magid adds that a lot of the submissions are closer to memoirs of Jewish experiences than to fiction. *Commentary* is looking for crafted, professional stories.

Publication time: varies, but generally within one to three months.

ABOUT THE STORY: "We would like the caliber of the fiction we publish to be as distinguished, original, and unconventional as our nonfiction. We don't abide by many of the current social views. Our reputation is for controversial and thought-provoking essays—we do our best to describe reality in all its complexity.

"Fiction can have a news-bringing function, among other things, illuminating reality in a way that nonfiction cannot. The way it is here and now for this particular character, accurately rendered, is fascinating."

Much of the fiction *Commentary* has published has been Jewish in theme; the magazine also brings relatively unknown Israeli and Yiddish authors to the readers' attention. High-quality Jewish fiction is welcome, but the magazine is entirely open to fiction with no Jewish content. "We are open to any fiction about the way we live now," Magid says, "about contemporary reality." Length: 2000-6000 words.

REJECTION: A standard rejection form is used only for the pieces about which it is impossible to say anything good. If anything is found interesting or promising in a story, it will be returned with some sort of note. If a story is found really interesting and promising, though still unsuccessful, the editors will ask to see more work.

COSMOPOLITAN

224 West 57th Street
New York, NY 10019
(212) 262-5700

FICTION AND BOOKS EDITOR: Betty Nichols Kelly

SOURCE: Donna Jackson, editorial assistant, fiction and books

IN SHORT: Uses mostly agented material

ABOUT THE MAGAZINE: Monthly; approximately 25 stories a year. The typical *Cosmopolitan* reader is between 18 and 35, has a job or career, and is unmarried. The magazine offers self-help, self-exploration, guidance in beauty, fashion, and careers, and entertainment features. The major subject is women and men together —how they get together and what happens after. *Cosmopolitan*'s reader is apt to be a young woman who is concerned about relationships and finding the right one. This is strongly reflected in the fiction. Circulation: 2.8 million.

GETTING PUBLISHED: Rates: begin at $750; can go as high as $2000 for a very well-known writer. Payment: on acceptance. Rights: first North American serial. Reply time: about a month, longer if story is being considered. Guidelines: available.

Close to 100 unsolicited manuscripts are submitted every week. In a year, approximately four of these pieces will be published. Most of *Cosmopolitan*'s fiction is found among the agents' submissions.

The editors believe the magazine has a clear identity. They stress that if writers would bother to look at *Cosmopolitan* before sending stories, it would save time for everyone.

Editorial assistant Donna Jackson is the first reader. If a story has possibilities, she passes it to the fiction editors. She estimates that on a good week as many as ten stories might make the first cut. Editor Helen Gurley Brown reads the stories chosen by the fiction editors and has final say about what is published.

Stories are not always read all the way through. Because *Cosmopolitan* has very specific needs, a page or two is often enough to show that a story will not do. Cover letters that include credits also get minimal attention, since even established writers often miss the magazine's particular market.

Editors will ask for rewrites and resubmissions on spec if a story has very high potential but major problems. If a story has minor problems, it will be bought and edited in-house. If the author requests, the changing and/or cutting will be shown.

Once a story is accepted, it should be in print in from three months to a year.

THE STORY: *Cosmo* stories must be very high in reader identification. The heroine should be between 20 and 30 and should be a modern young woman. The focus is on stories of man-woman relationships. These stories have to be both sophisticated and sensitive. That is, the heroines are independent and sexually liberated, but they are not tough. They care deeply about love and relationships and are capable of being hurt.

Because the reader is usually single, *Cosmo* is more interested in the meeting and marrying phase of a relationship than settled married life. If a story is set after marriage, it still must concern romantic problems, as opposed to parenthood or economic difficulties.

Certainly, not all *Cosmo* stories are love stories. Other subjects of interest to young working women—dealing with jobs, friends, and so on—are possible. The recognition factor is the important part.

Editors screening unsolicited manuscripts often find that a quick skim will be enough. If the story is about refugees or a chronicle of family life, it is rejected without being fully read.

Editors also insist on fully realized stories with positive resolutions. Readers want to know how things turn out. The story is meant to be an entertainment experience.

Two stories taken from the slush pile in the recent past are "Connections," by Kathleen Leverich (Nov. '80), and "As I Was Going to St. Ives," by Eileen Kolb (Mar. '82). "Connections" was notable for its precise writing; *Cosmo* receives too many stories with wordage that does not forward the action. Further, the story was different because it concerned two women instead of a man and a woman. A twist ending made it more interesting. "As I Was Going to St. Ives" was described as being beautifully written—a case where the piece was bought more for the writing than for the plot.

Short-shorts should run 1500-3000 words, stories 4000-6000 words.

REJECTION: Standard form used for most stories. Editors may write back to express admiration, suggest other markets, or ask to see more work. Any story that has been given any consideration—that is, more than one reading—will probably be returned with some personal acknowledgment.

ESQUIRE

2 Park Avenue
New York, NY 10016
(212) 561-8100

FICTION EDITOR: Rust Hills

SOURCE: Bruce Weber, assistant fiction editor

IN SHORT: Difficult to sell

ABOUT THE MAGAZINE: Monthly; 10 to 12 stories a year. Provides entertainment and service for the man who wishes to be well informed and cares about good writing. Most readers are college-educated, success-oriented, interested in being up-to-date, between 24 and 40. "Our reader is the person who not only wants to know what's going on," says assistant fiction editor Bruce Weber, "but also why it matters."

Esquire has gone through a change of ownership and editorial policy in the recent past. It considers its editorial identity to be neither that of conventional "men's" magazines nor that of a "highbrow" magazine, but rather that of a sophisticated hybrid. Circulation: approximately 650,000.

GETTING PUBLISHED: Rates: $1000 and up. Payment: on acceptance. Rights: first North American serial. Reply time: tries for a month. Guidelines: available.

Close to 100 unsolicited manuscripts come in every week at *Esquire*. In the last two years, two have made it into the magazine. Most of the fiction comes from agents' submissions.

Still, everything that is submitted is considered. Weber begins with the cover letter: "I am looking for a reason to consider a story with care." Possibilities include previous credits, recommendations from known writers, writing-program affiliations, or possibly just good persuasive writing in the letter itself. But worse than no cover letter at all, he adds, is the voluminous letter about the author's life, the letter with story synopsis, or the ill-written, misspelled letter. He emphasizes that cover letter or not, stories are read.

Weber estimates that he passes along five stories a week to fiction editor Rust Hills. If Weber and Hills agree on the merits of a story, it is read by other senior editors and discussed at a weekly editorial meeting. Final decisions are made by the editor-in-chief. Editors might ask for a rewrite on a promising story, but it will be on spec. Effort is made to publish stories as soon as possible after a sale. But because of space restrictions, it can take up to a year, and possibly longer.

THE STORY: "*Esquire* has been in publication for 50 years," Rust Hills says, " and fiction has always had a place. Its role is unique, out of proportion to the number of pages it fills. It is central to the magazine's image as literary and literate."

Esquire publishes traditional stories—that is, where the emphasis is on characters who are altered by action. Genre fiction, no matter how well written, is not considered. Nor are mood pieces, vignettes, sketches, or experimental prose.

Asked to name a quintessential *Esquire* story, Weber chose "Rock Springs" by Richard Ford (Feb. '82). It's the story of a petty grifter, on the run, in a stolen car, with his little daughter and her dog and the woman he loves. "It has strongly drawn characters, a unique point of view, identifiable plot. It is contemporary," Weber says. "It expounds a code of behavior that makes sense today."

Talking about his reading of the slush pile, Weber adds: "The first thing I look for is surety of voice. Sensitivity to the sound of sentences and how the voice typifies the narrator's point of view. Second, a sense of purpose. A feeling that the story begins in the right place and that the writer knows where he is going. Language and control: those two qualities immediately winnow out 90 percent of what comes into this office."

The two stories that went directly from the unsolicited pile into the magazine were "Watching TV with the Red Chinese," by Luke Wishnant (Mar. '82), and "My Livelihood," by Charles Dickinson (May '82). The first is the story of three mainland Chinese exchange students and the American who is trying to pilot them through the complexities and craziness of American life. The second is about a man, with wife and children and in-laws, who loses his job. His first unemployed act is to buy a set of golf clubs. He's a man with everything but work on his mind. Both these stories are very much about how men act in the face of a society that at best is difficult and can often seem a little mad.

Weber adds that stories do not necessarily have to be from a man's point of view and certainly not from male writers. But, he points out, *Esquire* is a man's magazine and a writer has to remember that. It is a circumstance that narrows possibilities. Stories can run between 1500 and 7000 words.

REJECTION: In most cases a standard form is used. Rejected stories considered to have quality are returned with a personal letter, perhaps asking to see more work. The extent of personal response might solely depend on how much time the editors have. "But," Weber says, "we correspond with many writers. Naturally, we are interested in finding new writers." He estimates that something like 12 personal rejection letters might go out in a week.

ESSENCE

Essence Communications, Inc.
1500 Broadway
New York, NY 10036
(212) 730-4260

SOURCE: Susan L. Taylor, editor

IN SHORT: Looking for high-quality fiction

ABOUT THE MAGAZINE: Monthly; approximately three pieces of fiction a year; would like to do more. For black women aged 18-49. Most are married, have children, and are college-educated. *Essence* carries normal service features on fashion, beauty, diet, etc. It also covers the large and difficult range of issues associated with being a black woman in America. Articles can concern politics and economics, as well as social issues.

Editor Susan Taylor would like nothing better than to run fiction regularly. But she needs, and is not getting, the kind of fiction that will stand up to the nonfiction. Circulation: 700,000.

GETTING PUBLISHED: Rates: $450-$1000, depending on celebrity of author. Payment: on acceptance. Rights: reverts to author. Reply time: approximately three months. Guidelines: available.

Taylor says she receives too little fiction in the mail to make even a rough count. She is willing to read all submissions—either unsolicited or from agents.

THE STORY: "We want fiction that is powerful and provocative," Taylor says. "Work must mirror contemporary black women's experience. We receive too much work that mirrors the experience of people who no longer exist, with archaic dialect and outmoded events that deny the complex inner life of our reader. We also want fiction with purpose, not simply shouts of pain and suffering. There has to be a structure and character growth. There is room for love stories, but they cannot be trivial. They have to deal with the real and serious problems of identity and society that black women and men have in coming together."

Taylor suggests the writer look at "Widow Woman," by Jenée Gaskin (Aug. '81), as an example. "It is a story in which the quality of the writing holds your interest," Taylor says. "It's a black woman's story. The character is alive in an alive setting of colors and smells."

Taylor will read stories up to 3000 words.

REJECTION: Standard forms are generally sent to those contributors who are unknown to the editors. If the contributor is a writer known from previous work, or through reputation, or if it's someone the editors would like to encourage, a personal note will be sent.

FAMILY CIRCLE

488 Madison Avenue
New York, NY 10022
(212) 593-8000

SOURCE: Diane Hynd, books and features editor

IN SHORT: Looking for new writers, but not a break-in market

ABOUT THE MAGAZINE: Published 17 times a year; uses as many as 12 short stories a year. Women's service magazine, covers beauty, diet, exercise, health, crafts, food, fashion, consumer news, and articles of interest to a reader who is likely to be middle-income, married, a mother, often living in the suburbs, with a job but not a career. Material targeted for all ages, but average reader is in mid-30s. Newsstand and supermarket distribution. Circulation: 8.4 million.

GETTING PUBLISHED: Rates: varies widely according to author; first sale from unknown writer about $300; much higher for well-known writer. Payment: on publication. Rights: exclusive rights in all domestic and foreign editions. Reply time: four to six weeks. Guidelines: available.

Most of the fiction is chosen from agents' submissions. Between 50 and 100 unsolicited manuscripts are submitted every week. Occasionally a piece is pulled from the slush pile, but, according to books and features editor Diane Hynd, it's very rare.

Editors are eager to find stories; they would like to be using more fiction. Every manuscript sent in is at least scanned. In many cases it is immediately obvious that the story is from someone who has no idea what writing is supposed to be. Anything written competently is read. First readers are all staff editors. Anything with publication possibilities, or anything very good even if not right for the magazine, is shown to Hynd. Several top editors look at a story seriously considered for publication.

If a story has only minor problems, editors will clean it up in-house. If the problems are more extensive they might ask for a rewrite and resubmission on spec.

Hynd adds that a cover letter listing credits does generate

interest. Editors are looking for more work from professional writers.

THE STORY: Fiction in *Family Circle* is intended to provide an entertainment experience for the reader. Conclusions are always positive, problems are usually resolved. Stories should be high in reader identification—about reasonably young, married women with children or about their families. (Contemporary mysteries are also welcome.) Most popular are stories of husbands and wives refinding each other in the face of temporary misunderstandings, or stories concerning children—children with friends, brothers and sisters together, and so on. True-life problems are dealt with, but not problems that are too grim or past solution.

"We are looking for simple, uncluttered direct writing that has style, sets a mood, gives good characterization," Hynd says.

"The Little Girl Who Wanted to Skip Christmas" by Louise Shivers (Dec. '82) is about an 11-year-old girl who is embarrassed by her five rowdy younger brothers. She envies her friends who live in neater, well-ordered houses. But the night before Christmas she has a dream: She is asked to choose which of her too-many brothers should be sent back. The next morning she realizes how she loves them all and how lucky she is. In "Rapunzel, Rapunzel," by Loretta Strehlow (July '82), a wife and mother wants nothing more than a weekend alone with her husband; when he ruins her plan by inviting another couple to join them she takes a vacation of her own by withdrawing—with food, a good book, and a sleeping bag—to the family tree house. Her husband gets the message, cancels the other couple, and joins her in her leafy nest.

Stories can run between 500 and 2500 words with 1500 words about ideal.

REJECTION: Standard form used in most cases. If a story is well done, but not right for the market, Hynd might ask to see more work. "We are trying to find new writers," she says, "and that's one good way of doing it."

GALLERY

800 Second Avenue
New York, NY 10017
(212) 986-9600

SOURCE: John Bensink, senior editor

IN SHORT: Not very open to new writers

ABOUT THE MAGAZINE: Monthly; one story an issue. A men's magazine combining explicit photo spreads and erotica with investigative reporting, features on subjects of interest to men (mountain climbing, boxing, stereo equipment), and pieces seriously exploring man-woman relationships. Readers: 70% are 18-34; 23% have attended or graduated college; 66% are married; the median independent income is $18,279, the median household income $24,025. Circulation: 500,000.

GETTING PUBLISHED: Rates: $350 for up to 1000 words; $600 top for unknown writer. Payment: half on acceptance, half on publication. Rights: first North American serial. Reply time: two weeks for rejection, five to six weeks if story is being considered. Guidelines: none available. Simultaneous submissions: will read.

Most of the fiction published in *Gallery* is chosen from agents' submissions. Approximately 7500 unsolicited stories are submitted annually, two of which will make it into the magazine.

The stories are read by an associate editor. Maybe 1000 every year come close enough to be given to senior editor John Bensink. A much smaller number (maybe six a year) are given to the editorial director, and associate publisher Eric Protter, who has the final say on what gets printed.

Major rewrites are not asked for. Editors do find that minor rewrites are necessary on many accepted pieces.

Bensink adds that cover notes are fine, but cover letters unnecessary. He is interested in credits but definitely not résumés, schools, or details of travels abroad.

Publication usually follows acceptance in two to three months, but there is no guarantee and the wait can be much longer.

THE STORY: Gallery has a separate monthly feature for sexually explicit fiction called "Private Lives." These pieces (2500-3000 words, paying $400) are written to formula by regular writers, but editors will consider unsolicited submissions. Address "Private Lives Editor."

Short stories in *Gallery* do not need any sexual theme or content. Fiction ranges from mysteries to science fiction (tends to be big names only) to horror and even to serious introspective pieces on contemporary man. Writers include Lawrence Block, Harlan Ellison, Stephen King, Bruce Jay Friedman, Jack C. Haldeman II, James Sallis, and Peter Meinke, who just won an O. Henry Award.

"It would be hard for a person who has only read a writer's guide to figure out how to write a story for *Gallery*," Bensink says. "It's a man's magazine, so we do want action/entertainment stories. But there are exceptions. For instance, Bruce Jay Friedman. And more introspective work from Ivan Praksher. We are open to anything a man between 24 and 35 might like. We do not think our reader will look at a piece of writing and say, 'No shoot-outs, no escapes, this is no good.' "

In the genre fiction published, Bensink wants writing and characterization that will make the stories rise above the genre.

Editors will read pieces ranging from short-shorts to novellas, but novellas, published in special inserts, have been from writers like Stephen King. Ideal length is 2500-3000 words.

REJECTION: Standard form used in most cases. Letters are written (maybe one a month) if stories are good but not right for *Gallery* or if there is something promising in a piece. Bensink adds that a note of praise about some aspect of a story attached to a letter of rejection is not an invitation to the author to rewrite and then resubmit. If the editors want a rewrite, they will ask for it.

GENTLEMAN'S COMPANION

Larry Flynt Publications
2029 Century Park East
Suite 3800
Los Angeles, CA 90067
(213) 556-9200

SOURCE: Jim Gregory, fiction editor

IN SHORT: Very open to new writers

ABOUT THE MAGAZINE: Monthly; uses 12 stories a year. A men's magazine with a mix of reporting, profiles, interviews, explicit photo spreads, and sex-related articles. This magazine is published by the same company, though with different editorial staff, as *Hustler* and *Chic*. It is similar in format and has similar needs. Like those two magazines, its major source of fiction is the unsolicited pile. For details, see the *Hustler* and *Chic* listing. Circulation: approximately 100,000.

GETTING PUBLISHED: Rates: $300. Payment: on acceptance. Rights: exclusive magazine first and second, English and English translations, worldwide publication rights; includes permission to reprint in "Best of . . . " editions (for an additional 20% payment). Reply time: a month or less. Publication time: three to four months.

Gentleman's Companion receives approximately 50 unsolicited submissions a month.

THE STORY: Fiction should run between 3000 and 4000 words. Adventure stories are primarily wanted, but other types will be considered if they have a tight plot. Fiction editor Jim Gregory comments that the difference between a *Hustler* story and a *Gentleman's Companion* story is that *GC* is "more erotic, has fewer taboos, and is more open to varying topics that are barred from *Hustler*." Still, the magazine is not looking for pornography; it wants fully realized characters, exciting, fast-paced plots, and erotic scenes that grow realistically out of the action.

GOOD HOUSEKEEPING

959 Eighth Avenue
New York, NY 10019
(212) 262-5700

FICTION EDITOR: Naome Lewis

SOURCE: Arleen L. Quarfoot, associate editor

IN SHORT: Rarely buys from unknown writers

ABOUT THE MAGAZINE: Monthly; uses two to three pieces of fiction per issue, including novel excerpts. A service magazine for a middle-income woman with a traditional life-style. The average reader is married, has children, and puts family and home above her job. She is conservative in her values. "We don't push modern values on our readers," associate editor Arleen Quarfoot says. "At the same time, we try to move with the times. In fiction, our heroines have changed and grown. They still put family and home over job, but they don't chase after men. They have more pride." Circulation: 5.5 million.

GETTING PUBLISHED: Rates: $1000 for short-shorts; $1250 for stories; $250 more on second story, then for every fourth story until $3000 top is reached. Payment: on acceptance. Rights: first North American serial. Reply time: approximately six weeks. Guidelines: none available.
   Good Housekeeping receives 1500 unsolicited manuscripts a month. In the past several years, none of these have been purchased; 60% of the fiction comes from agents, the rest from regular contributors. Top money makes this market even more competitive.
   Still, editors read unsolicited submissions and consider them important. Though they have bought no first stories in recent years, they have seen work they liked enough to write back with suggestions and requests for further work. "We correspond with a large number of writers," Quarfoot says. "We are a difficult market to define, and writers rarely understand our needs in the beginning. Sometimes, after several submissions, something develops and a sale is made."
   A first reader looks at all submissions. Possibilities are passed to senior editors. Any story accompanied by a cover letter listing credits is automatically passed on. If editors are interested in a

story, they might ask for a rewrite on spec. They also will do extensive in-house rewriting when necessary.

The average time between acceptance and publication is three to five months. Seasonal material can expect a longer wait.

THE STORY: *Good Housekeeping* fiction is intended to entertain. There has to be a strong recognition factor for the reader in character and plot. Stories are built around some problem or conflict, but the message is always hopeful. Problems are always solvable and do not include such matters as real poverty, basic incompatibility, and rejection of the underlying values of family life in America.

A light touch and humor are very welcome. Two staple subjects of stories are relationships among family members, friends, and neighbors, and romance. The key is to find a fresh way to handle subjects like the 20-year-old marriage that appears to be going stale, the father coming to terms with his daughter's marriage, a mother helping her daughter through the social embarrassment of being a teenager, and so on.

The contents of most unsolicited submissions have convinced editors that writers are sending in stories without reading the magazine. Quarfoot mentions harrowing stories of rape or strange pieces like the story of an abortion from a fetus's point of view. There is no place for any of this in *Good Housekeeping*. The editors think writers should stop wasting everybody's time.

Writers who regularly sell to the magazine and exemplify what it needs include Marlene Fanta Shyer, Adele Glimm, and Rosamunde Pilcher.

Needed are short-shorts of about 2000 words and stories up to 4000 words. Editors warn that short-shorts are a more skilled form of writing in which not a single word can be wasted. Plots should generally be light.

REJECTION: Standard form used in most cases. A letter asking for revision is very rare. "But," Quarfoot says, "in the case of any writer with previous credits, or any manuscript that shows any promise at all, we will put a small encouraging note on the rejection form." Calling it a very rough estimate, Quarfoot says 50 such notes are mailed a month.

HADASSAH

50 West 58th Street
New York, NY 10019
(212) 355-7900

SOURCE: Roselyn Bell, associate editor

IN SHORT: Open, but specialized market

ABOUT THE MAGAZINE: Published ten times a year; seven or eight stories a year. Magazine of Hadassah, the Women's Zionist Organization of America. Circulation is 370,000, readership 1 million—mostly Hadassah members. Articles cover all aspects of Jewish life in America, Israel, and around the world. Hadassah looks like a magazine supplement in a Sunday paper. Averages 50 pages an issue. Sample copy: $1.50.

GETTING PUBLISHED: Rates: 15¢ a word up to 3000 words with a $300 minimum. Payment: on publication. Rights: first North American serial. Reply time: four to six weeks for rejection: up to ten weeks if story is being considered. Guidelines: available.

Most fiction is chosen from the approximately 20 unsolicited stories submitted monthly. Associate editor Roselyn Bell reads everything and estimates that two stories a month are good enough to be given to the executive editor for further consideration.

A rewrite might be asked for if a story's problems are easily identifiable. Publication time varies but is not always within a year.

THE STORY: "We use stories with a clear Jewish or Israeli theme," Bell says. "We want to hit our readers where they live, but we want to entertain as well. We try to avoid any didactic quality. We want straightforward stories, with strong characters that our readers will identify with and care about. We avoid fiction for women only."

Bell cited two stories in particular. "After the Revolution: An American Passover Story," by Sylvia Rothchild (Apr. '81), is a mother's tale of dealing with the problem of American Jewish children who turn away from their heritage. "The Carp," by Barry Hyams (Aug./Sept. '81), was called "unusual" by Bell. "It is a less straightforwardly Jewish story." Set in Louisiana, it's a child's-eye view of new neighbors, a Jewish couple who have fled from Europe during the Second World War. Its problems are more universal than specifically Jewish. It is a particularly sensitive piece, very evocative of time and place.

Stories run 1000-2500 words; 1500 is ideal.

REJECTION: A standard form is used. Hadassah members, known figures in the Jewish community, and people who have sold to the magazine before receive personal letters with their returned stories. Bell also writes if she is impressed with a story and can suggest another possible market.

HARPER'S

2 Park Avenue
New York, NY 10016
(212) 481-5220

SOURCE: Helen Rogan, associate editor

IN SHORT: Looks at but does not necessarily read unsolicited mss.

ABOUT THE MAGAZINE: Monthly; approximately 12 pieces of fiction a year. *Harper's* is a magazine that has chosen quality even at the expense of quantity. One of the country's oldest continuously published magazines, *Harper's* was in serious financial trouble not long ago. The decision was to tighten up and give the magazine a clear identity for rigorous and thoughtful writing on a variety of political, cultural, and social subjects. The circulation was allowed, even welcomed, to fall to its present level of approximately 140,000. This gives the editors, few for a major magazine, room to experiment. One decision was not to look for big-name novel excerpts, but to concentrate on short stories and to take chances on the stories chosen. Readers are described by associate editor Helen Rogan as highly literate, tending not to be New Yorkers, and heavily academic. They feel strongly about the magazine and write in angrily when they disapprove of something in it.

GETTING PUBLISHED: Rates: $500-$1200 for an unknown, depending on length. Payment: on acceptance. Rights: first North American serial. Reply time: over a month is not uncommon. No guidelines.

Printed in the masthead every month is a disclaimer: "*Harper's* does not publish unsolicited fiction or poetry." In fact, this is not exactly true.

Between 100 and 150 unsolicited short stories are received at *Harper's* every week. It is extremely rare that any of these stories are published in the magazine. But these envelopes are not returned unopened. Someone, probably an assistant editor, glances at every manuscript, looks over every cover letter. "It's really a question of a manuscript or letter catching someone's eye," Rogan says. "And that process is not to be discounted. Editors develop intuition about stories."

What might catch the eye is hard to pin down. Certainly a

cover letter listing quality credits will win a full reading. A fine, engrossing first page might do it as well.

The *Harper's* position is that very few writers produce stories of the quality the magazine requires. The editors do not want to be deluged by manuscripts. Expectations for the unsolicited pile are slight.

If a story passes the first reader, it is given to Rogan. She estimates that she sees 20 manuscripts a week. If she is impressed by a story, she will pass it on to other editors. Stories are chosen more or less by consensus; not everyone has to like a piece, but everyone does have to admire it. Rogan adds that agents' submissions are often just as "off" as slush pieces.

Once a manuscript is purchased, publication is apt to follow in two to three months.

THE STORY: "We are terribly committed to fiction in *Harper's*," Rogan says. "In a way it is a kind of centerpiece of the magazine. Stories have to be strong to hold up against the nonfiction. People read us for ideas and writing, and the fiction has to live up to that.

"At the same time, stories have to be accessible. We have turned down some classy stuff because it was obscure. We like stories to care and to engage the reader quickly. We are not looking for sketches, or the simple evocation of mood that just tails off, or the story with the little epiphany ending. We like movement, a strong sense of character. We need work to be sturdy."

The variety of the fiction published is tremendous. Three stories by Robert Walser ran in July 1982. Walser was born in Switzerland in 1878. In 1929, suffering from schizophrenia and extreme poverty, he committed himself to a sanatorium. He did not write again, though he lived until 1956. He left behind 15 books, innumerable poems, and over a thousand short prose pieces. Though admired by Hesse, Kafka, and others of his age, Walser was a forgotten writer. In 1982, Farrar, Straus and Giroux published *Selected Short Stories of Robert Walser,* translated by Christopher Middleton, and *Harper's* reprinted three of the pieces. Only one of the stories is long enough to fill a page. They are difficult, intense, and powerful. Even the publishers were surprised when *Harper's* asked for reprint rights.

"Sugar Among the Freaks," by Lewis Nordan (June '82), is

another matter entirely. The story is Southern, offbeat, quirky, full of energy. Rogan describes it as "Southern grotesque, yet touching and delicate." *Harper's* published Nordan's first story and four others since then.

In the November 1982 issue is "My Own Earth," by Jane Hamilton. It is the author's first published story, and it was found in the slush pile. A childhood reminiscence, it mixes conventional narrative with letters written by the characters attesting to past events.

In October 1982, *Harper's* published "Granted Wishes," by Thomas Berger—three short-short comic (black-comic) pieces. Anne Tyler and Paul Theroux were also published in 1982, as well as Portuguese writer Jorge Amado, André Dubus, and Tova Reich, among others.

REJECTION: Most stories are sent back with a standard form. Rogan will write if she wants to encourage an author. She warns that she writes very rarely, perhaps in one out of 20 cases.

HUSTLER and CHIC

Larry Flynt Publications
2029 Century Park East
Suite 3800
Los Angeles, Ca 90067
(213) 556-9200

SOURCE: Ted Newsom, fiction editor

IN SHORT: Very open to new writers

ABOUT THE MAGAZINES: Monthly; 12 stories a year in each publication. Men's magazines published by the same company, edited by the same staff. Both run documented exposé articles, profiles, and interviews with well-known personalities as well as explicit photo spreads and sex-related articles. There are differences in the two magazines. *Hustler's* circulation is 1.4 million; *Chic's* nearer 300,000. *Hustler* pays over twice as much for stories and most articles. *Hustler* demands a higher level of complexity, writing, and research in both fiction and nonfiction. The demographics (1980 figures) are similar. The typical reader is 18 to 34, blue-collar (60% at *Hustler*; 65% at *Chic*), and at least a high school graduate.

GETTING PUBLISHED: Rates: *Hustler* pays $1000, *Chic* $300. Payment: on acceptance. Rights: exclusive magazine first and second, English and English translations, worldwide publication rights; includes permission to reprint in "Best of . . . " editions (for additional 20% payment). Reply time: a month or less. Publication time: three to four months.

Almost all fiction published in *Hustler* and *Chic* is chosen from the unsolicited submissions. Fiction does come from authors who have sold to the magazines before, but seven or eight new writers are likely to appear in each magazine every year.

Approximately 150 stories are submitted every month, and fiction editor Ted Newsom looks at everything. "I read as long as I'm interested, then I stop," he explains. "If I'm not interested, the reader won't be." He estimates that less than 10% of the manuscripts are worth any consideration at all.

If a story catches Newsom's attention, it might not matter which magazine it was addressed to. Stories sent to *Chic* may be upgraded to *Hustler*; stories sent to *Hustler* may be accepted for

Chic if the author will accept the lower rate. Newsom also might, if the story seems right, give it to the editors of *Gentleman's Companion* (another Flynt publication, also listed here) to read.

A cover letter listing previous publications does not hurt a story, but neither does no letter at all. Everything is read and starts with an equal chance.

THE STORY: *Hustler* buys only adventure stories; *Chic* buys adventure and humor. Neither magazine buys pornographic fiction. There are differences in the *Hustler* and *Chic* stories. A *Chic* story is sheer entertainment, sheer adventure. The story generally moves from beginning to end with a minimum number of complications and sidetracks. A *Hustler* story is expected to be more complex, more significant. Things are not always what they seem at first; characters lie to each other and plots unravel in more complex ways. The story is entertaining, but the stakes tend to be higher, have more meaning. For both magazines, there should be a twist ending that surprises and satisfies the reader. There should also be an erotic scene (specified as being one and a half pages long) that grows out of the characters' desire for each other and fits in naturally with the terms of the story. The major problem with most submitted stories is a lack of adventure—simply, not enough happens.

Neither magazine buys any science fiction. Neither magazine will accept any story with homosexuality, drugs, incest, kinky sex, or sex with minors as a theme, or that includes any blasphemy ("damn" is okay; "goddamn" is forbidden). Stories set in bordellos or massage parlors should also be avoided.

Stories are expected to be fast-starting and fast-moving. Flashbacks should be avoided.

The characters have to be more than stock figures. They have, besides heroic attributes, personal lives of some sensitivity or interest, and personal quirks that make them individuals. Heros can be adventurous types—soldiers, policemen—or more average citizens who get caught up in unexpected events and (to their own surprise) find the strength to carry the adventure through to a successful conclusion. "An ordinary guy doing his best in an extraordinary situation is much more exciting," Newsom says, "than another 007 clone saving the world again."

Women should not be passive "damsels in distress" or "sex objects." They should be active, bright, and independent and often are the man's partner in the adventure, exhibiting bravery and resource. Women have also appeared as prime movers of stories—a heroine instead of a hero.

Locations can be exotic—Monte Carlo, the jungles of Brazil—but they can also be midwestern or small-town America. Newsom particularly likes stories in which the familiar can be made exciting.

The adventure itself can be merely amusing (as in a treasure hunt), but if the adventure has some significance—against a resurgent Nazi movement, for example—it is even better (particularly true for *Hustler*). Stories should run around 4500 words.

REJECTION: Stories that miss the form entirely and do not appear to be from writers with any skill are rejected with a standard form. If the story misses the form but appears to be from someone with writing skills, the guidelines will be sent back. If the person is a professional writer, who misses on a close call, a personal note will be written. Newsom does ask for rewrites and resubmissions (on spec) if a story comes close, but will only work through one rewrite.

LADIES' HOME JOURNAL

3 Park Avenue
New York, NY 10016
(212) 872-8000

SOURCE: Constance Leisure, books and fiction editor

IN SHORT: Does not read unsolicited mss.

ABOUT THE MAGAZINE: Monthly; used six short stories and seven novel excerpts in 1982. Readers are women with families and a whole range of outside interests—70% work full- or part-time. The average reader is around 37 years old and has two children. Service features include health, fashion, beauty, and more substantial journalistic topics like crime prevention and dealing with retardation. The celebrity interview is the major entertainment feature. A lot of coverage is given to ordeal stories—true-life accounts of personal and medical crises. According to reader surveys, the most popular feature is the monthly "Can this marriage be saved?" column. Food is next in popularity, then beauty and/or fashion. Though unsolicited manuscripts are not read, editors are actively soliciting short fiction. Circulation: 5 million.

GETTING PUBLISHED: Rates: from $500 to an infrequent high of $3000 depending on writer's celebrity and regularity as a contributor. Payment: on acceptance. Rights: first North American serial. Guidelines: none available.

Almost all the fiction published in *LHJ* comes from agents' submissions or from known writers. Unsolicited manuscripts are returned to sender *unread*. Most of the time, not even a cover letter with impressive credits gets a manuscript through. However, every now and then a story does get through almost accidentally. The receptionist who opens envelopes is not expected to read cover letters, but she occasionally decides to hold on to story.

It is possible, however, for an established writer who does not have an agent to make contact. This can be done either by a letter or a phone call to Constance Leisure. A writer with credits and an interesting idea should feel free to get in touch.

Invited submissions are read first by the assistant editor. Leisure reads the possibilities, and the editor-in-chief makes the final decision. Editors ask for rewrites only if they are very sure they will use a story. If a story's problems are simple—for instance, too long—it will be edited in-house.

Publication time can be slow, as short stories are not carried in every issue.

THE STORY: First and foremost, fiction at *LHJ* is entertainment. The editors stay away from subjects too serious or too unhappy. In general, there is no place for violence, or very intense problems with children, death, old age, religion, or infidelity.

Story subjects should be high in reader identification: going back to work; marriage versus career; balancing home and work. Divorce, separation, and second marriage are possible topics, but the ending must be upbeat. Stories of married couples working out problems are always wanted. Romance, or meeting-and-marrying, stories are welcome, but must have a catchy, contemporary hook. In general, heroines should be no older than 35. Stories about animals and about children, especially when an adult helps a child to face the crises of adolescence, are popular with readers.

LHJ has recently gone through major editorial changes. A new editor-in-chief has been putting her own stamp on the magazine. Two recent stories have been more sophisticated than previous fiction and might indicate a direction for the future.

"February Roses," by Virginia Fassnidge (Feb. '82), was a favorite of the editor. It's a story of suspected infidelity, based on a bouquet purchased by a husband but not given to his wife. The wife at first is sure the husband was unfaithful, then finds evidence that she is wrong. Then, perhaps, that she was right initially. Or maybe not. And finally, does she even want to know? The clear evidence is that after a long married life he still cares for her as she still cares for him.

"Getting it Straight," by Rhoda Tagliacozza (July '81), shows the same kind of ambivalence. A divorced woman, working for a Ph.D. in literature, moves into a suburban neighborhood of housewives and kids. She has more than her share of problems and insecurities, but her drive to make something of herself, her concentration on her work, gives her neighbors pause and makes them reexamine their own lives. "Ten years ago we wouldn't have done a story about feeling ambivalent about husbands, even with a happy ending."

LHJ will consider stories of all lengths, but between 3000 and 3500 words is most salable.

LADY'S CIRCLE

Lopez Publications
25 West 26th Street
New York, NY 10010
(212) 689-3933

SOURCE: Ardis Sandel, editor

IN SHORT: Very open to new writers

ABOUT THE MAGAZINE: Monthly; one or two stories an issue. Women's service magazine. The readers are usually high-school-educated, and many have graduated from college; they usually do not work outside their homes. Half the readers are 18 to 35; the other half are over 40. The magazine covers a lot of medical news, crafts, and money-saving ideas, and runs pieces about people helping others. It is centered on the woman who is primarily a homemaker and mother.

GETTING PUBLISHED: Rates: $125; may be $75 for a very short piece. Payment: on publication. Rights: all rights, but will return on request. Reply time: rejection in one or two weeks but if a story is being considered, it may take several months for an answer. Guidelines: available.

Most fiction is chosen from the over 50 unsolicited stories submitted every week. Editor Ardis Sandel is the first reader. She passes the possibilities (an estimated five a week) to the publisher, who makes the final decisions on acceptance.

Send stories related to specific holidays six months in advance. Once purchased, a year can pass before a story is published.

THE STORY: Sandel is looking for what she describes as "emotional fiction"—stories that will touch and move the reader, and leave behind a feeling of warmth. Emotional fiction does not mean stories of death, alcoholism, or retardation. It means fiction that celebrates the small things that can produce joy in the average homemaker and mother's life. Stories are supportive, and show the pleasure and significance in the average kind of happenings that make up day-to-day existence.

Story characters should be very close to the readers—average women, married, with children, home-centered, not too affluent. The reader has to be able to feel for and identify with the heroine.

Sandel does not want stories about divorce, infidelity, or separation. She also does not want light romances. Stories should show the positive side of family life. Though a heroine might have a passing problem, she has no doubt about the basic goodness of her life. The most common subjects are marriage and the parent/child relationship. In one story a woman comes to terms with her desire to work (her desire for identity) and her family's desire to have her at home by starting a home baking business. In another story, a bed handed down through the generations symbolizes continuity and stability, and is the focus of a woman's reverie.

The ideal length is 2000 words; stories should not run over 2500.

REJECTION: A form letter is usual. Sandel occasionally adds a note if she liked a particular piece. She rarely asks to see more work, and rewrites are requested very infrequently.

MADEMOISELLE

Condé Nast Publications
350 Madison Avenue
New York, NY 10017
(212) 880-8800

SOURCE: Susan Schneider, fiction editor

IN SHORT: Mostly agented material

ABOUT THE MAGAZINE: Monthly; generally uses one story an issue. *Mademoiselle* has always had a reputation as a thinking woman's fashion magazine, and fiction has always been part of that reputation. Coverage of fashion, beauty, self-help, and self-exploration for the young career woman is central to the magazine. But *Mademoiselle* also does more substantive reporting. Fiction editor Susan Schneider adds that recent reader surveys show that fiction is becoming a more and more popular part of the magazine. There is even some possibility of using more than one story per issue in the future. Circulation: 1.5 million.

GETTING PUBLISHED: Rates: $1250; goes as high as $1500 for a known writer. Payment: on acceptance. Rights: first North American serial. Reply time: two months or longer. Guidelines: available.

An estimated 100 unsolicited manuscripts are submitted every week. In the last two years or so, one story from the slush pile has been published. Most *Mademoiselle* fiction is chosen from agents' submissions.

Manuscripts are opened and read by one of the fiction assistants. Stories with cover letters listing credits are read first, but everything is read. First readers are encouraged to pass anything with even a hint of promise to Schneider. The number of stories that Schneider reads varies tremendously. Some weeks there might be none; six or seven is probably the top figure. Schneider's choices are read by the articles editor and the editor-in-chief, both of whom have to approve before a story is purchased. Very few manuscripts make it this far.

Rewrites are asked for only if the problems are minor and the editors are very sure they want the story. Schneider adds that she would never turn down a fine piece because it was written by a man, but that "*Mademoiselle* is a woman's magazine and I like the idea of making it a forum of the best from women writers."

Mademoiselle works on a six-month lead time, and Schneider tries to use stories as soon after that as possible. But space limitations can make the publication wait stretch out much longer.

Mademoiselle runs a yearly short-story contest for writers 18-30 years old whose work has not previously been published in a magazine with a circulation over 25,000. Each entrant is allowed to submit one original story under 5000 words. First prize is $750 plus publication in the magazine. Second prize is $300. The dates of the contest and other entry requirements are announced in the magazine; the contest usually closes in mid-March. For further details contact *Mademoiselle*.

THE STORY: "Most of the submissions we get," Schneider says, "are from people who are not writers. Something has happened to them; they have a story to tell of death or violence or love. They put it down on paper as a way to deal with it. These people don't read; they don't study writing. They are not for us.

"Most of the stories we do publish deal with young women involved in the search for identity. In the 1980s, the old rules don't work anymore. Women are searching for ways to be, in work and relationships. We want thoughtful and provoking stories."

Mood pieces, character sketches, or vignettes are not automatically rejected. But Schneider suggests that these are harder to do than stories. "It's a mistake," she says, "for a writer just starting out and struggling to get published to make things harder for herself by submitting these kinds of work."

Some of the authors recently published whose work Schneider particularly liked include Janette T. Hospital, Linda Arking, Jane Smiley, and Susan Harper.

The stories of these writers have in common the sensitivity of their main character. She may be a young woman with a glamorous job, or a young Navy wife. She may be struggling with unrequited love or watching someone else's struggle. She may have gone through a terrible fire and be waiting for the bandages to come off her face. In every case, she is a woman whose inner life is as important as her outer. She is a person in touch with her feelings. She tries to use her intelligence to make sense out of what is going on in and around her, and she is closely observed as she does it. These are very much stories of the inner landscape of the person who might read *Mademoiselle*.

The one unsolicited story published in the period 1981–82 was "The Secret Lives of Dieters," by Perri Klass (July '82). "It's a nice story," Schneider comments. "It's steeped in the reality of concrete detail, and characters are deeply related in secret and subtle ways." The story since has won an O. Henry Award.

One other point that helped the story: It was short. *Mademoiselle* will read longer stories, but over 20 manuscript pages is hard to sell because of space limitations. The editors are glad to see shorter pieces.

REJECTION: Almost all stories are returned with a standard printed form. In a small number of cases, Schneider will write back to an author and either ask for a revision and resubmission on spec or ask to see further work. "I don't do this lightly," Schneider says. "It's not fair to encourage a writer for work that is only mediocre. Nor do we want to see stories from people whom there is very little chance we will ever publish."

McCALL'S

230 Park Avenue
New York, NY 10017
(212) 551-9500

SOURCE: Helen DelMonte, fiction editor

IN SHORT: Uses a lot of agented material; open to new writers

ABOUT THE MAGAZINE: Monthly; uses one or two stories an issue. *McCall's* editors describe their readers as sophisticated, active women. The median age is 37 (editorial material often slanted for younger reader); the audience is heavily suburban, married, with children. Approximately one-half work outside their homes. There is a strong commitment to fiction at the magazine. Circulation: 6.2 million.

GETTING PUBLISHED: Rates: $1250 for a short-short, $1500 for a short story. Payment: on acceptance. Rights: first North American serial. Reply time: four to eight weeks. Guidelines: available.

Close to 150 unsolicited manuscripts come in every week. "In 1982, five of the fiction contributors originally came to us by sending an over-the-transom submission," fiction editor Helen DelMonte says. "Three are now represented by agents.

"Though agents are our largest source, many no longer handle short stories. Many writers, even established writers, handle their own short-story submissions. We're not sure of the reason, but we're finding more talent in slush then we once did."

Stories are read by freelance readers and the assistant fiction editor. Their choices, usually somewhere between 15 to 20 a month, go to DelMonte. Stories she likes go to the managing editor and then to the editor-in-chief for approval before purchase.

DelMonte emphasizes that the freelance readers are carefully chosen. They are often writers themselves who understand what the magazine needs.

A cover letter is important only if it lists professional credits. A résumé detailing the writer's nonwriting life is not of interest.

There is no in-house rewriting at *McCall's*. But editors are willing to cut a too-lenthy piece and work with the writer on a revision. Lead time is four months and the illustration process takes time, so count on about six months (sometimes longer) from purchase to publication.

THE STORY: *McCall's* needs short-short stories with a 2000-word top, and longer pieces averaging between 3000 and 5000 words. Short pieces tend to be lighter than longer ones, but all stories have believable story lines. "Stories are not divorced from reality," DelMonte says. "There is no subject that is automatically taboo if it is handled well. But a writer trying to break in should avoid sending a piece on incest or homosexuality."

McCall's wants subjects that relate to their readers' lives. Stories must provide a sense of recognition and have characters the reader cares about.

The quality that *McCall's* looks for is a fine sense of detail, writing that makes characters and situations come alive. There is no place for experimental exercises, slight mood pieces, or sketches. Substantial stories with recognizable characters and situations are needed. Endings do not have to be happy, but they should be positive, affording a sense of hope and affirmation. Something should happen that gives the characters insight into themselves. Stories should have a discernible point.

McCall's would "love to have more love stories," DelMonte says. She adds that those are precisely the stories that are very difficult to do in a fresh way.

A recent story pulled out of the slush pile and published was "Seventeenth Summer," by John Kilgore (July '82). It concerns a father's disapproval of his teenage daughter's first serious love. It's not a particularly original plot, but the treatment is fresh. The focus is not so much on the daughter as on the father and what the episode makes him realize about himself. "The story is written with a keen observation," DelMonte says. "The situation is one that readers can easily identify with. The father exasperates us, but we care about him."

Most stories at *McCall's* are rejected because of poor writing and familiar themes that are handled with no freshness or insight.

REJECTION: For most manuscripts there is a standard rejection form. If there is anything about a piece that stands out, or if a writer is considered to have potential, editors will ask to see more work. "Very often," DelMonte says, "the first submission is not the perfect story. It is the second or third we take." If there is a specific small problem with a story, the editors will sometimes ask for a rewrite on spec.

MOMENT/FORTHCOMING

Moment:
462 Boylston Street
Boston, MA 02116
(617) 536-6252

Forthcoming:
P. O. Box 11210
Tel Aviv, Israel

SOURCE: Nechama Katz, assistant editor, *Moment;*
Nessa Rapoport, associate editor, *Forthcoming*

IN SHORT: Not very open market

ABOUT THE MAGAZINES: *Moment* is published ten times a year
and uses three to four stories a year. *Forthcoming* is published
twice a year. *Moment* covers a variety of aspects of Jewish life
here and in Israel. "Its goal is to contribute to the development,
examination, and celebration of Jewish life, to inform and to
enrich Jewish debate." The magazine is open to stories of high
literary merit on Jewish subjects, but fiction is not a top priority.
Circulation: 25,000. Sample copy: $2.50.

Forthcoming is an editorially independent magazine published twice a year (Jan./Feb., July/Aug.) in partnership with
Moment and sent to *Moment*'s subscribers. *Forthcoming*'s editor, David Rosenberg, works in Israel. The magazine is heavily
fiction-and-poetry-oriented, but has a small staff and is not
geared for the handling of unsolicited submissions from unknown writers. Further, the magazine's editorial plan calls for
concentrating on well-known authors.

GETTING PUBLISHED: *Moment* only: Rates: $100-$400, depending
on length, complexity, writer, and subject. Payment: on publication. Rights: first North American serial. Reply time: three to
eight weeks. Guidelines: available.

Moment's fiction is generally chosen from the unsolicited submissions. Assitant editor Nechama Katz reads all manuscripts
(about ten a week) and gives possibilities to the managing editor
and editor. She adds that many weeks nothing is good enough to
pass on and it is rare for more than one story a week to be
seriously considered.

A cover letter is found helpful, and Katz would prefer writers unsure of the suitability of their work to send a query before submitting a manuscript.

Because fiction is not used in every issue, publication can be slow to follow purchase. Three to six months is an average wait, but it can go one to two years.

THE STORY: "Fiction is not a top priority at *Moment*," Katz says. "We feel no obligation to print it every issue. But we do feel a need for Israeli (Hebrew) fiction to be read more widely, so we are particularly partial to such fiction in translation. We do feel that a percentage of our readers enjoy (and read) fiction, so we are happy to use stories that contribute to our goal of adding to Jewish discussion and debate. Also we are trying to celebrate Jewish culture in all its different manifestations, and fiction certainly has a place in this."

Editors will consider "anything that expresses some aspect of Jewish life in a *fresh* way." They are open to traditional and more experimental approaches. They are looking for literary distinction as opposed to formula ethnic stories.

Katz cites "Wheels of the World," by Amnon Shamosh (Jan./ Feb. '82). "Shamosh is a respected Israeli writer, and *Moment* is committed to publication of Israeli fiction in America. It is a charming story about a period of time which many of us know little of." "Me Tor Nisht," by Lori Lefkovitz, was published in March 1982. "She writes well and we are happy to publish someone who has great promise but isn't yet published. And the story adds something to discussion of Judaism/womanness and how Jewish women can find a place for themselves within Judaism, but as women."

Stories should run around 3500 words; the magazine will accept longer works only in exceptional cases.

Forthcoming is a magazine of "Jewish Imaginative Writing." In the first issue, the editors wrote: "The authors in *Forthcomings*'s first issue are not unknown writers looking for a place to publish. Their books are on the trade market. What is unique is that they have never been published together. Put side by side, something is being said that goes unheard when each author appears in isolation."

Included are both Israeli and American writers. The editors see "a renewed interest on both sides to explore a common past.

Forthcoming will bring together the best of these writers, who until now remain scattered." The magazine's intention is "to broaden the audience for this generation's forthcoming books— as a way of building a place for the younger generation to emerge."

Nessa Rapoport adds, "We are very unlikely to publish an unsolicited story from an unknown writer."

REJECTION: *Moment* does use a standard rejection form, but Katz will write to authors whose work the editors admire.

MS.

119 West 40th Street
New York, NY 10018
(212) 719-9800

SOURCE: Rhoda Katerinsky, editorial research

IN SHORT: Specialized, high-quality market

ABOUT THE MAGAZINE: Monthly; between 12 and 24 pieces of fiction a year—including reprints, excerpts, condensations, and children's stories. *Ms.* is dedicated to the serious consideration of women's self-awareness, their changing roles in society, the reasons for the changes, and their consequences. Like all women's magazines, *Ms.* assumes a woman who is challenging old ideas and stereotypes and is looking for a fulfilling way to live in a world that often insists on traditional values.

Ms. fiction has been nominated for national magazine awards. In 1981, Scribner's published a short-story collection, *Fine Lines: The Best of Ms. Fiction;* there is a special fiction issue every year as well as a fiction contest for college students. Circulation: 500,000.

GETTING PUBLISHED: Rates: pays competitive rates. Payment: on acceptance. Rights: first North American serial. Reply time: four to six weeks. Guidelines: available.

Ms. receives approximately 75-100 unsolicited stories a week. In the past several years, two of those have been published. Most of the fiction comes from agents' submissions and contacts with well-known writers.

Still, all manuscripts are read, and read seriously. Any story addressed to "The Editors" goes to the unsolicited-submissions department for a first reading. Possibilities are passed around to other editors. If three or four people like a story, it goes to Suzanne Braun Levine, who makes the final decision.

Editors take care of their own mail. If you know the work of someone at *Ms.* and want her to read your story, it only needs a name on the envelope. In the end, the story still must go the rounds of several editors.

Publication is apt to follow purchase within six months to a year.

THE STORY: "Discovering new voices has always been a priority at *Ms.* In the first five years we published many new writers and poets, including Erica Jong, Ntosoke Shange, Alice Walker, Mary Gordon. Many were published for the first time in *Ms.*"

Editors want stories about a woman's understanding of herself, dealings with the world, growth, pain, and so on. *Ms.* prints neither true-life cries of pain disguised as fiction nor political arguments dressed up as fiction. The editors want stories exhibiting artistry and craft on a highly literate level.

What is not wanted is "women's fiction"; its typical subjects—romance, aging marriages, dealing with adolescents—are acceptable, but they have to be handled as the complex subjects they are. There is no place for that rosy outlook that assumes all problems can be solved and "all's well with the world." Further, *Ms.* stories are about women who are interesting as individuals, not only in their roles as wife or mother.

Every year *Ms.* runs a short-story contest for college (and graduate school) students. The winning entry is published. (Check with the magazine for rules and dates.)

The winner of the 1982 competition was Shannon Richards for her story "Granny's Boy" (Sept. '82). It tells of the meeting between an angry, disaffected black woman and a child who has lost his grandmother and is now in the care of the state. He is obsessed with religion; she wants only to be left alone. Without sentimentality, the characters reach each other in deep ways.

Ms. also runs a feature called "Stories for Free Children." These pieces recognize that young girls are as adventurous, energetic, and intelligent as young boys are supposed to be, and that they have ahead of them the same range of opportunities. A lovely example can be found in the August 1982 issue: "Need a House? Call Ms. Mouse!" by George Mendoza, illustrated by Doris Susan Smith. It's about a mouse architect who builds wonderful homes for all the creatures in the forest.

REJECTION: There is a standard rejection form. But there are many reasons why editors might write back personally. First, if a work is admired, if more work should be sent, or if a rewrite, on spec, is wanted. But *Ms.* also receives a tremendous amount of writing described as "a cry of pain thinly disguised as a story." In these cases, editors try to make some kind of personal response.

THE NEW YORKER

25 West 43rd Street
New York, NY 10036
(212) 840-3800

SOURCE: One of the fiction editors

IN SHORT: A possibility for very few writers

ABOUT THE MAGAZINE: Weekly; over 100 stories a year. *The New Yorker* is a national magazine based in New York City. *The New Yorker* has been and is the home of a distinguished group of writers and editors, and there has always been a certain mystique and an anecdotal quality about its workings and practices.

The New Yorker is a dense magazine, to be read, not merely browsed through. Art stands on its own merit, not as illustrations for articles or stories, and text is not considered in need of illustrations to explain it or make it more alluring. There is a feeling in *The New Yorker*'s pages that writing can and does have power all by itself. Editors' names are not listed in the masthead. There are six editors who handle fiction; one of them was interviewed for this book. In keeping with the magazine's policy of editorial anonymity, he asked that his name not be used. Circulation: over 500,000.

GETTING PUBLISHED: Rates: payment is according to a word rate; editors prefer not to specify the exact amount, but say it is very good. Payment: described as very quick. Rights: author can request return of copyright; the magazine's permissions department will act as the writer's intermediary on reprints, with all payments going to the writer. Reply time: generally two to eight weeks. Guidelines: none available.

There are 200 to 300 unsolicited stories addressed "To the Editors" submitted every week. Others come in addressed to specific editors by name. In a year, anywhere from none to ten slush-pile stories might be purchased.

New Yorker fiction is most often written by past contributors, though these writers can have a piece turned down if the editors don't think it's right for the magazine. Work is rarely solicited, though editors do read the literary reviews and sometimes follow up on an impressive piece of work. There is a commitment to publishing new writers. There was a time when *The New Yorker* was not finding a lot of new fiction, and the number of new contributors was low. In recent years that number has risen. Now, out of 110 or so stories, anywhere from 10 to 20 may be by writers who have not previously published in *The New Yorker*.

The processing of a story depends on the name on the envelope. If it is addressed "To the Editor" or "To the Fiction Editors," it goes to one of the readers who work for the magazine. If it is addressed, by name, to one of the fiction editors, it goes directly to that person. Readers are described as "experienced and conscientious"; their instructions are to pass along to the editors anything that shows promise. The story then might be circulated among the editors, who add written comments. Eventually, if there is a chance that a story is good enough to be taken, the story and the written comments about it go to the editor-in-chief, who has the final say. Readers might write back to an author, but encouraging letters are not written lightly. Care is taken not to raise hopes too high.

If an editor likes a story sent directly to him, he circulates it, collects comments on it, and, if there is a generally positive response, passes it to the editor-in-chief. If a writer sells a second piece to the magazine it is usual for him to continue working with the same editor. When an editor rejects a story that has been sent directly to him, the reply may be anything from strong encouragement to something like "Thank you, but no," or even a rejection slip.

A cover letter listing previous publications does not change the handling of a manuscript by moving it past the readers. As far as cover letters are concerned generally, the advice was: "Avoid lengthy self-introduction. There is nothing wrong with no cover letter. It makes no difference in the evaluation of the story. The work is what you are offering, and that's all that has to be enclosed."

Editors do not usually encourage major revisions and resubmissions for the simple reason that they rarely work. "Significant overhauls tend not to work, and everyone ends up feeling bad. An editor might say, 'Look, this has serious problems, but there is some good stuff here. If you want to take the risk of revision, we'll look at it again.' The tendency is away from stories needing a great deal of work." Small changes are asked for, and humor—

much wanted—is agreed to be a slightly more editable form than serious fiction.

The time between acceptance of a story and publication can vary from two months to a year. It depends on the amount of editing involved, the size of the inventory, the length of the piece, and so on. A writer's wishes on the subject are taken into account.

THE STORY: *The New Yorker* publishes both serious and light high-quality fiction. Regular contributors include (or have included) John Updike, John Cheever, Donald Barthelme, Ann Beattie, Jorge Luis Borges, Isaac Bashevis Singer, J.D. Salinger, Frederick Barthelme, Bill Barich, Ursula K. LeGuin, Edna O'Brien, V.S. Pritchett, Mavis Gallant, Raymond Carver, Bobbie Ann Mason, Woody Allen.

The editor interviewed for this book spoke of wanting to be surprised by a story. He admires stories that make him look at the world in a new way. "Good fiction makes you see things differently. Every writer's perspective is different, and he must make it become part of the reader's own world view. And the writer has to have not only an original or distinctive way of looking at things but also a true one. I guess we're asking for a thinker, an observer, and an artist in one person."

A lot of the stories submitted are written in styles popularly but mistakenly identified with the magazine. One is the story without affect. Sparse prose, alienated characters, and the premise that the world is incomprehensible and neither characters, writer, nor reader should be expected to make any sense out ot it—all these characterize many submissions by writers who are trying to tailor their work for *The New Yorker*. The inconclusive ending is another device popularly but mistakenly attributed to the magazine's fiction.

There are a number of subjects that are done and done again in submissions. They are not necessarily played out, but they are so frequently written about that it is hard to come up with something new to say about them. Without originality of subject, style has to bear an even larger burden. Among the familiar types: first-person family reminiscences; terminal cancer; aging parent; boy meets girl; coming of age. Further, a lot of this material was described as strictly autobiographical in feeling. The events in the story never transcend the writer's personal experience and so fail to become part of the reader's life. They contain no original insights and observations about human existence in general.

Use of profanity and graphic sex will not cause a story to be automatically rejected, but their use is definitely the exception. "We use such material only when it is powerful and entirely justified."

Length varies from 250 or 500 words to novellas.

PEN SYNDICATED FICTION PROJECT

% National Endowment for the Arts Literature Program
Washington, DC 20506
(202) 634-1558

SOURCE: Donna Phillips, project coordinator

IN SHORT: Originally funded for one year; check with NEA for project status and eligibility requirements

ABOUT THE PROJECT: The Syndicated Fiction Project is designed to encourage the use of fiction in newspapers by making quality short stories readily available to interested editors. The project chooses the material, pays for it, and offers it to newspapers participating in the program. The project was made possible by a special agreement between NEA and PEN American Center. In its first year manuscripts were read between Feb. 21, 1983, and Mar. 11, 1983, with publication of chosen stories begun in June. The project was open only to writers with NEA grants or who are members of PEN. However, project coordinator Donna Phillips does hope the program will be extended for at least another year and that eligibility will be widened to include more writers.

Authors who are interested in the program must check with the NEA for information as to its status and eligibility requirements. Manuscripts sent in before or after designated reading times or by writers not eligible for the program will be returned unread.

GETTING PUBLISHED: In its first year, 104 stories were chosen to be submitted to newspapers. The selections were made by a panel of four writers including Russell Baker, Ann Beattie, Robert Stone, and Kurt Vonnegut, Jr. Each of the judges chose 26 stories. Every month, each of the newspapers participating in the project received eight stories to read. From these they chose two to four to publish. Winning authors were paid $500 on selection by the panel with an additional $50 paid for each newspaper that accepted the story.

Phillips commented that in preparing the project it was found that there was a broad, though not universal, movement toward using fiction in newspapers, with many editors feeling it was appropriate. In press releases about the project it is noted that

Charles Dickens, Bret Harte, O. Henry, Mark Twain, F. Scott Fitzgerald, Langston Hughes, and John Steinbeck all published fiction in newspapers. Frank Conroy, novelist and director of the endowment's Literature Program, commented, "Through the early part of this century, fiction flourished in newspapers. The rise of magazines ended that long tradition. The current decline of general audience magazines in this country suggests that a return to the original system is appropriate. Both newspapers and writers will benefit."

PENTHOUSE

909 Third Avenue
New York, NY 10022
(212) 593-3301

SOURCE: Kathryn Green, fiction editor

IN SHORT: More interested in novel excerpts; difficult market

ABOUT THE MAGAZINE: Monthly; uses three to four short stories a year; nine novel excerpts. *Penthouse* is an entertainment magazine for men 18-34 years old, with the heaviest concentration of readers in the 25-34 group; 54% of the readers are single. The education figures are 33% high school, 32% some college, 20% college graduate. The readership is predominantly white-collar, with 38% blue-collar. The magazine covers a range of subjects of interest to men, including investigative reporting, service features, and celebrity interviews. These are combined with sexually explicit photo spreads. Circulation: 5,350,000 worldwide.

GETTING PUBLISHED: Rates: competitive with top magazines. Payment: on acceptance. Rights: world rights. Reply time: within a month. Guidelines: none available.

Penthouse is more interested in novel excerpts from known writers of entertaining fiction—Jimmy Breslin, Gael Greene—than short stories.

Still, editors do read everything that comes in unsolicited. "From an editor's point of view, it's the best part of the job," says fiction editor Kathryn Green. "The hope that you will find something good. It is true the odds are not good for getting published in *Penthouse,* but if one writer gets a start, can find an agent, begin a career, it's worth it."

Approximately 60 unsolicited manuscripts are submitted every week. In 1982, one of those made it into the magazine.

The slush pile is read by an editorial assistant, who passes the possibilities to Green. She estimates she sees maybe three unsolicited stories a month. The few pieces she likes are given to the managing editor. Most of the short fiction, like the novel excerpts, is from known writers and submitted through agents.

Once a story is purchased, it should be in print in six months to a year.

THE STORY: "The fiction in *Penthouse* is not pornography, soft-core or otherwise," Green says. "We are looking for quality, sophisticated fiction. It doesn't even have to be sexual in theme. We are not particularly looking for humor, but a lighter tone is more salable than gloom.

"We like to run fiction about active men in the world, rather than introspective men. We want the male point of view, a balance between action and narrative and strong characters. We want men grappling with concrete problems that have real solutions. The problems can be with women, but that is only one alternative. We want professional-caliber stories that are fun, interesting, and make the reader think."

What *Penthouse* does not want, and gets too much of in its slush pile, is personal experience thinly disguised as fiction. A man meets a pretty girl, has a few drinks with her, and an odd sexual experience that really affects him, writes it up, and sends it off to *Penthouse*. "This is not a story," Green says. "It's not crafted. Some of these manuscripts even come in handwritten." Green also mentions that more experienced writers make a similar mistake in sending pieces that are reveries about, or descriptions of, sexual experiences that, no matter how well done, are not crafted stories.

Penthouse is open to mysteries, science fiction, and other genre types.

The one story taken off the slush pile recently was "The Victorian," by Stephen Wolf (Sept. '82). It was chosen, says Green, partly because of its very unusual subject. It's the story of T. J. Phelps, a gymnast obsessed with physical prowess and being the best. His goal is the Victorian, a trick on the rings long dreamed of but never accomplished. He brutalizes his body to master the feat; his mind comes through with a trick of its own in response. "A first-person narrative, it draws you in with a sparse style and no unnecessary words," Green says.

Penthouse can use stories from 3000 to 6000 words.

REJECTION: Most unsolicited manuscripts are rejected with a standard printed form. Green writes back to an author only if she admires a story very much and either wants to see more work or to suggest another market. However, the assistant editor writes back frequently, explaining the rejection and perhaps suggesting further submissions.

PLAYBOY

919 North Michigan Avenue
Chicago, IL 60611
(312) 751-8000

SOURCE: Alice K. Turner, fiction editor

IN SHORT: Difficult and not very open market

ABOUT THE MAGAZINE: Monthly; averages two stories an issue. *Playboy* is a magazine for men 18-35 years old. The reader is usually urban, white-collar, well-to-do, and educated. Circulation: 5 million.

GETTING PUBLISHED: Rates: $1000 for under 1200 words; $2000 base rate for longer pieces; actual fee depends on how steady a contributor the writer is expected to be. Payment: on acceptance. Rights: all rights until publication; holds an option for sale to foreign editions. Reply time: tries for a month. Guidelines: available.

About 80 unsolicited short-story manuscripts arrive at *Playboy*'s offices every day. These are immediately divided into two piles. Those from unpublished writers go to freelance readers. Those with a cover letter listing previous publications are read by a staff editor. In the past two years, fiction editor Alice Turner says, nothing has been bought from the unpublished-writer submissions.

Sales have been made, however, by unagented, published writers with no previous connection to the magazine. "*Playboy* constantly publishes new writers," Turner says. "We are hoping to find people with whom we can establish a regular working relationship."

Though cover letters are important, there is no advantage to including a long biography. Only professional writing credits or degrees from well-known writing workshops count.

Turner says most unsolicited submissions are not from real writers—people who work at it on a regular basis. She adds this category includes not only the insurance executive who has had an interesting experience, but also the university professor who thinks general literacy is enough to produce a good story. "We are not interested in hobbyists," Turner says.

"Their work generally lacks the professional patina of a *Playboy* piece."

Playboy has often published stories from people who write regularly in addition to doing another job—for instance, professors. "But what an editor really wants," Turner says, "is a partner, someone to work with, to count on to send in first-class stories on a regular basis."

Once a story is accepted, publication can be slow to follow. Lead time is four to six months; frequent book excerpts geared to meet publication dates can hold up short stories. A year's publication wait is not uncommon, and it might go longer.

THE STORY: "Thirty years ago when Hugh Hefner started *Playboy*," Turner says, "he wanted naked girls, but he wanted respectability too. Quality fiction was the way to get it. We still make that effort. We look for serious, quality stories on contemporary life and pure entertainment pieces, including genre fiction. Even the entertainment has to be done on a highly skilled, fast-paced level.

"A writer who wants to know about *Playboy* fiction might look at the stories of Paul Theroux." Donald Westlake is another first-class *Playboy* contributor. "Light, frothy, but skillful," Turner says. "A real old-fashioned storyteller."

Playboy wants stories; it is not interested in mood pieces, sketches, vignettes, or extremely experimental prose. Pornographic fiction is not published. At the same time, it is a men's magazine and it does cover subjects and themes of interest to men. Turner would be happy to publish more women writers, but finds they rarely submit the kind of story *Playboy* needs.

There is a 7500-word maximum length. Turner suggests that length is something a new writer trying to interest *Playboy* should consider. "We use two pieces of fiction every issue," she says. "One is apt to be a major piece from a well-known writer. Sometimes there is not enough room left for another long short story. Shorter pieces are very welcome."

REJECTION: The vast majority of stories submitted by unpublished writers are rejected with a form letter. Stories from published writers are usually rejected with a personal letter: "A courtesy to professional writers." Editors take a great deal of time to encourage writers they think are promising. "I correspond with several writers from whom I have never bought a story, but whose work I admire," Turner says. "I think every editor has writers he is spending time on, nursing along, just because they have so much talent." Turner will also occasionally suggest other markets for a piece *Playboy* cannot use.

PLAYGIRL

3420 Ocean Park Boulevard
Suite 3000
Santa Monica, CA 90405
(213) 450-0900

SOURCE: Mary Ellen Strote, fiction editor

IN SHORT: Very open to new writers; does not publish pornographic fiction

ABOUT THE MAGAZINE: Monthly; average of 14 stories a year. A woman's version of a man's sex/pinup magazine. The focus is on men, in words and pictures. But *Playgirl* also does entertainment features and celebrity interviews, researched exposé articles, offbeat self-help pieces, fashion, beauty, and, occasionally, recipes. The readers are 18-40 years old; half are married; half have children. They are interested in sensuality and sexuality. Circulation: approximately 850,000.

GETTING PUBLISHED: Rates: $500-$600 for longer stories; from $250 for a very short piece. Payment: within 30 days of receipt of signed contract. Rights: one-time English language. Reply time: six to eight weeks; longer if a story is being considered. Guidelines: none.

Approximately 150 unsolicited stories are submitted every month. Each year, six or seven of them make it into the magazine, accounting for half the published fiction.

"We are a wonderful market for a new writer," fiction editor Mary Ellen Strote says. "We are very open to the offbeat story, something a little different that might not fit in at other magazines."

A practical consideration adds to *Playgirl*'s openness. Editors want the kind of quality found in the top magazines but do not quite match the top prices.

Strote reads every submission. She estimates that 50 to 60 stories a year are good enough to consider for publication. Stories Strote likes are read by the editor-in-chief, who makes the final decisions.

Strote is interested in a cover letter listing credits, awards, or other credentials. "When you read over 30 manuscripts a day," she says, "you get jaded. If a letter says the writer has published in a prestigious literary journal, it wakes you up."

In theory, Strote does not like to ask for rewrites, but admits to having done so three or four times this year. "Sometimes something in a story is fabulous," she says, "with wonderful suspense developed. You turn the page and find it has all trickled off into some esoteric graduate school ending. I will ask for a new ending."

Strote will also ask an author for minor deletions when there is too much explicit sex or violence. All rewrites are on spec.

Publication usually follows within six months of acceptance.

THE STORY: "People think *Playgirl* wants graphic sex in its fiction," Strote says. "This is not true. There is enough of that in the magazine. We don't want violence, we don't want raw sex, we don't want anything scatalogical, no child abuse or molestation, no murder, no science fiction, no mysteries, no Westerns."

Strote complains that she gets too much material from men that is nothing more than distasteful male sexual fantasy about victimizing women. She will use no story in which a woman is physically brutalized. If she uses a story on rape, it is how a woman was strong enough or clever enough to avoid it.

Writers published in *Playgirl* include Thomas Tryon, Tennessee Williams, Anais Nin, Alice Adams, Margaret Drabble, and others of equal caliber.

"We have published many writers, for instance Jane Smiley and Raymond Carver, who have gone on to win awards and appear regularly in prestigious magazines. It is a fact we are proud of."

Playgirl wants stories with a strong story line, preferably but not necessarily told through a woman's eyes and, again preferably, with an upbeat ending.

Most stories are about human relationships, particularly about contemporary male/female relationships: romance in a world in which old rules no longer apply. There is an openness to sensuality and sexually liberated characters. Humor is much welcomed.

But Strote makes it clear that there is room for the offbeat story —the one that steps even further away from usual women's fiction.

"Generic Love," by Maureen McCoy (Nov. '82), is a manic,

hysterical romp about a sexually obsessed woman chaser who "does it in the road" and everywhere else till he meets a woman who is more than his match. "Made me laugh out loud," Strote says.

In "The Elephant Story," by O. Henry winner Daniel Asa Rose (Apr. '82), a young woman introduces her new boyfriend to her father, a man who has suffered a stroke and has nothing left but his daughter. The meeting takes place at the breakfast table, where the father informs the young couple that when he closes his eyes he sees elephants—elephants marching, roaming free, in zoos, mutilated and starving to death. In a strange way, the old man's bizarre fantasies bring the young people closer together. "I bought this story because it was startling and touching," Strote says.

The fiction editor at *Playgirl* has had four pages to fill every month as a self-contained section (eight in December; none in June). However, management is considering moving fiction to the body of the magazine. Strote will read stories up to 4000 words. She prefers stories running from 1000 to 3500 words.

REJECTION: Standard form used. Strote is careful about encouraging writers: "Once you say a kind word they begin to inundate you with material." Still, if she likes a story that is not right for *Playgirl*, she will write. Or if she sees something good in a piece not up to publication, she will ask for more work. If a story has been at all seriously considered for publication, she will tell the author.

REDBOOK

230 Park Avenue
New York, N.Y. 10169
(Watch out for possible address change)
(212) 850-9373

SOURCE: Mimi Jones, fiction editor

IN SHORT: Welcomes new writers

ABOUT THE MAGAZINE: Monthly; number of stories per month varies. In 1982 *Redbook* was acquired by Hearst. Subsequently there were changes in staff and editorial emphasis, including changes in the fiction. *Redbook* now has allotted 16 magazine pages to fiction each month, accommodating around 100 manuscript pages. Occasionally the space will be used for a condensed novel, but more often for a combination of original short stories, novellas and novel excerpts. The mix of the different types of fiction will vary month to month. Fiction editor Mimi Jones says that issues carrying only condensed novels and no stories or excerpts will be rare.

Readers are between the ages of twenty and forty, but the editors describe their target reader as a young woman in her twenties, who either is married or may expect to be in the future, who has children or plans to, and who is working or has worked outside the home. Since the *Redbook* reader is a bright, well-informed woman, whose interests are varied, she is not solely concerned with fiction that affects her own life. *Redbook*'s fiction may be about a wide variety of situations and characters.

Redbook twice has been winner of the National Magazine Award for fiction and has had many selections in *The O. Henry Award Prize Collections* and *The Best American Short Stories*. Fiction is a favorite feature among the magazine's readers. Circulation: 3.8 million.

GETTING PUBLISHED: Rates: $850 for an unsolicited short-short; $1000-$1500 for first short story purchase. Payment: on acceptance. Rights: first North American serial. Reply time: four to six weeks for a first reading. Guidelines: available

Fiction editor Mimi Jones estimates that one-third to one-half of the stories published in *Redbook* come directly from the slush pile or come from authors who originally came to the attention of the editors in the slush pile. Approximately 36,000 unsolicited manuscripts are received a year.

All stories are seriously considered. Each of the editors in the fiction department devotes some time to reading unsolicited stories. *Redbook* also uses freelance readers, "but only after they have passed a strenuous reading test," Jones says. If a story is liked, it will receive several readings within the fiction department before going on to the editor-in-chief who makes all final decisions on purchases.

Cover letters are not necessary. The story will be judged on its own merits. If you do wish to send a letter, include only fiction credits. Only those stories accompanied by self-addressed stamped envelopes large enough for the manuscript will be returned. If an SASE is not included, you will not hear from the magazine unless editors are interested in buying the story. Manuscripts should be addressed to the Fiction Department.

Most stories are scheduled for publication within a year of purchase. Prior to publication, galleys are sent to the author.

THE STORY: *Redbook* is open to a wide variety of types of stories. Since the magazine is targeted to young women, many of the stories it publishes are about young women and deal with topics of specific interest to them: courtship, marriage, parenthood, in-laws, career situations, money problems, etc.

"We also like to give our readers stories about characters unlike themselves," Jones says. "We feel our readers enjoy having a chance to see the world through someone else's eyes, whether it's a matter of witnessing a marital conflict from the husband's point of view, or seeing life from a treetop with a beekeeper, or getting an insider's view of life among different ethnic and social cultures. A sharp satire, a charming fantasy, a well-done mystery or horror story, can also appeal to us. Such stories must be accessible—that is, they have to provide in the story itself a way for the reader to relate to what is going on, a way for the reader to understand things she might not have been familiar with before the story began."

It is by exposing the reader to something new that *Redbook* differs from other women's magazines. *Redbook* assumes the reader will enjoy an offbeat, ground-breaking story, as well as the more regular kind of story with which she can readily identify.

Pure adventure stories (where plot overshadows characterization), tall-tales, unforgettable-character sketches, and stories with surprise endings, are not likely to find a home at *Redbook*. In the guidelines, editors say that highly oblique or symbolic stories that come to no conclusion and stories with obviously contrived plots will not suit their needs. "A successful story does not have to have a happy ending," Jones says, "and the ending does not have to tie the story up in a neat package. But something should have been resolved by the time the story ends. If we come to the end of a piece of fiction and feel nothing has changed—we haven't learned anything, the characters haven't gained any insights, we haven't grown to care about or understand the characters—then the story has failed for us."

The *Redbook* Novel is a condensation of a full-length novel. Most of the novels published have already been accepted by hardcover book houses; however, editors do read and buy original novels and novellas. For further information, send a SASE to Ficton Guidelines.

Redbook sponsors an annual short-story contest. It is open to women and men, 18 to 28, who have not published fiction in a commercially published book or magazine with a circulation over 25,000. Each entrant is allowed to submit one story, no longer than 20 typed (double-spaced) manuscript pages. For complete rules, see the March issue of the magazine or send a SASE in the spring when copies of the rules will be available. First prize is $1,000, plus $1000 more for publication in the magazine. Second prize is $500; there are three third-prize winners of $250.

The winner of *Redbook*'s Fourth Young Writers Contest was David Downing, whose "Anorexia Machismo" was published in the March, 1982 issue. Catherine Brady's "Home" was the first-prize winner in the Fifth Young Writer's Contest; her story appears in the March, 1983 issue.

Short-shorts run nine manuscript pages or less; short stories are over nine pages and preferably under 20; 15 pages is considered the average length. Longer fiction will be considered, although space limitations make the editors look at it all the more critically.

REJECTION: A standard rejection form is used. About 5 percent of the unsolicited stories are considered good enough to receive notes on the rejection slips or letters from one of the fiction editors. If it is felt that a story might be publishable with further work, the editors offer critical feedback and encourage revision. All revision is on spec.

ROLLING STONE

745 Fifth Avenue
New York, NY 10022

SOURCE: David Rosenthal, managing editor

Rolling Stone is no longer reading unsolicited fiction or carrying short stories on a regular basis. When *Rolling Stone* does publish fiction it will be solicited from regular contributors.

THE SATURDAY EVENING POST

Curtis Publishing Company
1100 Waterway Boulevard
Indianapolis, IN 46202
(317) 634-1100

SOURCE: Ted Kreiter, fiction editor

IN SHORT: Difficult, not very open market

ABOUT THE MAGAZINE: Published nine times a year; one to two stories an issue; may be one story and one short-short.

A general-interest family magazine mixing news, service, and entertainment features. Fiction editor Ted Kreiter describes *The Post* as "upbeat, a little patriotic, and slightly conservative." Readers' median age is under 40. Circulation: 700,000.

GETTING PUBLISHED: Rates: from $500 to $1500, depending on length and author's credentials. Payment: on publication. Rights: either first North American serial or all rights. Reply time: four to six weeks and often faster. Guidelines: available. Simultaneous submissions: editors will read them, but prefer not to receive them.

Over 100 unsolicited manuscripts (fiction and nonfiction) are submitted every week. Kreiter says, "Very, very few of those make it into the magazine; 10% or fewer of what comes in is publishable by anyone. Of those that are of professional caliber, many seem to come from writers who don't look at the magazine. Some would be more appropriate for *Playboy* than a family publication. A lot of them are much too grim and downbeat. Bittersweetness is acceptable, but nothing more. We get a lot of trite material such as the grandmother-in-a-nursing-home story. I would say maybe five stories a week get more than a cursory reading."

Submissions are looked over by an assistant fiction editor. The possibilities are passed to other editors. A cover letter listing credits may make a difference. "However, judging by what we see," Kreiter says, "I think some people must be making the credits up."

Increasing the difficulty of selling to *The Post* are the magazine's archives. *The Post* owns work by William Saroyan, Booth Tarkington, Kurt Vonnegut, Mary Roberts Rhinehart, Ray Bradbury, Shirley Jackson, and others, all from the days when it was the country's leading magazine for contemporary fiction. Readers request reprints of these stories, and at the moment the archives are providing most of the fiction.

Kreiter adds that he still would like to find new writers. There is a possibility of increasing the fiction per issue. He envisages one old and one new story each month. He adds that the slush pile rarely provides the kind of new work he needs.

Seasonal fiction can take up to a year before it is published.

THE STORY: *Post* fiction has to be professional entertainment. Editors are open to Westerns, romance, suspense, humor, science fiction, and mystery. In all genres, they want pacing, plot and characterization. Professional is the key word.

Stories must have clear resolutions that, at least, are upbeat. Kreiter often sees stories that are very readable up till the end. The writer has been working toward a climax and does not fulfill the promise.

Kreiter also sees much competent but lifeless writing. Stories have to touch and involve the reader, and make the reader care about what happens to the characters.

Besides genre fiction, *The Post* likes coming-of-age stories, bridging-the-generation-gap stories, all stories full of positive human feelings. Sentimentality is not out of place. Stories can be about orphans who find abandoned kittens or little boys in hospital charity wards. This kind of writing takes considerable technical expertise. The twin chasms of mawkishness and triteness are easy to fall into.

Stories also must be accessible. Nothing in them should be so difficult—including plot, language, and characters—as to make them more than entertainment. Yet, they should not be simple. The overall effect should be of a highly crafted piece of writing with no excess and no loose ends.

Stories have an upper length of 3000 words.

REJECTION: Standard form used in most cases. Personal letters are sent if the author has worked for *The Post* before or if the editors admire a story they cannot use. Editors may ask for rewrites followed by resubmission.

SUNSHINE

Sunshine Press
Litchfield, IL 62056
(217) 324-3425

SOURCE: Peggy Pinkerton Kuethe, assistant editor

IN SHORT: Open to new writers; important to get sample copy

ABOUT THE MAGAZINE: Monthly; five adult and one children's story per issue. *Sunshine* is a small (5¼ x 7¼), 42-page magazine for family reading, most often subscribed to by an older, retired female. It carries no ads and is available only by subscription. In both its typeface and editorial content, it is easy to read. Each issue includes one personal-experience piece, one reminiscence, ten poems, and a selection of inspirational sayings, meditations, and quotes from famous people. No piece runs over 1200 words. *Sunshine* does not publish overtly religious material, but it is an inspirational magazine promoting traditional concepts of family, Americanism, and the Christian way of life defined as charity, neighborliness, and love. Circulation: 100,000. Sample copy: 50¢.

GETTING PUBLISHED: Rates: $20-$100; the more a story has to be rewritten by editors, the less money. Payment: on acceptance. Rights: first North American serial; reprint rights in other Sunshine Press publications. Reply time: two months. Guidelines: available.

Of the fiction published in *Sunshine*, 60% comes from regular contributors; everything else is from unsolicited submissions.

Approximately 80 stories are submitted every week. Everything is looked at by two readers. Promising pieces, roughly eight a week, are passed to senior editors. Final decisions are made by the director of publications.

Because *Sunshine* uses very simple material, the idea can sometimes be more important than the writing. If a well-conceived but badly written story comes in, the editors might be willing to rewrite, with author approval. If a piece is too long, but otherwise fine, a rewrite might be asked for. Since everything is read, a cover letter is not important.

Assistant editor Peggy Keuthe adds that there is a high turnover of writers and work from new authors is constantly being published. Once a story is purchased, it may be published anytime from five months to a year.

THE STORY: Adult stories should run between 400 and 1200 words, children's stories between 400 and 700. The professional background of many of the writers who successfully submit to *Sunshine* is from youth or religious magazines. Though no overtly religious material is used, the fiction has a clear message that happiness is a function of having proper values and treating fellow beings with tolerance and love. Stories are always about ways in which people, especially family and neighbors, should get along.

The children's stories involve a learning experience for a youngster (4-14), especially through a happy and successful interaction with an adult. Children's material may also include fables, story-type poetry, fantasy or humor, or true-to-life experiences.

Kuethe cites two recent stories as exemplary. In "Summertime Santa," by Carole Joyce Davis (June '82), a couple is called unexpectedly away from home. Their primary worry is the effect of the hot sun on their lovingly tended lawn. They come home to find that a new neighbor, a man they never met, has noticed the problem and been watering their lawn every day. His motive is only goodwill and disinterested friendship. In "A Dance with Father," by Mary Catherine Wilds (July '82), a young, grieving widow is persuaded to go to a community dance by her father. That night on the dance floor, she realizes that she is not really alone.

The stories are simply written, both in vocabulary and structure. There is no room for anything concerning violence, sex, retardation, alcoholism, and so on. *Sunshine* is about a world in which problems come up, but underneath everything is fine.

REJECTION: Standard rejection form. A note will be added if a piece is considered to be promising.

VANITY FAIR

Condé Nast Publications
350 Madison Avenue
New York, NY 10017
(212) 880-8800

When we went to press, *Vanity Fair*—described as "a magazine of literature and the arts, politics and popular culture"—had published only its first couple of issues; the editors felt it was too early to discuss the kinds of fiction submissions that would be considered.

While the first issues contained fiction by name writers, the editors stressed they were planning to read unsolicited submissions and were hoping to use fiction in every issue. All submissions, with SASE included, should be sent to Leo Lerman, editor-in-chief.

In updates of this book, more detailed information will be included. Studying back issues is recommended.

WOMAN'S DAY

1515 Broadway
New York, NY 10036
(212) 719-6492

SOURCE: Eileen Herbert Jordan, books and fiction editor

IN SHORT: Interested in finding new writers, but not a break-in market

ABOUT THE MAGAZINE: Published 15 times a year; has been using nine or ten stories a year (fiction bonus issues in December and August); may use more fiction in the future. *Woman's Day* is a nonsubscription women's magazine with a circulation over 8 million. The typical reader is probably married, probably works, but is essentially a homemaker. Many have children. Age range is broad, but much material is targeted for the early-30s group. The aim is to keep the reader abreast of the newest trends in decorating, exercise, health, beauty, and so on. Eileen Herbert Jordan is actively looking for fiction; she would like to be using more in the magazine, but is not finding the slush pile helpful.

GETTING PUBLISHED: Rates: no published rate scale; meets current market standards. Payment: on acceptance. Rights: first North American serial. Reply time: six weeks.

Jordan estimates that 50% of the fiction comes from agents' submissions, the rest from writers the magazine has worked with for years. The slush pile is considered increasingly important because many writers who could have agents are choosing to represent themselves and agents are increasingly refusing to handle short stories.

Jordan estimates over 4000 unsolicited manuscripts come in every year. Stories have been taken from the slush pile, but almost all have been from previously published writers. Most of the slush has not been of professional caliber. Jordan would like to be seeing more submissions from professional writers.

A manuscript from a writer with credits gets pulled for immediate reading. The rest of the unsolicited pile is shared out among the editors. Any story approved by the first reader goes to Jordan. Her choices are passed to the editor-in-chief.

A writer may have to wait over a year to see a story in print.

THE STORY: In December, three stories with a Christmas theme are regularly run; three stories are again used in August as a "summer reading issue."

Editors are looking for stories women can relate to. They should be entertaining and uplifting. Serious subjects are not taboo, but problems should be resolved and characters should experience some sort of growth either in themselves or in their knowledge of those around them. Violence, unrelieved depression, and obvious sex are all unacceptable. Editors would particularly like to see more humor.

Length is important. Anything over 4000 words can be a problem. Jordan considers between 1500 and 3000 words ideal.

The three stories run in August 1982 are exemplary of *Woman's Day* fiction. "Blood Sisters," by Mary Emblad, is about childhood friends who have gone their separate ways—one to marriage and motherhood, the other to a medical degree and an important job. Six years later they meet again and have to learn how to cope with mutual jealousy and the fact that people do change. "Beauty and the Beast," by Richard Horberg, is about a dog and his human family. When Beast stunningly fails a canine IQ test, his young owners are very distressed. Then their father points out that Beast has other things such as loyalty, warmth, and generosity, perhaps qualities to be preferred over intelligence. "The Oasis," by Gerald Lewis, is a woman's childhood reminiscence following her mother's death. The story focuses on one incident in her family's life: the acquistion of a beautiful pastel-colored rug that created an oasis of softness and loveliness in the family's otherwise hardworking and often hard life. It was the mother who introduced this symbol of a more beautiful world into the family's existence, and it was a simple act that had reverberations through the years.

REJECTION: Most stories are returned with a standard form. If Jordan is impressed with a peice of work she cannot use, she will write and say so, perhaps suggesting another market. If a story has minor problems, editors will suggest changes and a resubmission on spec.

WOMAN'S WORLD

Heinrich Bauer North America, Inc.
177 North Dean Street
Englewood, NJ 07631
(201) 569-0006

SOURCE: Nancy McCarthy, fiction editor

IN SHORT: Excellent break-in market

ABOUT THE MAGAZINE: Weekly; two pieces of fiction an issue. Service magazine sold mostly in supermarkets; directed at low-to-middle-income women who are 25-60 years old. Patterned after a successful German magazine, *Woman's World* began publication in 1981. Circulation is close to 1 million; at present no advertising is carried. The editorial content is targeted at the blue-collar worker's wife. She is probably less affluent and less educated than readers of some of the other women's magazines. She may have a job, but not a career. The magazine is not available in all areas. Sample copy: $1.

GETTING PUBLISHED: Rates: $1200 for stories; $500 for mini-mysteries. Payment: on acceptance. Rights: first North American serial for six months. Reply time: four to eight weeks. Guidelines: available. Simultaneous submissions: acceptable.

Woman's World uses over 100 stories a year, 50% of them from the slush pile, the rest mostly from agents.

Fiction editor Nancy McCarthy receives close to 200 unsolicited manuscripts a week. Because the slush pile is such an important source, she at least looks at all manuscripts herself. She estimates that 80% are immediately rejected because they are not the type of story she needs.

McCarthy passes the possibilities to the editor-in-chief, who makes the final decision. She estimates that one to two stories a week are good enough to pass on.

McCarthy does no major rewriting. If a story has only minor problems she will ask for a rewrite and resubmission on spec. She adds that the magazine has a high turnover of writers and is a good market for the newcomer.

Stories are usually published approximately three months after acceptance.

THE STORY: *Woman's World* needs light romances of approximately 6000 words and mini-mysteries of 2000 words.

A romance should have a heroine no older than 40 who provides a sense of recognition for the reader. The heroine might work, for instance, but she should not be a Wall Street lawyer. The romance can take place in a boy-meets-girl setting, within a marriage, or after a divorce. Story plots are never complex: The heroine has a romantic problem that she solves. In every case, there is a happy ending. Story settings should not be too exotic. Explicit sex, violence, or seamy settings are unacceptable.

Most rejections are due to trite plots. McCarthy lists several that are submitted over and over again: the married woman attending her high school reunion where she will see the exciting basketball star she could have married instead of her dull, steady, but loving husband; the frazzled, drowning-in-babies wife meeting her childhood friend who has a glamorous New York career. Of course, both characters find out they are happier as they are. Further, *Woman's World* does not use any story that demeans a woman. The kind of story that ends: "At last she got what she wanted. A man who would dominate her." Although heroines may consider men the most important part of their lives, they are lively and bright. Freshness and believable characterization is the key.

One romantic story recently published in *Woman's World* tells of a young woman, hurt by love, who is determined to have nothing to do with men. A friend tricks her into taking a vacation at a dude ranch, where she meets a charming cowboy. It turns out the cowboy is the friend's brother and it was all planned. Another story is told from a man's-eye view: He falls in love with a spoiled rich girl, leaving behind a girl of his own background who loves him. He soon realizes he has been seduced by style and given up substance. He makes amends.

These stories are simply written and meant to be nothing more than entertainment.

Mini-mysteries, McCarthy warns, are harder to sell than romances. Because they are short, many writers make the mistake of assuming they are also easy. In fact, it is hard to pack crime, solution, comeuppance, and character development into 2000 words. The major demand on a mini-mystery is a well-worked-out plot. There is no need for romance in the mysteries and the writer is free to use police, private eyes, or sleuthing housewives. The crime does not have to be either murder or attempted murder, but it does have to be major enough to compel interest. A missing loaf of bread will not do.

Minis usually fail, according to McCarthy, because of the ending. It is easy, she says, to set up a challenging situation. But by the end, the situation has to be resolved and all the loose ends tied up. McCarthy mentioned one submission that had her on the edge of her seat as one character after another came into a police station and claimed to have killed a wealthy man. But the story had no ending; it simply faded away in a sort of dream. Put simply, mini-mysteries have to be clever.

REJECTION: Most stories are rejected with a standard printed form. McCarthy estimates that for roughly 12% of the submissions she will add a personal response. She might ask to see more work or enclose guidelines and suggest the writer try again.

YANKEE

Main Street
Dublin, NH 03444
(603) 563-8111

SOURCE: Deborah Navas Karr, fiction editor

IN SHORT: Publishes little-known writers; has a regional slant

ABOUT THE MAGAZINE: Monthly; 12 stories a year. *Yankee* is a general-interest magazine about the northeastern United States. Distribution is national: people interested in New England as well as those who live there. Subjects include history, architecture, antiques, crafts, current politics, and people. The average reader is approximately 54 years old, is more likely to be a woman, is fairly well educated, and has an income in the mid-$20,000 range. *Yankee* is digest-sized and runs approximately 176 pages. Circulation: 950,000. Sample copy: free.

GETTING PUBLISHED: Rates: $750 for first story; $100 raises after each third sale until top price of $950 is reached. Payment: on acceptance. Rights: usually buys all rights but will negotiate. Reply time: standard rejection in two weeks; over a month if the story is being considered. Guidelines: available. Simultaneous submissions: will read.

Yankee receives 30 to 40 unsolicited stories every week. Six of them are likely to make it into the magazine each year. The rest of the published stories come from regular contributors, some of whom made their first sales through the slush pile. *Yankee* occasionally buys from agents, and work is sometimes solicited.

Everything submitted is looked at by a first reader, who passes an estimated four to six stories a week to fiction editor Deborah Karr. This number includes stories from previous contributors, whose work is passed on automatically. Of the six stories Karr might read, one or two will generally be given to other editors. Stories are chosen by staff consensus. "Not everyone has to love a story," Karr says, "but it does take approval from two or three senior editors."

Once a story is sold, publication can take up to a year. Editors try not to prolong it further.

THE STORY: "Fiction is important here," Karr says. "It is only in the last four or five years that we have looked for first-rate literate fiction, as opposed to formula pieces. Ideally, we would like to have a reputation for discovering young New England writers."

While particularly happy to receive a story based in New England from a local writer, editors are open to authors from any part of the country and stories about a wide range of subjects. The only type of writing automatically barred is regional fiction set outside New England.

Other kinds of stories always rejected include women's-magazine formula pieces, stories with explicit sex and/or violence, and trite pieces about stereotypical New England characters.

Yankee editors are most interested in seeing character portrayal and development. They want to read about sensitive, thinking people trying to make sense out of what life has handed them. "Catering," by Elinor Lipman (Oct. '81), is a woman's description of her erring, absent, about-to-return husband whose fatal charm manages to excuse hurtful behavior. "The Appaloosa House," by Sharon S. Stark (Mar. '82), is a daughter's reminiscence of her parents' marriage—her flamboyant, noisy mother and her roaming father, two people who couldn't live together and couldn't stay apart. "Hello, Love, Goodbye," by Peter Meinke (Feb. '82), is the story of a woman confronting her first and still most important love after 17 years. She's a spinster; he's an alcoholic poet. It's for her to decide whether to stay or go. The magazine is also open to humor.

Stories run from 2500 and 4000 words; 3000 words is about ideal.

REJECTION: Standard form used. Karr will write to the author of a rejected piece to express admiration, to ask to see more work, or to suggest a rewrite and resubmission on spec.

The
Specialty
Magazines

The magazines in the following section are specialized. They are written for a narrowly defined audience (teenagers, farm wives, etc.) or they publish only one kind of material (science fiction, mystery, Western). For the unconnected, unagented writer, they are the most accessible type of magazine.

The science fiction, Western, and mystery magazines are almost solely devoted to fiction They use up to ten stories an issue and stand or fall on their quality. The editors need fresh, new material, and the slush pile is very important. Editors take real pains with rejected stories that come close; they are often willing to guide an author through several rewrites. They are hoping not only to find good stories, but to find writers they can count on for regular contributions.

At one magazine (*Analog*) the editor is the first reader. Another (*Amazing*) does not use standard rejection forms. One editor (at *Fantasy and Science Fiction*) points out that at SF conventions writers can meet editors. There is a magazine (*Ellery Queen*) with a department of first stories. The editor of another (*Hitchcock*) says that mystery writing is one of the few forms of fiction that can be done successfully part-time. And so on.

The teen magazines are not as open as the genre publications. But they do have a high turnover of writers. Many of their best pieces come from authors who only occasionally handle teen fiction. Editors are constantly on the lookout for writers who can reach teens without talking down to them.

Other specialty magazines (for farm wives or military wives) have trouble finding authors who can both write a good story and make it believable for the specialized audience. Agents rarely submit to these markets, and editors are always on the lookout for new writers.

The most important hint to reading this section is: Take the listings seriously. If the editor says no sword and sorcery, or no light romances, or no Sherlock Holmes parodies, believe it! Do not tell yourself, "My story is so good that the editor will forget his stupid prejudice and print it anyway." What is much more likely to happen is that the editor will look over the manuscript, see that it is sword and sorcery, or a light romance, or a Holmes parody, and return it *unread*.

ALFRED HITCHCOCK'S MYSTERY MAGAZINE

Davis Publications, Inc.
380 Lexington Avenue
New York, NY 10017
(212) 557-9100

SOURCE: Cathleen Jordan, editor

IN SHORT: Very good break-in market

ABOUT THE MAGAZINE: Published 13 times a year; eight to nine stories an issue.

"Our aim is to publish original fiction concerned with crime and detection," editor Cathleen Jordan says. "We want the kind of quality that Alfred Hitchcock stood for, but the stories don't necessarily have to have twist endings."

Two or three anthologies are published every year. Because the magazine is published by the same company as *Ellery Queen's Mystery Magazine*, a manuscript submitted to one may be read by the editors of both. Circulation: around 200,000.

GETTING PUBLISHED: Rates: averages 5¢ a word. Payment: on acceptance. Rights: first North American serial; some foreign rights; anthology options. Reply time: tries for four weeks; manuscripts can get backed up. Guidelines: available.

About 100 to 150 unsolicited manuscripts are submitted every week. Jordan often buys work from two to four new writers an issue. "We are a very good break-in market," she says. "We are really looking for new material. A lot of our stories come from amateurs who write as a sideline. In the mystery field it is probably more possible to do this than in other areas of writing."

Everything that comes in is read by either Jordan, the assistant editor, or a part-time reader. "We have real hopes for our unsolicited pile," Jordan says.

Publication should follow acceptance within seven months.

THE STORY: Jordan wants stories of detection. "There has to be a crime that can be solved," she says. "We get too much material in which a death occurs but doesn't require solving, atmospheric pieces that only marginally have to do with crime, or psychologically based character dissections in which the crime is lost. We do not want occult stories, werewolves, vampires, and so on. We also will not publish unnecessarily violent stories or stories with gratuitous sex."

This does not mean the story can't be from the criminal's point of view, or about threatened, thwarted crime, or about odd, out-of-the-way crimes. Stories can concern police, private eyes, or innocent bystanders pulled into events beyond their control. One way or another, a mystery has to be created and solved.

Poor writing is the most common reason for rejection. But two other problems crop up with regularity. First is the trite plot. Jordan says they are overloaded with manuscripts in which that hoary old story of husband and wife planning to murder each other comes up. The second problem is endings: Jordan rejects stories that set up interesting characters in interesting situations, but tail off with a weak resolution. Mystery readers expect stories to come to a definite conclusion with all the questions raised by the story reasonably answered.

What Jordan would most like to see are intriguing crime stories, with interesting characters, written in a way that makes both plot and characters come alive. She names as examples two recent stories that fulfill those requirements. "To Catch a Wizard," by Walter Satterthwaite (Mar. '83), is set in Africa and tells of a local police officer who searches for the killer of a journalist. "The Marley Case," by Linda Haldeman (Dec. '82), answers the question "Who murdered Jacob Marley?" (from Dickens's *A Christmas Carol*).

Stories run up to 15,000 words. The most salable length is about 8000 words.

REJECTION: A standard form is usually used. Rewrites and resubmissions on spec will be asked for if a story has easily identifiable problems. Jordan does write back if stories show special promise and she would like to see more work.

AMAZING SCIENCE FICTION STORIES

(Combined with *Fantastic*)

Dragon Publishing
P. O. Box 110
Lake Geneva, WI 53147
(215) 382-5415

SOURCE: George Scithers, editor

IN SHORT: Very open to new writers; personalized response on all submissions

ABOUT THE MAGAZINE: Bimonthly; uses six to eight stories an issue. *Amazing Science Fiction Stories* first saw print in 1926, edited by Hugo Gernsback, one of the founding fathers of science fiction. It has changed hands several times since, but now has a new publisher and editor who are determined to bring it back to what it once was. The two immediate changes were to go from quarterly to bimonthly frequency and raise story fees to competitive levels. (There is also a future possibility that *Amazing* and *Fantastic* will again be separate magazines.) The goal is to increase circulation to the 100,000 mark. Editor George Scithers is hoping to attract a large teenage readership, a group that has slipped away from other SF magazines. He warns, however, that teen readers and unsophisticated writing do not go together. The teens today, with movies and computer games, are used to very sophisticated entertainment. Circulation: 15,000-16,000.

GETTING PUBLISHED: Rates: 4¢ to 6¢ a word on a graded scale depending on length. Payment: on acceptance. Rights: first North American serial; anthology options. Reply time: often within a week. Guidelines: available for $1.

Approximately 70 manuscripts from unpublished writers are submitted every week. Editors estimate they buy one or two of them per issue.

"We live by manuscripts," Scithers says. "We want to see more and more." All stories are read by a staff editor who makes written comments that are used in the rejection letter. Stories that are considered possibilities are read by several editors. Scithers has the final say.

Scithers is serious not only about finding stories to publish in *Amazing*, but also about developing writers who will bring new vitality to the field. He has put together a 29-page pamphlet that is nothing less than a guide to writing science fiction. It starts with manuscript preparation and goes on to consider what an SF story should be, what some of the best writers in the field have said on the subject, and some obvious traps to avoid. It is concerned with *Amazing*'s specific needs, but it talks about writing in general as well. It recommends further, more detailed sources. The guide is available for $1 (to cover postage and handling), and Scithers suggests that if writers would send for the guide before they send in manuscripts they might save themselves a lot of wasted time.

Cover letters are not necessary. If included they should be short and should not include a synopsis of the story. The only information the editors are really interested in is past credits and, if there has been previous correspondence, a reminder of what was said.

Publication usually follows acceptance in something over five months.

THE STORY: *Amazing* is interested in science fiction and fantasy (about one-third of the fiction). It is one of the few science fiction magazines that is open to sword and sorcery. Horror will also be considered, although not much is published. (Definitions of all these forms of SF are given in the writing guide.)

One of Scithers's major points is that it is almost impossible to come up with a completely new plot. The end-of-the-world story, the first-contact story, the time-travel story—all these have been done and done again by masters. Scithers strongly believes that in order to *write* science fiction, in order to come up with a new treatment of these classic plots, you have to *read* science fiction. If you don't know what has been done, the chances are your clever "new" idea will already have been published, republished, and copied.

There are three types of stories that are always rejected. First is simply the weakly told story—whatever new world the writer is trying to create never becomes believable. Another is the surprise-ending story that totally rests on a tricky little twist at the end (two aliens on a planet turn out to be Adam and Eve). The third is the convoluted, impressionistic story so murky and opaque that the editors can't figure out what is supposed to have happened.

To quote from the guideline booklet: "We are looking for the widest possible range of imaginative subject matter and approach, from hard science and high technology to myth, from gritty realism to extravagant surrealism. We do ask that stories hold the readers' interest, give them something to think about afterwards, and take those readers from the present into the imaginary worlds that you—the writer—have wrought."

REJECTION: No standard printed rejection forms. Every story is returned with some sort of critique that the editors promise will be very frank. In fact, some manuscripts are so bad that the critique may be a suggestion that the writer get hold of a book on English grammar and usage.

ANALOG SCIENCE FICTION/SCIENCE FACT

Davis Publications, Inc.
380 Lexington Avenue
New York, NY 10017
(212) 557-9100

SOURCE: Stanley Schmidt, editor

IN SHORT: Very open to new writers

ABOUT THE MAGAZINE: Published 13 times a year; uses five or six stories per issue. *Analog* is the oldest continuously published science fiction magazine. Editor Stanley Schmidt has a clear idea of what *Analog* has been and is and what makes it different from other science fiction magazines.

"In *Analog*," Schmidt says, "we publish only what is called hard science fiction. Not sword and sorcery, not fantasy. This does not mean the story should be primarily about gadgets or science or technology. It means that the scientific speculation or the technological idea has to be integral to the story so that if the science were removed, there would be no story. By this definition, the movie *Star Wars* is not science fiction. It is an adventure story that happens to be set in outer space. A movie that is science fiction is *Charly*. No science, no story."

Readers are 75% male; almost 70% are college graduates and 30% have at least one postgraduate degree. Nearly 49% of the male readers and 35% of the female readers have their degrees in engineering or one of the hard sciences. Circulation:100,000.

GETTING PUBLISHED: Rates: 5.75¢ a word to 7500 words; 3.5¢ a word for over 12,500 words; flat fee of $430 for stories between; regular contributors 1¢ more a word in all categories. Payment: on acceptance. Rights: first North American serial; nonexclusive foreign; nonexclusive anthology option. Reply time: usually three weeks or less; can get backed up. Guidelines: available.

Most fiction comes from regular contributors and agents' submissions. Schmidt estimates that 15% of the magazine, or approximately ten stories a year, are from the unsolicited pile.

About 100 unsolicited stories are submitted every week. Schmidt reads them all. "Everything that comes in is considered," he says. "Roughly 5% of the stories are good enough to provoke real interest. Another sizable group tends to be competent but not interesting."

Schmidt adds that he wants to find new writers and that the slush is particularly important because many of the regular writers started there.

Schmidt sees no need for a cover letter. A list of previous credits doesn't hurt, but stories are judged on their merit.

Analog uses no more than four serials—of 40,000-80,000 words—a year. On these, Schmidt wants a query first. Anthologies published three times a year. Publication usually follows acceptance within five months to a year.

THE STORY: *Analog* wants real stories in which believable characters come to grips with compelling problems. One of the most common reasons for rejection is that the story is not science fiction as *Analog* defines it. Another problem is the downbeat, no-hope ending. *Analog* does not insist on happy endings, but it does insist that characters make a real and reasonable effort to solve their problems. The price might be high in the character's personal life, but problems are dealt with. Another frequent failing is the overworked plot. These include "scientific retelling of Biblical stories; time travelers who unwittingly change their world; stories in which the alien world turns out to be earth." A similar problem is the too-slight plot; a story in which not enough happens and nothing is resolved.

Two stories which Schmidt thinks exemplify the best of *Analog* are "Emergence," by David R. Palmer (Jan. '81), and "Petals of Rose," by Marc Stiegler (Nov. '81).

"Emergence" came from the slush pile and was voted best 1981 story by *Analog*'s readers. The story is in the form of a journal kept by an 11-year-old girl who has survived a biological holocaust. In it, she comes to terms with the qualities in her own nature that allowed her to survive when almost everyone else died. She then begins the process of starting over again. Schmidt says: "There is not an awful lot of new idea there, but there is a very, very vivid depiction of an interesting character in an interesting situation."

"Petals of Rose" concerns the clashes inherent in the meeting of aliens whose life spans range from 36 hours to 80 years (that's us) to 25,000 years. Schmidt says, "It's an extremely original, thought-provoking idea with a whole range of consequences considered."

"Interesting character in an interesting situation";"thought-provoking idea with a whole range of consequences." "For a story to interest me," Schmidt says, "it has to have one of those two qualities."

Analog can use stories of from 2000 to 20,000 words.

REJECTION: In an effort to make rejection useful to the writer, Schmidt has prepared five different standard forms, each directed to a common problem. Points include: the story is not science fiction; problems with the ending; not a real story; good writing, but too weak a plot. There is also a generalized "Thank you, but no" form.

Schmidt will ask for more work from an interesting writer. He would like to respond personally to everyone, but because of time, writes only to those few whose work is almost what he needs (maybe 5%).

BOY'S LIFE

1325 Walnut Hill Lane
Irving, TX 75062
(214) 659-2000

SOURCE: Kris Imherr, fiction editor

IN SHORT: Uses few new writers a year

ABOUT THE MAGAZINE: Monthly; one story an issue. The magazine is for boys 8-18, but the fiction is geared toward 12-14-year-olds. Published by the Boy Scouts of America; includes coverage of scouting activities. Editorial emphasis is on the outdoors—camping, sports, nature. There is a monthly interview with major sports figure, and there are regular columns on books, cars, nature, stamps, coins, magic. *Boy's Life* also includes features on taking care of yourself and handling emergencies when parents are not home. Distribution is mostly by subscription; editors suggest writers see back issues at libraries. Circulation: 1.5 million.

GETTING PUBLISHED: Rates: start at $350; top price depends on length and author's reputation. Payment: on acceptance. Rights: one-time rights. Reply time: two weeks for rejection. Guidelines: none. Simultaneous submissions: will read.

Most of the fiction published in *Boy's Life* is from regular contributors who have a following among the readers. Fiction editor Kris Imherr estimates that there are usually only three or four new authors published every year and they are most likely to be solicited.

Around 100 unsolicited stories are submitted every month. Editors have generally found the unsolicited pile unrewarding and are hesitant about being too encouraging to authors. At the same time they are looking for good stories and do read whatever comes in. When a story has been pulled from the slush pile, it has tended to be from an established author.

Imherr has no interest in cover letters, and credits make no difference in how a story is handled. Imherr is the first reader. She finds an estimated one story out of every 200 submissions good enough to pass on to the editor-in-chief, who has final say on publication.

Stories are usually published within several months of purchase, but Imherr warns that it can go much longer.

THE STORY: *Boy's Life* publishes a wide range of stories; types include adventure, contemporary, humor, suspense, mystery, Western, science fiction, and sports.

Fiction is primarily entertainment; action generally is as important an element as introspection. Pacing is the problem on which most submissions fail.

The stories are neither mindless nor simple. Characters confront real-life problems and find ways to deal with them—sometimes by themselves, sometimes with the help of an adult. Many stories fail because the writer is too heavy-handed on moral or teaching aspects and forgets that a story must be entertaining.

"It takes a certain deftness to handle," Imherr says. "A writer has to know the magazine well to catch its viewpoint and pacing. That's why we don't have guidelines. We tell writers to read back issues."

Stories should be about characters (teenage boys—though a girl's point of view is acceptable) the readers will recognize and like. Boys in the stories have interests and a certain competency; they are active. Stories must always have clear resolutions. Stories about sex, hunting, crimes, and the occult are not published. But serious themes—death, peer pressure—are possibilities. Pure-entertainment stories are certainly welcome.

"The Crossover," by Edna Corwin (Jan. '83), is the story of a teen boy who has to cope with moving to a new home. "Shadow in the Sky," by E. J. Neely (Nov. '82), is about a teen who lives on a ranch, and must learn to deal with his rage against the horse that causes his sister's death. "The Lesson," by Raboo Rodgers (Oct. '82), is about a boy who helps a mistreated dog by teaching the dog to take care of himself. "The Case of the Chinese Restaurant," by Donald J. Sobol (Aug. '82), is a purely entertaining tale, a solve-it-yourself mystery in which a teen in trouble goes to a ten-year-old detective.

Imherr adds that one problem with submissions is their repetitiveness; if a cowboy story appears in November, in December she is besieged by cowboy manuscripts much too similar in feeling, scope, and plot.

Acceptable length is 1000-6000 words.

REJECTION: A standard form is usually used. Imherr has written to authors of promising stories, but adds she does it rarely. Rewrites are asked for, but usually on spec.

CO-ED

50 West 44th Street
New York, NY 10036
(212) 944-7700

SOURCE: Elizabeth Forst, senior editor

IN SHORT: Looking for writers but needs carefully targeted work

ABOUT THE MAGAZINE: Published ten times a year; uses one story an issue. *Co-ed* has a circulation of 1 million (about 80% female, 20% male) and no newsstand sales. It is distributed through home economics classes in schools across the country. Subscriptions are paid for either by the school or by teens through the school. The magazine serves the dual purpose of entertaining and providing a teaching tool. Readers' ages range from 13 to 18, with 14-15 the average.

Most of the readership is in the Midwest and South, and a lot of it is rural. To a great extent, readers are planning on vocational training and/or marriage rather than college. It is a magazine for teens who will soon be entering adult life.

Besides the usual fashion and beauty, celebrity interviews and recipes, *Co-ed* handles issues like pregnancy, runaways, and suicide in a down-to-earth, practical manner. Fiction is touched with the same kind of realism. Sample copy: $1.

GETTING PUBLISHED: Rates: $300. Payment: on acceptance. Rights: all rights. Reply time: usually within six to eight weeks. Guidelines: available.

Almost all of the fiction comes from the 60 to 80 unsolicited manuscripts submitted every week. The first cut is made by an assistant editor, who passes an average of one or two stories a week to senior editor Elizabeth Forst. Her selections are passed to the editor-in-chief, who makes the final decisions.

Neither a cover letter listing previous publications nor an agent's imprint move a story past the assistant editor. "I sometimes think people, including agents, don't bother to look at the magazine," Forst says. "We get some very good writing, clearly from professional writers, that is much too old for our reader."

Forst emphasizes that *Co-ed* has a high writer turnover, usually using ten different authors a year. The unsolicited manuscripts are important.

A purchased story can usually expect to see print within a year.

THE STORY: Stories should run near 2000 words with a 3000-word top and should be about real problems facing teens with emphasis on personal growth. Subjects can include friends, dating, family, and issues like prejudice. Problems of coming of age, making life decisions, and handling dreams are all possibilities. *Co-ed* is on the lookout for stories with appeal to male readers, too. The challenge is to provide entertainment yet still offer the kind of substance that can be a basis for classroom discussion. The editors regularly append questions concerning character motivation and value judgments to a story for classroom use. It is very important to avoid any kind of preachy moralism. *Co-ed* wants real characters in real situations.

Immediately rejected are formula boy-meets-girl stories or any kind of pat romance, highly melodramatic adventure stories, and any explicit sex or violence.

In "Becoming a Man," by Mary Dunham (Apr. '82), a Hispanic teen washing dishes in a diner after school dreams of college though his family barely has enough for food and rent. It is a real-life problem and the end of the story is neither happy nor sad. The boy's way of coping is to accept the necessity of helping his family without losing hope for something better for himself in the future.

"Bringing Up Stepmother," by Ann Edwards-Cannon (Mar. '82), is about a teen coping with her father's constant remarriages. The story is mature in its appreciation that human relationships can't be understood by stereotypes. In it, the adults act like children; it is the teen who must act like an adult.

These stories are challenging and realistic while still managing to be hopeful in outlook. The editors would also like to see humorous stories.

REJECTION: Standard form used in most cases. Editors do not usually ask for major rewrites. Encouraging letters, asking for further submissions, are sent only to people the editors feel are talented writers who missed the market. Forst estimated between three and five of these letters are sent a week.

ELLERY QUEEN'S MYSTERY MAGAZINE

Davis Publications
380 Lexington Avenue
New York, NY 10017
(212) 557-9100

SOURCE: Eleanor Sullivan, editor

IN SHORT: Very open to new writers; excellent break-in market

ABOUT THE MAGAZINE: Published 13 times a year; an average of 13 stories an issue. *Ellery Queen's Mystery Magazine* has published mystery fiction since 1941. The Ellery Queen character, created by Frederic Dannay and Manfred B. Lee, has appeared in scores of novels and short stories. According to editor Eleanor Sullivan, the *EQ* novels have been one of the formative influences on the modern detective story in their blending of a classically constructed plot with a psychological view of character. The magazine tries to meet these standards.

Approximately 73% of *EQ*'s readers are female; 30% of them are 35-54 years old and 55% are 55 or older. Four anthologies are published every year; one of them consists of stories never before published in the U.S. Submitted manuscripts may also be read by the editor of *Alfred Hitchcock's Mystery Magazine*, published by the same company, if *EQ*'s editor thinks they might be of interest. Circulation: 250,000.

GETTING PUBLISHED: Rates: start at 3¢ a word; can rise to 8¢ depending on writer's credentials and regularity as a contributor. Payment: on acceptance. Rights: first English language rights; translation rights for foreign editions and first anthology rights. Reply time: within a month. Guidelines: available. Simultaneous submissions: will read.

EQ's fiction is 60% from agents, 30% from regular contributors. The rest—15 to 20 stories a year—is from unsolicited submissions. Over 100 come in every week.

The magazine is well known for its "Department of First Stories" feature. The 600th "first" was published in 1982. The editors are actively looking for new and/or unpublished writers; they read the slush pile with care.

Stories are read by either the editor or the assistant editor. A cover letter listing previous publications will move a story directly to the editor's desk for a quick reading.

If a story is marred by only a few easily identifiable problems, Sullivan will ask the writer to rewrite and resubmit on spec.

Publication usually follows within six to eight months of acceptance.

THE STORY: *EQ* is open to suspense, psychological study, deductive puzzles, police procedurals, locked rooms, and so on. Sullivan prefers contemporary stories, but will look at stories set in the past. She has found that readers do not like parodies or Sherlockiana; she will still read them, but has to find them outstanding.

"The shape of mysteries has changed," Sullivan says. "At one time it was all technique: clocks, train timetables, and so on. Now there is a more psychological approach. While plot is still of first importance, there is more room for exploration of character."

Not considered for publication are supernatural stories, horror stories, or stories of sex, sadism, and gratuitous violence. *EQ* almost never uses stories concerning murder of or by children, or stories in which a child commits a murder.

Most often rejected is the story in which the end is obvious from the second page. At the same time, a writer has to play fair with the reader, giving him all the clues leading to the solution. And the story does have to come to an end. Problems must be resolved.

The January 1983 issue shows *EQ*'s range. Contributors include James Powell, Florence V. Mayberry, Janwillem van de Wetering, Christianna Brand, Carol Clemeau, and Jean Bowden. Plots run from a murder among dolls (who—as everyone knows —come alive for a few hours each Christmas morning) to a story in which the victim protects the murderer. There is a story about a Japanese detective, a corpse, and a stamp collection. Another story includes a murderer who confesses to a crime he has gotten away with. In yet another tale a classics professor stops a blackmail scheme. And in one story a little old lady's expertise on the subject of laundry solves a crime. Best advice to writers: Read a few issues.

REJECTION: A standard form is used in most cases. A story marginally better than most, but still not of professional caliber—what Sullivan calls "showing a little promise"—gets a "But thank you" on the note. A work that is admired will be returned with a letter explaining the rejection.

FANTASY AND SCIENCE FICTION

Box 56
Cornwall, CT 06753
(203) 672-6376

SOURCE: Edward L. Ferman, editor

IN SHORT: Very open to new writers

ABOUT THE MAGAZINE: Monthly; approximately eight stories an issue; anthologies every 18 months. The editors are interested in hard and soft science fiction, supernatural stories, and even marginal fantasy—the contemporary story touched by only a hint of strangeness. "We are more accessible to the casual reader of science fiction as opposed to the hard-core fan," editor Edward Ferman says. "We tend to use less hard science fiction. In fact, we would like to do more. For an unknown writer that would be the best chance. Most of what we get is fantasy. The competition is tougher."

Readers are 65% male, mostly between 23 and 45 and well educated. Almost all have some college and 37% have some graduate school. Circulation: 60,000.

GETTING PUBLISHED: Rates: 3¢ to 5¢ a word depending on author's celebrity and regularity as a contributor. Payment: on acceptance. Rights: first North American serial; nonexclusive foreign serial; anthology options. Reply time: one month. Guidelines: available. Simultaneous submissions: will read.

"The slush pile is important," Ferman says. "It's one of our jobs to find new writers. And if we find a writer who goes on to become famous, we have a source of quality work for years to come."

Ferman receives approximately 100 manuscripts a week. He estimates he might buy from 6 to 15 of these a year. Ferman initially sorts all submissions. Anything with a cover letter listing previous credits, or from a writer he has heard of, he reads himself. Everything else goes to the assistant editor, who makes the first cut. Every week, three to five stories make it back onto Ferman's desk. He emphasizes that the assistant editor is a science fiction fan, a writer, and a teacher of writing. Manuscripts are looked at seriously.

An accepted story will see print in from four to 18 months.

THE STORY: "There are basic plots in science fiction that are continually redone," Ferman says. "Deals with the devil, after-the-bomb stories, first-contact stories. We have no objection to this if a writer can come up with a fresh angle. But old themes are dangerous for the writer who doesn't know the field well. He's liable to duplicate what's already been done."

The possibility of coming up with something new is increased at *F&SF* by its broad definition of science fiction. Ferman emphasizes that the magazine is open to stories set in the present as well as the future and on earth as well as in space and to stories that have only a hint of the unusual in them. "We get stories from very fine writers who are not science fiction people," Ferman says.

Ferman will consider mood pieces, character sketches, and vignettes if the author "hits it exactly right." He warns that a writer has a better chance with a well-plotted story line. He is not a fan of sword and sorcery.

In most unsolicited submissions, poor writing is the major problem. Trite plots also lead to rejection, but less frequently. "From a new contributor, good writing and character development are more important than plot. A clever idea badly written will not sell."

Illiteracy is not the major writing problem. Often there is nothing wrong with a piece on a sentence-to-sentence basis. "But it doesn't go beyond routine literary competence," Ferman says. "It has no grace and no life."

Two stories pulled from the slush pile illustrate the range Ferman is looking for. "Dinosaurs on Broadway," by Tony Sarowitz (Sept. '82), is an example of marginal fantasy chosen because "it was so well written." The piece is a character study with a slight overtone of fantasy. It is about a woman who imagines seeing dinosaurs on the city's streets. This story was originally published in *Transatlantic Review*, a literary quarterly.

"Healer," by P. E. Cunningham (July '82), is the story of an alien youngster whose talent for healing is blocked by adult disbelief and jealousy. "A solid, straight science fiction story. I wish we had more," Ferman says. "What sold me is not the writing, though that is good, but the inventiveness. An alien culture is presented in a convincing way."

Ferman will read stories of from 500 to 20,000 words; most salable is 5000-10,000.

REJECTION: A standard form is used in most cases. Stories with promise, or stories admired but wrong for the magazine, may be rejected with suggestions for improvement or requests for more work. Almost all stories passed by the first reader receive some sort of acknowledgment. Rewrites (on spec) are asked for if a story's problems are minor.

FAR WEST

Wright Publishing
P. O. Box 2260
Costa Mesa, CA 92626
(714) 545-2118

SOURCE: Scott McMillan, editor

IN SHORT: Excellent break-in market

ABOUT THE MAGAZINE: Quarterly; approximately ten stories an issue. A magazine of Western stories and art. *Far West* is devoted to the frontier between 1840 and 1920, but occasionally does contemporary stories. Readers are both interested in Western lore and knowledgeable about it; a high degree of historical accuracy is necessary. Half of the readers are female; age ranges 35-65 and circulation is national. There is a possibility of monthly publication in the future. Sample copy: $2 plus SASE with 50¢ postage. Circulation: 50,000.

GETTING PUBLISHED: Rates: based on length with $150 minimum; average payment runs $350-$450. Payment: on publication (actually pays after 90 days if publication is held up for any reason). Rights: all rights; 50% assigned back to author after publication. Reply time: within six weeks. Guidelines: available. Simultaneous submissions: will read.

Almost all of *Far West*'s fiction is chosen from unsolicited submissions, and 70% of the stories published are from authors new to the magazine. Editor Scott McMillan is on the lookout for fresh, new material and will work with promising writers.

"This is an excellent start-up market," McMillan says. "Of the 50 or so writers who have published first stories here recently, 10 went on to write novels and 6 are ongoing successful novelists."

Every week, 30 to 50 manuscripts come in. They are read by the associate editor, who rejects about 65% of them immediately. McMillan reads all the rest.

"We get a lot of material from beginning writers," he says. "It is often interesting in content but weak in craft. If a writer shows talent and ability we will work with him—15% to 20% of what we publish is based on rewrites (all done on spec)."

McMillan has gone through as many as four rewrites with one

author, though he does add that was an unusual case where the story's potential was "terrific."

Cover letters are not necessary; credits make no difference. Publication usually follows acceptance in three months but it can go over a year.

THE STORY: *Far West* wants stories about the people who lived on the frontier between 1840 and 1920, and their experiences.

Generally, McMillan says, the readers want action. A major problem with the "close failures"—stories considered but not taken—is lack of movement, lack of getting on with the story. "If I'm not interested by the end of the second page, the reader won't be," McMillan says.

At the same time, the characters have to have depth. Too many submissions feature stereotyped characters that do not come individually alive. They never get past the tough marshal, the lonesome cowboy. Situations and locales are stereotyped also. Too much concentration on the lawman who rides into the desert to get the outlaw, too much emphasis on Texas and Arizona.

McMillan wants stories about storekeepers, farmers, and schoolteachers as well as lawmen and cowboys. One very successful story was about a soldier's wife at a Wyoming fort. He would like to see the West from something other than the white or Hispanic point of view: the Chinese immigrant; the black cowboy. Writers are too narrow in locale; they forget about Canada, Minnesota, Idaho. One of the magazine's most successful stories was about a Wild West show that travels to Europe.

Stories have to be realistic. Because the West was a frontier society, survival is a major (though not the only) topic. The problems and dangers have to be believable.

Historical accuracy is absolutely demanded. McMillan says that both he and the publisher are Western historians. The readers, too, are very knowledgeable about the period: they will catch anything phony or anachronistic.

Occasionally a modern story is published. One concerned an older traditional American Indian and his relationship with young activists.

Writers can expect editing on their work; McMillan sees a lot of overwriting and he has to do quite a bit of cutting and tightening. He does not show changes to the author before publication. He adds that his editing never changes structure or characterization; if the actual substance of the story needs work, the author is asked to rewrite.

The ideal story length is 2500-4500 words, but *Far West* has published both short-shorts and novellas. "Tell the story," McMillan says. "I do not turn down great stories because of length."

REJECTION: A standard rejection form is used, but if a story shows any promise at all, a few encouraging lines will be added. This is particularly the case if a story is being rejected only because the idea has already been covered. From time to time, McMillan will write a real critique of the story. This depends first on the author's asking for comments, then on McMillan's finding the time, and finally on the story's promise. If the story really does have potential, the writer is likely to get some in-depth, extensive criticism and suggestion.

FARM WIFE NEWS

P. O. Box 643
Milwaukee, WI 53201
(414) 423-0100

SOURCE: Ruth Benedict, managing editor

IN SHORT: Open, but very specialized market

ABOUT THE MAGAZINE: Published 11 times a year; approximately eight stories a year. For rural American women, especially those living on farms and ranches. Not an agricultural journal, but a forum in which readers can air their problems and discuss the pleasures and pains of their style of living. "Loneliness is a pivotal point in a farm woman's life," managing editor Ruth Benedict says. "The magazine tells the reader she is not alone." *Farm Wife News* publishes recipes, craft news, profiles, and so on, but it also considers the problems in leading a physically grueling, rarely luxurious life. It discusses the satisfactions of working the land, but also the drawbacks. A great deal of the writing is done by readers—farm wives sharing their experiences. Benedict describes the average reader as in her 40s, although readers include all age groups, and men. No advertising is carried and the magazine is available only by subscription. Circulation: 328,000. Sample copy: $2.

GETTING PUBLISHED: Rates: $75-$200; the more editorial work required, the less money. Payment: between acceptance and publication. Rights: first North American serial. Reply time: six weeks. Guidelines: available. Simultaneous submissions: will read, but wants to be informed of other submissions.

"This is a great, wide-open market," Benedict says. "We would publish more fiction if we could get it. The readers write in asking for it. But where do you find writers with rural experience?"

All the fiction published comes in unsolicited. Benedict estimates she receives five stories a week—half from readers and half from professional writers who rarely have bothered to look at the magazine and consider its special needs.

Benedict reads everything herself. She likes to see a short cover letter with a little background on the writer's contact with rural life. "Something that will help me gauge the truth of the experience in the story," she explains.

In 1981, *Farm Wife News* ran a writing contest for its readers. There were 3224 entries (stories, nonfiction, poetry), and winning pieces were published. Further contests are being considered.

Once a story is purchased, publication should follow within six months.

THE STORY: "We get some decent fiction," Benedict emphasizes, "that we cannot use because it does not relate to our reader. We are interested in the life of the farm wife or ranch wife. Our readers are down-to-earth women. They will reject anything too fantastic or far-fetched."

FWN writing tends to be straightforward and steeped in accurate detail. Stories are short, with a 1000-1500 word top, and tend to have few characters. The action often takes place in the heroine's mind as she tries to come to grips with some aspect of her life.

When fiction is about farming and is still rejected, it can be for a variety of reasons. Most common is a misapprehension about agricultural life. A farm wife is rarely just a homemaker now. She also works part-time and is active in community and church affairs. Even if she is confined to the farm, her role is one of business partner. She helps with the planning, makes decisions on major purchases, does the books, and so on. A lot of the fiction submitted suffers from an overdose of sentimentality. Farming is hard work and a business. Benedict describes many stories as "syrupy and saccharine," with an idealized television view of farming.

A common subject of published stories is a woman learning how to deal with the hardship of her life, reminding herself how to find joy in the face of backbreaking labor or the vagaries of the weather, or children who leave the farm, or men too tired even to watch TV at night.

"The Spring Ritual," by Carol McMullen (May '81), is a meditation about working the land. It was inspired by the grueling, endless, year-in, year-out labor of clearing rocks from fields. As the heroine lifts the heavy stones, her mind ranges from anger to self-pity to a consideration of rocks and their place in the scheme of things. She thinks of Japanese rock gardens and "The

Rock of Ages." Finally, she realizes that rock clearing is only a problem in a life that is essentially satisfying.

"The Key," by Susan Lindau (Sept. '81), is a personal favorite of Benedict's. A young farm wife, worried by serious financial troubles, is horrified to find herself pregnant. Then she comes across her grandmother's diary. She reads the story of the birth of her grandmother's first child during a blizzard, without a doctor, and with barely enough to eat. That raw picture of life so many years before brings a dose of perspective and strength.

REJECTION: Standard form used in most cases. Rewrites are not requested, but if a rejected story is admired, Benedict might ask for more work. She warns that she writes back only six to eight times a year for all material, and so not even that often for fiction.

IDEALS

Ideals Publishing Corporation
11315 Watertown Plank Road
Milwaukee, WI 53226

SOURCE: Colleen Callahan Gonring, editor

IN SHORT: Very open to new writers; very specialized material

ABOUT THE MAGAZINE: Published eight times a year; two to three stories an issue. An illustrated poetry magazine that uses a few very short, simple pieces of fiction. Full-color, full-page photos and drawings are integral to the magazine, taking up close to half the pages. Each issue is devoted to a theme. The following is a list of the themes, with the submission deadlines in parentheses. February: Valentine issue (June). April: Easter (end of August). May: Mother's Day (early October). June: Friendship (end of November). July/August: Countryside (early January). September/October: Autumn (late February). November: Thanksgiving (early April). December: Christmas (middle of May).

Ideals has a preponderance of female readers, but considers itself a general-interest family magazine. Its purpose is purely to entertain with light, sentimental writing and picturesque art. The reader is probably in her 40s or older. Available by subscription and in bookstores. Circulation: 200,000.

GETTING PUBLISHED: Rates: $50 to $125 depending on length. Payment: on publication. Rights: first North American serial. Reply time: four to six weeks. Guidelines: available.

Most fiction is chosen from the unsolicited submissions, though occasionally a piece is assigned. Approximately five stories are submitted each week. Assistant editors pass the possibilities on to editor Colleen Gonring. Major rewrites are not asked for, though editors will do a small amount of reworking if a piece is close to being acceptable. Time between purchase and publication depends on how far in advance of its special theme issue a piece is bought.

THE STORY: Length is very important; each piece has to fit into, at most, a two-page spread with room for the usually elaborate illustration. Lengths of 800 to 1000 words are most salable.

Stories should be light, entertaining, about rural rather than urban subjects, family-oriented. The "Autumn" issue included a forest vignette about an acorn deciding to leave its parent oak and start out for itself. In the "Friendship" issue was a story about a boy who finds an injured bird and goes to great trouble to save it. In the "Mother's Day" issue was the story of a little girl who—with her grandmother's help—makes a dress for her mother; the mother wears the dress even though she knows it looks terrible. The "Valentine" issue included a humorous piece about a woman who is constantly rejected by her plants despite her attempts to give them loving care.

Most common reasons for rejection, Gonring says, are stories too long or too trite. Stories are also rejected if they are dully written or meander without coming to any conclusion.

REJECTION: Standard form used in most cases. If editors want to consider a piece, they make a copy for themselves and return the original. The writer is free to submit elsewhere. If the editors eventually decide to use the story, they will get in touch with the author. Holding a piece does not necessarily lead to buying it.

ISAAC ASIMOV'S
SCIENCE FICTION MAGAZINE

Davis Publications Inc.
380 Lexington Avenue
New York, NY 10017
(212) 557-9100

SOURCE: Shawna McCarthy, editor

IN SHORT: Very open to new writers

ABOUT THE MAGAZINE: Published 13 times a year; uses approximately ten stories an issue. Editor Shawna McCarthy defines science fiction as fiction with any element of the fantastic in it: "The magazine is for the reader in search of entertainment, not just the regular science fiction fan." McCarthy wants the magazine to develop a reputation for literary excellence with an emphasis on character development over adventurous plot or wealth of scientific detail. "The writer should think of science fiction," McCarthy says, "as literature with fewer boundaries. The concerns and feelings should be the same as in other forms of writing, but the writer can go further. He is not bounded by time or space or even species." Circulation: 100,000. Isaac Asimov is a regular contributor.

GETTING PUBLISHED: Rates: begin at 3¢ a word; go to 5½¢ for regular contributors, and go still higher as writer gains more recognition. Payment: on acceptance. Rights: first North American serial; some foreign rights; options for anthology use. Reply time: editors try for two weeks, but it may be longer. Guidelines: available.

As in other SF magazines, most of the published stories come from established writers who are regular contributors. McCarthy estimates that 35 to 45 unsolicited manuscripts are submitted every day. Out of every 100, possibly one will make it into print.

Manuscripts are sorted into two piles. Those from recognized authors and those accompanied by a cover letter listing previous credits are read by McCarthy. She also looks at the unsolicited, unknown, unpublished pile, reading at least the first two pages and the last page of everything. Anything that has captured her attention (the "culls") is passed to the assistant editor for a complete reading. Those that the assistant editor finds to be "possible" go back to McCarthy.

On an average week, the assistant editor will probably find three or four stories from the "culls" good enough to give to McCarthy.

"When you look at the figures," McCarthy adds, "it may seem as if it's impossible to be published. But for the beginner, science fiction is the best place to start. Novelists tend to lose interest in short stories, and there is a constant need for new writers."

Publication follows within two to seven months of acceptance.

THE STORY: *IAsfm* can use stories ranging from short-shorts to 15,000 words for the newcomer and 20,000 words for the established writer. McCarthy wants fully plotted stories, not character sketches or mood pieces. But she objects to plot at the expense of character development. "We like to see characters illuminated and changed. The plot is the device to put a character through its paces.

"Our readers are not necessarily science-oriented, and though we want some element of the fantastic, some element above the mundane, there is no need to ground it in science or technology. Science fiction is first and foremost fiction, and its job is to illuminate the human condition!"

McCarthy objects to what she calls "cute" or "juvenile" science fiction. In these categories she includes elves and goblins, damsels in distress, most sword and sorcery, space opera, and pure action stories. Worst of all is the trite plot—the story in which the primitive couple turn out to be Adam and Eve, or the one in which a time traveler tries to stop the assassination of Lincoln.

An example of what McCarthy wants is "Firewatch," by Connie Willis (Feb. '82), one of the most popular stories ever run in the magazine. The story uses the familiar going-back-in-time theme. This time the traveler is a history student from Earth's future. The author tells us that sometime between our present and that future, nuclear holocaust has laid our world to waste. From there, she considers what history is to the generations who inherit it and the relationship between history's cold facts and the people who live and die as part of it. The result of the story is the coming-of-age of the young student.

Another example is "The Boarder," by Madeleine E. Robins (July '82), a first SF sale pulled out of the slush pile. It's the story of an elderly widow, alone except for a canary, who is forced by the authorities to board an alien pensioner. It shows how a human and alien fulfill each other's emotional needs even though they are so physically different that direct communication is impossible.

REJECTION: Stories in the "pro" pile are always rejected with a personal note. Stories rejected after a first reading are returned with a standard printed form. A more encouraging rejection form, often with a personal note added, is used for stories that the assistant editor found to be possibly publishable, or that struck the editors as having promising features. Rewrites and resubmissions (on spec) are asked for only when the problem with the story is very minor.

LADYCOM

Downey Communications
1800 M Street, N.W.
Suite 650-S
Washington, DC 20036
(202) 872-0960

SOURCE: Sheila J. Gibbons, editor

IN SHORT: Very open, but very specialized market

ABOUT THE MAGAZINE: Published ten times a year; eight stories a year. Women's magazine for military wives; distributed in commissaries here and abroad. The magazine is privately owned—not controlled by the military or the government. "We're trying to make the magazine a very good mirror of military domestic life," editor Sheila Gibbons says. "We are trying to provide military wives with a magazine that will help them interpret and cope with service life." Also covered are food, fashion, crafts, health, and child care. Reader age is 22-34; half have attended college; two-thirds are married to enlisted men, the rest to officers. About half the readers work full- or part-time, and most have small children. Circulation: 400,000 U.S.; 75,000 overseas. Sample copy: 75¢.

GETTING PUBLISHED: Rates: $200-$375, depending on the writer's credentials. Payment: prefers to pay on publication, but will negotiate. Rights: first North American serial. Reply time: tries for three weeks. Publication time: usually within six months. Guidelines: available.

All *Ladycom* fiction is chosen from unsolicited submissions, as this is a market agents rarely cover. Gibbons receives about eight stories every month and reads all of them. Something like two stories a month are seriously considered.

Gibbons likes to see a cover letter, if only as a courtesy. She wants to know about previous credits, though she adds that unpublished writers are at no disadvantage.

Gibbons will ask for rewrites. If the problems are minor, she will make a commitment to buy beforehand. If the problems are extensive, she will suggest a rewrite and resubmission on spec. If a story comes back improved but still not right, she will work through another rewrite with an author.

THE STORY: "It is more apparent in fiction than in nonfiction that we are getting things from people who have never bothered to look at the magazine," Gibbons says. "We publish fiction that takes believable, real-life difficulties occurring in military life and develops them. We want our readers to finish a story and say, 'Oh, boy—is that true!'

"Believability is the key. For instance, we don't insist on happy endings with all the loose ends tucked away. Military life is not like that for most women."

At the same time, *Ladycom* fiction is entertainment. Most stories are about relationships, usually between husbands and wives, but also between friends or family members. Romances are always welcome, but the more successful are within a marriage as opposed to boy-meets-girl. Stories can be about women who are actually in the military themselves. But Gibbons points out that most of these women are also married to servicemen, and the story should grow out of possible conflicts in the dual careers. *Ladycom* does not want grim, overly psychological pieces about alcoholism, violence, or sex.

Gibbons says the two major problems confronting military wives are loneliness and rootlessness. Husbands are often away, creating both problems and temptations for wives and creating another whole set of problems for children. Compounding the difficulty, service families move almost every two years, often to bases abroad, and the burden falls most heavily on the wife and children. "There is a huge range of fiction possibilities to be explored here," Gibbons says.

Loneliness and rootlessness are problems dealt with by writers who know nothing of the military, but Gibbons finds they rarely capture the right flavor. They know nothing of the jargon or detail. "Military wives live almost in a culture all their own. This has to be captured in the story."

Some of the most successful submissions come from military wives themselves. "It is rare that a nonprofessional sends in a first effort and we buy it," Gibbons says. "But many of the women have done other writing, mostly nonfiction, and have worked up to trying a story. A lot of what we publish is based on things that really happened to these women."

There are common reasons for rejection—for instance, a dated, unrealistic view of today's military and its demands. Gibbons is not interested in historical fiction. Another common problem is the stereotyping of women. "I do not publish stories in which passive women are waiting around for some man to come along and make their lives wonderful. Heroines should not be super-women, but they should be bright, lively, and capable of dealing with their problems."

REJECTION: A standard form is used in most cases. Gibbons writes back when she wants to encourage a writer—probably in one out of ten submissions.

OMNI

909 Third Avenue
New York, NY 10022
(212) 593-3301

SOURCE: Ellen Datlow, fiction editor

IN SHORT: Very competitive market

ABOUT THE MAGAZINE: Monthly; two to three stories an issue. *Omni* is a science fact magazine published by the same company as *Penthouse*, and is particularly lavish in its use of color and elaborate graphics. Fiction is important at *Omni*, because the magazine intends to be entertaining as well as informative.

Reader studies show the audience splits into two groups. The larger is composed of science professionals who read the magazine for entertainment. The smaller group works in nonscience fields and reads to keep abreast of new technology. *Omni*'s audience is mostly male and under 34, and has attended college. The magazine occasionally uses book excerpts from well-known authors and publishes "Best of . . . " editions. Circulation: approximately 800,000.

GETTING PUBLISHED: Rates: $1250 to $2000. Payment: on acceptance. Rights: first world periodical rights in all languages. Reply time: tries for within a month. Guidelines: available.

Most stories are from well-known authors. The editors try to mix known and unknown writers, but because *Omni* pays well, the competition is stiff.

Around 100 unsolicited manuscripts are submitted every week. In 1981, *Omni* bought four manuscripts found in the slush pile—an unusually high number. In 1982, no stories were purchased from completely new, unconnected writers (although one story was purchased from a new writer who had a previous editor's recommendation and another was from a writer whose first sale to *Omni* was unsolicited).

Stories from known authors or stories with cover letters listing previous publications go directly to fiction editor Ellen Datlow. Everything else is read by the assistant fiction editor. Datlow estimates that two stories a week pass the first reader.

If a story has only a minor flaw, Datlow will ask for a rewrite and resubmission on spec. She will stick with the author through several revisions if necessary.

Despite the fact that it is hard to sell to *Omni*, Datlow does not discourage new writers. "I think very often the best writers are the new ones," she says. "They have more energy and less formula in their work. And in science fiction, some of the well-known writers save their best for novels. From an editor's point of view, finding a new writer is the best part of the job."

Editors try for publication within a year of sale.

THE STORY: Although there is no typical *Omni* story, the editors automatically reject sword and sorcery stories and Hobbit-type fantasies. They also reject mood pieces, sketches, and vignettes. They want plotted stories with movement leading to resolution of problems or situations.

One key to what *Omni* is looking for lies in Datlow's preference for the phrase "speculative fiction" over "science fiction." A story can be fantasy, or nuts-and-bolts technology, but it should always relate to the human condition. Stories, as well as being entertaining, should extrapolate from where we are to where we might be someday. "That's what makes science fiction believable and makes it matter to the reader," Datlow says.

In the April 1981 issue is a story pulled off the unsolicited pile: "The Hitmaker," by Cynthia Morgan, showing the world of TV soap operas gone mad. Powerful television networks have given up actors and scripts and simply hired whole towns. Their cameras are affixed to trees, houses, and doorways. The results are predictably tragic. "It's a story of how technology affects people, which is just what we want," Datlow says. "Further, it's gorgeously written, low-keyed and still packing a punch."

Omni can use stories between 2000 and 10,000 words.

REJECTION: Most rejections are handled with a standard form. Any story that passes the first reader will be rejected by a personal note, perhaps asking to see more work and/or explaining the reason for the rejection.

SEVENTEEN

850 Third Avenue
New York, NY 10022
(212) 759-8100

SOURCE: Dawn Raffel, fiction editor

IN SHORT: Very open to new writers

ABOUT THE MAGAZINE: Monthly; one story per issue. A general-interest magazine for young women aged 12-21, median age 15-16. The reader is probably from a middle-class family and planning on college. She is beginning to think more about the outside world and is very interested in knowing what other teens are doing and thinking. The editors are dedicated to fiction and proud of their tradition of publishing fine stories. Circulation: just under 2 million.

GETTING PUBLISHED: Rates $500 for first sale. Payment: on acceptance. Rights: first North American serial. Reply time: approximately six weeks. Guidelines: available.

"*Seventeen* is a good market for the first-timer," fiction editor Dawn Raffel says. "We read everything."

Most of the stories are commissioned from known writers, but the unsolicited pile is important as a source for developing these writers. Further, there is a high turnover. Many of the contributors are adult writers who only occasionally work on the subjects of adolescence.

Close to 600 unsolicited manuscripts are submitted every month. In 1982, one of these was published.

Stories are read by the magazine's assistant editors, who pass the possibilities (six to ten a month) to Raffel. A cover letter listing credits in a major magazine will send a story directly to the fiction editor's desk. Raffel might ask for a revision and resubmission on spec if a story is close. She has worked through three such revisions in the last year. Final decisions on stories are made by the editorial director.

Seventeen has a six-month lead time and uses a lot of seasonal material; it can be a long wait before a story is in print.

THE STORY: *Seventeen* fiction, Raffel says, is closer to adult stories than to juvenile writing. "Much fine adult writing is about adolescence. It is important not to talk down to the reader. Certainly, the concerns of the story have to be those of the teenager, but considered at a level that takes into account the true complexity of teen problems.

"Romances are always welcome, but not of the cheerleader–prom queen mold. They have to concern well-drawn, thoughtful teens confronting interesting complications. Humor is also welcome, but not when it is based on making a young woman look silly."

Seventeen wants traditional stories in which a well-delineated character confronts and deals with a problem. The magazine stays away from grim or hopeless endings, but is open to unresolved endings in which a happier outcome is dependent on the character's future growth.

Stories of death and sexuality are not taboo, though graphic violence and explicit sex are.

Most stories are from the heroine's point of view, but there have been exceptions. Editors want the reader to have a sense of recognition, but stories have been concerned with girls who work in gas stations, girls abandoned by shiftless parents, charming girls with jobs in Manhattan. In all these stories there is a heroine (in one a hero) of some sensitivity who is learning about life, having an experience—pleasant or not—that leads to growing up.

Barbara Wernecke Durkin has sold several stories to *Seventeen*. In "Commencement '82" (June '82), a teenage girl about to graduate high school writes an essay about the relationship of her mother, whose early pregnancy led to an unhappy marriage, and her mother's best friend, a famous writer. The girl acknowledges that she cannot judge one woman's life a success, the other's a failure. She has come to see that what counts is the lifelong sustaining affection these two women have for each other and for her. In characterization and in language use, this story is closer to adult writing than what might be expected in a teen magazine.

The average story runs 3000 words. Occasionally a short-short is used. There is an annual writing contest for teens.

REJECTION: Though not much comes off the unsolicited pile and goes directly into the magazine, Raffel will enter into a correspondence with a writer if she wants to see further work; she hopes to develop new sources and sends roughly six encouraging letters a month. Most manuscripts are rejected with a standard form.

'TEEN

8490 Sunset Boulevard
Los Angeles, CA 90069
(213) 657-5100

SOURCE: Carol Priest, editorial associate

IN SHORT: Open to new writers for fiction only

ABOUT THE MAGAZINE: Monthly; 12 stories a year. 'Teen is a service magazine for girls 12-19 (median age 16½). The focus is on self-improvement. It speaks to parents as well as teens and encourages reader involvement and participation in the magazine. Two major in-house features appear every month on social awareness, sexuality, and physical and mental health subjects, plus entertainment, fashion, beauty, and other subjects of interest to teen girls. Circulation: over 1 million.

GETTING PUBLISHED: Rates: $100. Payment: on acceptance. Rights: all rights. Reply time: tries for six to eight weeks, but can go longer; writers should not contact the magazine before two months. Guidelines: available.

Three or four stories every year are purchased from known writers; the rest are chosen from unsolicited submissions. Approximately 50 stories are sent in each week. Editorial associate Carol Priest is the first reader and estimates that out of every 50 stories, ten are good enough to pass on to the managing editor, who chooses what will be published.

Priest adds that most of the manuscripts do not have to be read all the way through before rejection because they clearly do not meet requirements.

If a story has only very minor problems the editors will make in-house changes; if more major changes are needed they might ask for a rewrite on spec. This may not lead to publication, and editors will not work through more than one rewrite.

Cover letters are not considered important, and a list of credits does not change how a story is handled. Once a story is purchased, publication usually follows in five to six months.

THE STORY: Stories should feature a teenage girl readers can identify with. The heroine should undergo a learning or growth experience, and the story should make the reader wonder how she would have reacted in the character's place.

Stories have to be both realistic and upbeat. Serious themes are handled, but stories should not be too ponderous in feeling. The total effect of the story should be uplifting; problems should concern questions of ethics, and the action should show the heroine ultimately behaving in an ethical manner.

Editors acknowledge that writing the kind of stories 'Teen wants is difficult but suggest that the key is to create situations that are real and important but that the teen can effectively control.

Immediately rejected are hackneyed or trivial themes, romances where romance is the only object, too adult themes, explicit language, too gloomy or depressing stories, or stories with casual references to sex, smoking, drinking, or drugs.

Stories should concern subjects like friendship, siblings, relationships with parents, dating, any activities common to teens.

Stories should run between 2500 and 4000 words.

REJECTION: Most stories are rejected with a standard form. If a manuscript is slightly more promising, the guidelines will be included. Editors ask to see more work only from writers they are seriously interested in pursuing.

ROD SERLING'S
THE TWILIGHT ZONE MAGAZINE

800 Second Avenue
New York, NY 10017
(212) 986-9600

SOURCE: T. E. D. Klein, editor

IN SHORT: Very open to new writers

ABOUT THE MAGAZINE: Bimonthly; seven to ten stories an issue. Not a science fiction magazine; does not want stories about technology or outer space or life on other planets, and is not interested in sword and sorcery or imaginary-world fantasy. *Twilight Zone Magazine* prefers stories about contemporary America in which ordinary people are caught up in extraordinary events—along the lines of the old *Twilight Zone* television series. *TZ* is relatively young—since March 1981. Average reader age is 27, but editor T. E. D. Klein says it is getting younger. "Best of . . ." anthologies are planned. Circulation: 150,000.

GETTING PUBLISHED: Rates: 5¢ a word; $150 minimum. Payment: half on acceptance, half on publication. Rights: first North American serial; nonexclusive foreign serial. Reply time: as long as four months; editors trying to speed response. Guidelines: available. Simultaneous submissions: will read.

"*Twilight Zone* is still very much a magazine for a newcomer to get into print," Klein says. Approximately 500 to 600 unsolicited manuscripts are submitted every month, plus another 5000 stories submitted to the annual short-story contest. In any issue, two to three stories will come from the unsolicited pile.

Stories are sorted into two groups. Agents' submissions and work from known writers or previously published writers are read by Klein. Everything else is read by assistant editors and outside readers. Anything they like is passed back to Klein, who makes the final decisions.

Once a story is purchased it will usually be published within six months.

THE STORY: Stories should consider the darkness that lurks on the edge of ordinary things. "Not invaders from space," Klein says, "but the devils within. Trips into the hidden worlds just outside of ordinary perception. We do not want sadism or violence. We get too many pieces in which kindly old couples get eaten by slugs in their garden. The horror has to be more interesting and more subtle. Other things we don't want include hard-core science fiction, detective stories, gothics, vampires, sword and sorcery, and Hobbit-like fantasies.

TZ emphasizes characterization, people reacting to events in a world gone askew. "But," Klein adds, "I'm a sucker for a clever plot twist."

Mood pieces or sketches are acceptable when the writing is good enough. Writing is the key. "We want specific, concrete imagery," Klein says, "making the reader see and hear what the character sees and hears."

TZ's annual short-story contest has been open to unpublished writers, but at this time it is uncertain that the contest will be continued.

In 1982 two stories tied for first place; both were published in the April issue. "I'll Be Seeing You," by W. G. Norris, is about a bereaved man whose grief lifts him out of the workaday world. It begins when a newspaper comic strip appears to mirror private incidents between himself and his dead wife. Is it a communication from the other side, a strange coincidence, or all in his own mind? "The River Styx Runs Upstream," by Dan Simmons, is also about death, this time death unaccepted. The new cult is the Resurrectionists. If your loved one dies, these people will bring him back to life, or almost. It's a story about what happens to one family—and the world—when nature's order is tampered with. The result is not pleasant, and the story is plain frightening.

Klein adds: "I like stories that touch me on an emotional level, that risk sentimentality and deal with deep human emotions through fantasy. That's what the magazine is about. They are not slick. They are vulnerable stories, very human."

TZ can use stories between 500 and 6000 words.

REJECTION: A standard form is usually used. A story admired but wrong for the magazine will be rejected with a personal note. Further submissions might be asked for if the writing is found promising. Rewrites on speculation are asked for only if the editors have concrete suggestions. They have worked through as many as four revisions on one piece.

YOUNG MISS

685 Third Avenue
New York, NY 10017
(212) 878-8700

SOURCE: Deborah Purcell, features/fiction editor

IN SHORT: Looking for new writers

ABOUT THE MAGAZINE: Published ten times a year; one story per issue, plus occasional "bonus fiction" issues. *Young Miss* strives to be a "second best friend" to its teenage reader. It offers support, information, and entertainment. Its readership ranges from 12 to 17 with a core group of 15-16. The magazine discusses boy-girl relationships, friendship, family problems, loneliness, and other subjects central to a young woman's emotional and personal life. It also offers fashion and beauty advice, movie reviews, and celebrity interviews.

The editors are very enthusiastic about their fiction. "Our readers love our short stories," Deborah Purcell says. "Good fiction offers them not only fun, but also the chance to identify with universal situations." Circulation: 700,000.

GETTING PUBLISHED: Rates: $350 for first sale. Payment: on acceptance. Rights: first North American serial. Reply time: six to eight weeks. Guidelines: available.

In 1982, five stories, half the magazine's published fiction, came from the unsolicited submissions, which come in at a rate of about 50 a week.

Purcell is interested in finding new writers for the young adult market, but also solicits work from known writers and literary agents.

Only 10% of the submissions are interesting enough to receive any consideration, but Purcell reads everything sent in. She estimates that she discusses five stories a month with the editor-in-chief.

Purcell feels strongly that a cover letter, even if the writer has no previous credits, should be included. "Only one or two lines to establish personal contact," she says. Rewrites are asked for only if a story is of considerable interest and has easily identifiable flaws; rewrites are on spec.

It will be at least nine months before a purchased story sees print.

THE STORY: *Young Miss* needs both entertaining stories and fiction dealing with serious aspects of a teen's life. Its needs are dictated by the age range of its readers. "Our older readers have a broader range of concerns," Purcell says, "whereas our younger readers find light entertainment, including animal stories, particularly appealing. Romances are popular with both."

Young Miss stays away from grim or offensive subjects but does address serious topics such as cheating in school, old age, coping with stepparents, and so on.

In the June/July 1982 issue is a story that Purcell cites as an example of how to handle the subject of death for a young adult audience. In "Fragile Images," by Mary Elizabeth Ryan, a teenage boy, bereft and despondent at his mother's death, reconnects with life through his feelings for a woman photographer he meets at the beach. Though at the end of the summer they part company, her presence has reconfirmed for the boy that life is interesting, fun, and worth living despite the passing hard times.

There are several factors that lead to immediate rejection. "We get too many stories that are predominantly dialogue," Purcell says. "These give no sense of a heroine's inner conflicts, emotions, and growth as a person. Our readers are at an age where they are very much exploring their feelings. We're looking for stories with richness and resonance.

"Another problem is lack of realism, stories with characters out of *Father Knows Best*. In today's world, it is not realistic for a young woman to come home and find her mother in the kitchen baking cookies. The mother is more apt to be out working. We want to see this."

"Just Friends," by Jane Scherer (Apr. '82), came from the slush pile. A romance with a light touch, it tells the story of a boy's love for a taller girl and his fear of rejection because of his lack of height. Since so many teenage girls worry about being too tall, seeing the problem from the other side works well. Further, the girl is a basketball star about to compete for a college scholarship. That is, she is a modern, competitive young woman, and in the boy's eyes that only makes her more attractive.

Genre fiction would be welcome if it could be done properly

for teens. *Young Miss* can use stories up to 3000 words and would like to see more short-shorts.

REJECTION: A standardized form is used for most submissions. Purcell writes back personally only if she thinks the writer has real potential for *Young Miss*. She estimates that she writes five personal notes a week.

The
Literary
Magazines

There are countless small-press magazines that publish short stories. Here is a selection of them. Included are the well-known, widely circulated journals that often have work chosen for awards and collections (see Appendix A). There are also feminist publications, political magazines, journals looking for experimental prose, magazines publishing short prose pieces that aren't quite stories, magazines that print fiction and poetry almost exclusively, magazines that include a story or two among the essays and articles. Some are published by universities; others are private efforts of editors and writers.

Magazines that solicit all their work are not included. Neither are journals that use very little fiction. Finally, a few much-admired magazines are not listed because their editors either did not have the time or did not want to participate.

Offered in each listing is some news about the publication: some of the things the editors say; names of authors who have been published; a look at how the editors find and choose. Use the guide to help you get a feel for the magazines and to help you decide which ones to read. It is necessary to read these magazines before submitting stories to them. Each has a personality of its own. The writer who is familiar with a magazine stands a far better chance of being published in it than a writer who sends out his stories hit-or-miss.

Are literary magazines an accessible market? The answer is a qualified yes. It is not true that literary magazines are "easy" to break into—they are only for writers doing quality, literate work. But there are a lot of literary magazines. A determined writer can keep trying. One editor's rejection can be another editor's prize story. And literary magazines can and do take chances. Their readers are presumed to be people who will put the kind of concentration into reading a story that the author put into its writing. Stories that are offbeat, experimental in approach, or difficult in language and concept can find a place in these magazines.

About the listings

SOURCE: Name of person interviewed or who filled out a questionnaire. When no name is listed it is by the editor's request. Information in the listings also comes from research into back issues.

PUBLICATION FREQUENCY: Often, quarterly magazines are published triannually; that is, in two single and one double issue. Irregular or occasional publication means just that; the magazine is published when the editors get material and money together. It does not indicate any less serious purpose; many of the irregular magazines have been in publication for years and are highly respected.

CIRCULATION: This is often an approximate figure; press runs differ issue-to-issue and some of the magazines don't have up-to-date figures.

DISTRIBUTION: Subscriptions—often both national and international—are the mainstay of most literary magazines. Many are also distributed through literary bookstores and large newsstands, and many can be found in libraries. Single issues can be obtained directly from the magazines.

SUBSCRIPTIONS: Magazines published irregularly often have no subscription price listed. In other cases, subscriptions are always listed at their one-year price; two- and three-year rates generally come out to less per issue.

READER FEES AND SUBSCRIPTIONS: Many of the literary magazines (in fact, most of the literary magazines) are just scraping by financially. The editors can't help but reflect that if the writers who were constantly sending in stories were also reading (and buying) the magazines, the financial situation would be much better. Many editors are considering reading fees or asking that a subscription order accompany an unsolicited manuscript. Though this is not general now, it might well be a coming thing. It is, after all, much to a writer's self-interest to support the small presses.

THE AGNI REVIEW

P. O. Box 229
Cambridge, MA 02138
(617) 491-1079

SOURCE: Sharon Dunn, editor

ABOUT THE JOURNAL: Biannual (fall and spring). Founded: 1972. Circulation: 1200. Distribution: subscription; literary bookstores. Avg. issue: 124-148 pp. Size: 5½ x 8½. Price: $3.50. Subscription: $6. Sample copy: $3.50. Back issues: available. Price: $3.50.

FICTION: Eight to ten stories a year. Rates: $5 a page and three copies. Payment: on publication. Rights: first North American serial. Reply time: six to eight weeks. Publication time: two to six months. Length: no limits; has published novellas.

The Agni Review is a lively, eclectic journal of poetry and fiction that is committed to mixing promising unknowns with award-winning authors. About half of *Agni*'s pages are set aside for fiction, including novel excerpts. Approximately one-third of its fiction is solicited; the rest is chosen from the over 900 unsolicited manuscripts submitted annually.

Agni publishes both experimental and traditional prose with the emphasis on traditional work. Published writers include David Bosworth, Mary Morris, John Griesemer, Corinne Demas Bliss, Joyce Carol Oates, Abby Frucht, and Robert Taylor, Jr.

"Each of these writers," editor Sharon Dunn says, "has an individual, unique prose style and voice. They concern themselves with elaborating the textures and complexities of living, of thinking and feeling, through the telling of stories."

Fiction in *Agni* 15 (Fall '82) included four novel excerpts from work by T. Corraghessan Boyle, George Garrett, DeWitt Henry, and R. G. Vliet and a story by David Bosworth. *Agni* 14 included stories by James Hanley, Robert Taylor, Jr., Allan Provost, and William Young and a first published piece by Ralph Lombreglia.

Dunn reads all submissions. She estimates that 5% are good enough for more than one reading. The most common reason for rejection is "undistinguished writing." A standard form is usually used. A note is returned when a piece shows real promise and the editor would like to see more work. Specific criticisms and requests for minor changes are made only when a piece has been accepted for publication.

A cover letter makes no difference in the way a story is handled. If an author wants to submit a group of stories, he or she must submit a sample story and a query letter first.

Dunn's advice to writers: "Read back issues of the magazine to see the quality and kinds of fiction we've published in the past."

THE AMERICAN POETRY REVIEW

Department A
Temple University Center City
1616 Walnut
Room 405
Philadelphia, PA 19103
(215) 732-6770

SOURCE: Martin Novelli, assistant editor

ABOUT THE JOURNAL: Bimonthly. Founded: 1972. Circulation: 26,000. Distribution: subscription; newsstands. Avg. issue: 48 pp.; possibility of increase to 56 pp. Size: tabloid. Price: $1.50. Subscription: $7.50. Sample copy: free. Back issues: available. Price: $2 and $5.

FICTION: Generally one piece of fiction per issue. Rates: $25 per printed page. Payment: on publication. Rights: copyright reverts to author. Reply time: at least six weeks for rejection. Publication time: usually within three issues. Length: 1500-2000 words ideal; will go longer in the case of very worthwhile work.

The American Poetry Review is the best-known and most widely circulated (26,000 copies; six times a year) poetry publication in the country. It was designed to offer the work of serious poets in an accessible form. The result is a newsprint tabloid selling for $1.50, as opposed to the $4 cover price of most quarterlies. *APR* does not concentrate on any style or type of poetry. It is interested only in quality.

Fiction became more important in *APR* in 1980, when editors decided to publish it regularly instead of sporadically. Fiction or some sort of fiction-connected prose has appeared in 12 of the last 14 issues. *APR* also publishes essays, articles, letters, photos, interviews, reviews, news items, and art.

To some extent *APR* is an open market for the short story. All submissions (approximately six a week) are read by assistant editor Martin Novelli. But a lot of fiction is solicited. There are a high number of submissions from agents and from well-known writers.

Further, there is no predisposition to either new writers or a representative or exhaustive approach to contemporary fiction. In some issues, no story appears—only a piece of fiction criticism or a piece about a writer. For instance, selections from

Mark Twain's letters were published. And a selection from Gunter Grass's work was nonfiction.

In the last three years, no unsolicited story from an unknown writer has been published. Novelli does add that he has received manuscripts promising enough to lead him to write back to the author and ask for more work.

Among the stories published in 1982 were a piece by Maria Luisa Bombal and a story by Bill Barich. Bombal, who died in 1980, was a Spanish writer considered to be an innovative stylist and a precursor of such contemporary Spanish writers as Marquez, Borges, and Cortázar. Barich is a young American writer whose work has appeared in many magazines and quarterlies.

Fiction and poetry submissions are handled similarly. All the editors read every piece being considered. A majority vote determines what is printed.

ANOTHER CHICAGO MAGAZINE

Box 11223
Chicago, IL 60611
(312) 951-0999

SOURCE: Lee Webster, editor

ABOUT THE MAGAZINE: Biannual; send manuscripts to Barry Silesky. Founded: 1977. Circulation: 1200. Distribution: subscription; newsstands; bookstores. Avg. issue: 80-128 pp. Size: 5½ x 8½. Price: $2.50. Subscription: $5. Sample copy: $2.50. Back issues: available. Price: issues 1-3, $5; all others, $2.50. Published by Thunder's Mouth Press, Inc.

FICTION: Occupies 25% of total pages; one to three stories an issue. Rates: currently pays in copies, but is hoping for small cash payments in the future. Payment: on publication. Rights: first North American serial. Reply time: 6 to 12 weeks. Publication time: three to nine months. Length: no formal limits, though it would be difficult to publish an entire novel.

Describing *Another Chicago Magazine*, editor Lee Webster says: "Highly literary, postmodern, rural and urban, nonregional, traditional and experimental, generally left-wing." Included are fiction, poetry, essays, and art. The editors like to see work that is socially involved. *ACM* 6, for instance, included "Places and Ways to Live," a marine's memoir of Vietnam; and "Rituals," by D. L. Klauck, which won the PEN 1980 Malcolm Braly Prize, awarded to prisoner-writers.

"Simon J. Ortiz, G.W. Kennedy, and James McManus are three writers we've published who I feel are exceptionally talented," Webster says. "There are, of course, many writers whom we admire. When a story works, the characters have dimension, the plot is credible, the themes are appealing, the language sparkles, the content in some way moves toward the impovement of the human condition."

Fiction is chosen from the 200 unsolicited stories submitted annually. All stories are looked at by a first reader. Immediate rejections are sent back with a standard form. If the reader has either mixed feelings or very positive feelings about a piece, it goes to another reader. About 10% of the manuscripts are generally found to be worth more than one look.

If both readers are strongly in favor of a story it is accepted. If the editors disagree, the story is discussed extensively. If both editors have mixed feelings the piece is rejected but the author is encouraged to submit more work.

"There are times," Webster says, "when some element of a written piece excites us enough to write a personal note. We would like to do this more often, but time is very scarce."

Rejection is most often because of writing. "Rarely, but on occasion," Webster says, "subject matter will be inappropriate for us."

The less information in cover letters the better. "Résumés and lists of publications are annoying. We judge the work, not the writer." Editors will read a group of stories.

ANTAEUS

18 West 30th Street
New York, NY 10001
(212) 685-8240

SOURCE: Daniel Halpern, editor

ABOUT THE JOURNAL: Quarterly; no submissions June, July, August. Founded: 1969. Circulation: 5000. Distribution: subscription; newsstands; bookstores. Avg. issue: 160 pp; double issues. Size: 6½ x 9. Price: $5. Subscription: $16. Sample copy: $5. Back issues: write for list.

FICTION: One issue a year with no fiction; often an all-fiction issue; can publish up to 50 stories a year. Rates: $5 a page; hoping to go to $10. Payment: on publication. Rights: copyright reverts. Reply time: three weeks for rejection; three months when ms. being considered. Publication time: not over a year. Length: up to 100 manuscript pages.

Antaeus is among the best-known of the quarterlies and has a particularly strong commitment to fiction. The magazine both solicits work and considers unsolicited manuscripts. "Out of a possible ten stories in an issue," editor Daniel Halpern says, "we like to have two or three from well-known, immediately recognized writers."

Somewhere between 200 and 300 unsolicited short stories are submitted every month. Halpern estimates that maybe five out of every 300 are worth serious consideration. Something like 10% of the fiction published, or five stories a year, is entirely unsolicited. A higher number of published stories are from writers who have been rejected several times but have been encouraged to keep submitting.

First readers are from the graduate writing division of Columbia University. They pull anything "interesting, unusual, or accomplished" and pass it to the editors. "Most are just too poorly written," Halpern says. "They are sent back with a form letter meant to discourage."

Once a story passes the first reader, it is considered by staff editors and collects an accretion of opinions. Final decisions are made by Halpern. Any story that is considered at all will be rejected with a personal letter asking to see more work. Cover letters make little difference in manuscript treatment, and Halpern advises against sending in several stories at one time. "If a reader doesn't like the first story it hurts the second. Wait a month and the second story gets a fresh reading."

Stories are commonly rejected for two reasons: The writing is not good enough and they are not interesting to read. "There are pieces that are immediately, obviously bad. It is the marginal pieces that are difficult. So I let them sit. See if I can remember them a few days later; see if anything has stuck.

"We get some well-written, boring stories. There is nothing to argue with in them. They are intelligent, well told. But they consume themselves. When you are finished reading there is nothing left of them in your mind. Writing well, while essential, is no substitute for not having something to write about."

There are certain pat stories, he adds, that they see too much of, particularly relationships (between men and women) falling apart and dissections of parent-child relationships.

Antaeus is not closed to any type of writing. But Halpern adds that too many writers seem to misunderstand what the term "experimental fiction" means, or even is supposed to mean. They are using it as an excuse to abdicate control and responsibility.

Besides fiction, *Antaeus* publishes poetry, interviews with writers, essays (one was on the edibility of mermaids), letters, and drawings.

Antaeus has published a four-part reading list, "Neglected Books of the Twentieth Century" (vols. 18, 19, 20, 27); a special essay issue (vol. 21-22) with contributions from Auden, Pound, Brodkey, Barthes, et al; an essay issue entitled "The Autobiographical Eye" (vol. 45-46) with contributions from Calvino, Dillard, Elkin, Fowles, Gordimer, Hesse, Merwin, et al; and a popular-fiction issue (vol. 25-26) with contributions from Raymond Chandler, Ross Macdonald, John D. MacDonald, et al.

Fiction contributors also include Tobias Wolff, Meredith Steinbach, Stephanie Vaughn, and Steven Millhauser. Writers who are recently new to *Antaeus* include Steven Minot, Christiane Bird, and Jonathan Penner.

THE ANTIOCH REVIEW

Box 148
Yellow Springs, OH 45387
(513) 767-1504 ext. 518

SOURCE: Nolan Miller, fiction editor

ABOUT THE JOURNAL: Quarterly. Editor: Robert S. Fogarty. Founded: 1941. Circulation: 4500. Distribution: subscription; better bookstores. Avg. issue: 80-100 pp. Size: 9 x 6. Price: $3.50. Subscription: $12. Back issues: some available. Price: $2.50. Associated with Antioch College, but college has no editorial control.

FICTION: About one-third of total pages; three to four stories an issue. Rates: $10 a printed page and two free copies. Payment: on publication. Rights: copyright reverts on request. Reply time: over a month. Length: no limits.

The Antioch Review is one of the best-known quarterlies; it publishes material in all areas of the arts and humanities. Fiction accounts for something like 30% of its pages; there have been special fiction issues. Also published are poetry, articles, essays, criticism, and reviews.

Upward of 2000-3000 unsolicited stories are submitted every year. According to fiction editor Nolan Miller: "Ninety-nine percent of what comes in is unpublishable." Possibly one out of 50 stories is good enough for more than one reading.

"Most of what we receive is poorly written, tired prose, conventional situations, too descriptive, too expository. We like fiction that has something to say, is intellectually satisfying and emotionally fulfilling. Mature characters and mature themes have the strongest appeal. The personality—the voice—of the writer should be appealingly distinctive.

"We have no preconceived notion of what we want. Anything that 'hits' we take. All fiction is 'experimental.' But it has to be an experiment that works. If it's good and commands attention, we're open to it, whatever the subject. We do tend to avoid scholarly work or material too special and limited in interest.

"Our special delight is 'finding' a previously unpublished writer. For example, 'Poor Boy,' by Lynda Lloyd, was a first story; it will appear in the 1983 *O. Henry Prize Awards* volume."

Writers published include Gordon Weaver, James Purdy, John Hermann, Carolyn Osborn, Stephen Dixon, Mary Gordon, Gordon Lish, Percy Seitlin, Oakley Hall, and Ira Sadoff.

Miller's advice to the writer is to read the review. The most common reason for rejection is that the writer has not looked at the magazine and is sending inappropriate material, for instance science fiction or mass-media formula fiction.

Stories are screened by three assistant editors, who pass the promising pieces to the fiction editor. Real possibilities are read by the editor. Both the fiction editor and the editor must approve a story before publication. In most cases, a standard rejection form is used. Editors write only when some revision would make the story acceptable or when a writer is found promising and editors would like to see more work.

"Actually," Miller says, "very few stories are accepted as submitted; even professional writers can use an editorial point of view. Writers who resist criticism are few; in our experience, the better the writer, the more he/she welcomes suggestions for improving a story. We like very much to bring new writers along and will often encourage submissions over a period of years."

A recent fiction issue, titled "Varieties of Literary Expression: A Gallimaufry," was vol. 40, no. 1 (Winter '82). Writers included Marc Stephen Zasada, Susan Lohafer, Paulette Bates, M.E. McMullen, Laurence N. de Looze, and Percy Seitlin.

A quote from the editorial by Robert S. Fogarty:

"The varieties of literary expression published in the United States are striking. . . . We are open to literary expression wherever we can find it and our current issue, I think, reflects that approach.

"Readers will recognize traditional narratives, epiphany stories, sketches, and the 'essay as fiction' in this issue. . . .

"Neophyte writers often query us: 'What do you look for?' or 'How long should it be?' and, on occasion, 'Do you pay?' In answer to the first question we usually answer 'good writing' and to the second 'long enough.' To the third question we are less ambiguous and say: 'Ten dollars a page.' Not enough to make anyone rich, but enough to assert the principle established at this magazine that writers should be paid for their work. Although we seek variety, we have our blind spots, pass over works of genius, and publish stories we later regret seeing in print. What we do see is considerable vitality in our prose and poetry.

We read work, on occasion, that produces in us reaction akin to a religious experience. . . . "

Editors only want cover letters if they list previous credits; this does stimulate special attention. Editors do not like to see group submissions.

APALACHEE QUARTERLY

P. O. Box 20106
Tallahassee, FL 32304
(904) 878-1591, 644-2440

SOURCE: P. V. LeForge, editor

ABOUT THE JOURNAL: Quarterly; send manuscripts to "the editors." Founded: 1972. Circulation: 400. Distribution: subscription; regional newsstands and bookstores. Avg. issue: 44-60 pp. Size: 6½ x 9¼. Price: $2.50. Subscription: $8. Sample copy: $2. Back issues: available. Price: $2.

FICTION: Occupies 75% of pages; 20 stories a year. Rates: two copies. Rights: first North American serial. Reply time: three to six weeks. Publication time: three to four months. Length: 30 typewritten pages maximum.

Editors at *Apalachee Quarterly* "hope to see writing that aspires to the very heights of literature. . . . The only basis of an acceptance is that the story be well written. Most are not." The magazine concentrates on fiction and poetry.

All of *Apalachee*'s fiction is chosen from the 500 unsolicited stories submitted annually. The contributors are almost exclusively unknown or little-known writers.

Editors are very open to differing style and techniques. "Any genre can transcend its stereotyped limitations, as Brontë did with gothic romance, Dostoevsky with detective fiction, Pynchon and Lessing with futuristic work. A story, however, should be a story and not a vignette or slice of life. We like experimental fiction, but not from writers who have not mastered traditional forms." Mastering, editor P. V. LeForge adds, means writing almost every day.

"Bad writing may be loosely defined . . . as not meeting common . . . standards in storytelling, grammar, syntax, point of view, character development, dialogue, resolution, and general cohesiveness."

All stories are read by all the magazine's seven editors. Any one of them can mark a story for reconsideration. Stories which interested no one (about 50%) are sent back with a standard rejection form. Many will have critical comments added at the editor's discretion.

The stories held are circulated for a second reading, then discussed at an editorial meeting. Finally, a vote is held. It takes a majority vote for a story to be accepted. Tied votes mean rejection, though with critical comments sent to the author. Suggestions are made only to help the author; resubmissions are almost never asked for. The only exception is when the editors make changes and accept the story if the author approves them.

Rarely used, but in place, is what the editors call their "trump system." That is, if an editor is outvoted, he can make one publication selection on his own. This can lead to acceptance of stories out of the mainstream.

Editors prefer to see only one story at a time. As far as cover letters are concerned, LeForge writes: "If an author must send a cover letter, it should be brief and casual. Nothing gives us greater delight than to sit in a circle and ridicule long vitas and absurd lists of previous publications—some of which are longer and all of which are funnier than the manuscript itself. We often wax them and roll them into paper logs, cutting down our price of winter heat."

LeForge has a long list of dos and don'ts for writers. Among the don'ts are query letters, sloppy manuscripts, stories with racist or sexist terms or stereotypes, and simultaneous submissions. "Do not," he also says, "send out stories about dying or dead grandparents; travailing the lives of faculty members; about rustic prepubescents told in the first person; about rustic prepubescents told in the third person; glorifying or even mentioning cruelty to animals; or stories that end with the words: 'It was only a dream!' "

Another don't he mentions is "don't give up." The two dos are: "Study fiction. Find out why the great stories are read over and over again. . . . Believe that we wish you the best of luck."

ARIZONA QUARTERLY

541-B Main Library
The University of Arizona
Tucson, AZ 85721
(602) 626-1029

SOURCE: Albert F. Gegenheimer, editor

ABOUT THE JOURNAL: Quarterly. Founded: 1945. Circulation: private information; state-supported. Distribution: subscription. Avg. issue: 96 pp. Size: 9 x 6. Price: $1.50. Subscription: $5. Sample copy: $1.50. Back issues: some available. Price: $1.50.

FICTION: One or two stories per issue. Rates: copies. Rights: quarterly is copyrighted by Arizona Board of Regents. Reply time: two or three weeks. Publication time: varies. Length: average is 15-20 pages.

Arizona Quarterly publishes fiction, poetry, essays and articles on literary and cultural subjects, and book reviews. It sometimes features an author and has done an issue on the family in literature and another on women's literature. It welcomes Southwestern material and is interested in "anthropological, English, folklore" material.

Authors published over the past three years include Pat Carr, Miriam Finkelstein, Miriam Wolfe Laughlin, Harold M. Robinson, Chin-Ye Shih, Sanford Goldstein, Brenda L. Newland, Marie Chay, and J. M. Ferguson, Jr.

"They represent the cross section we try to achieve," editor Albert F. Gegenheimer says. "There is a coming-of-age story, an oriental story depicting the universal con man, a regional story about a family we have read about for years, a story about pride brought down, a story about endurance and its breakdown, a story about an American abroad adapting to a foreign country, a story of Western concern with archaeological digs, and a story about adaptation to America."

When stories are rejected it is because they are "unsuitable for a literary journal aimed at a literate readership." Gegenheimer says, "A good story has something to say and says it well."

Fiction is chosen from the approximately 175-200 annual unsolicited submissions. An editorial assistant is first reader, followed by the editor and a member or members of the editorial board. Gegenheimer says 10% of the submssions are worth more than one reading. A standard rejection form is used if there is no question as to the unsuitability of a story. Letters of criticism, encouragement, and revision requests are sometimes written when the material warrants it. Otherwise, notation is made on the rejection slip: "The large number of manuscripts received precludes any personal comment."

Editors prefer that writers include a brief biographical sketch and a note on previous publications so that upon acceptance they do not have to write for the information. Editors will read a group of stories.

BENNINGTON REVIEW

Bennington, College
Bennington, VT 05201
(518) 584-5000 ext. 302

SOURCE: Robert Boyers, editor

ABOUT THE JOURNAL: Triannual; no manuscripts accepted during summer. Founded: 1978. Circulation: 2500. Distribution: subscription; newsstands and bookstores mostly in the Northeast. Avg. issue: 90 pp. Size: 8x11. Price: $4. Subscription: $12. Sample copy: $3. Back issues: available. Price: $4. Supported by Bennington College.

FICTION: Occupies 15% to 20% of total pages; two to three stories per issue. Rates: 10 copies; discount on further copies. Rights: one-time English language. Reply time: three to five months. Publication time: 6 to 18 months. Length: no limits; accepts novella-length important works.

Bennington Review describes itself as "a testing ground for contemporary arts and letters." It publishes poems, art, interviews, essays, and criticism as well as stories. The editorial advisory board of the review includes writers Bernard Malamud, Nicholas Delbanco, and John Updike.

Most of the up to nine stories published every year are found in the approximately 300 unsolicited submissions. Editor Robert Boyers says, " . . . we've published the first professional story of several writers. . . .

"We're looking for quality material. It can be highly 'experimental' or conventional in form. We're very interested in political fiction, though it is hard to find."

Published writers include Nicholas Delbanco, Joyce Carol Oates, George Garrett, Wright Morris, Leslie Epstein, and Graham Petrie.

An assistant fiction editor is first reader. Stories found promising (between 10% and 15%) are given to the senior fiction editor. His choices go to the editor-in-chief, who makes the final decisions. A standard rejection form is used in most cases. Occasionally, editors will recommend revisions or cuts.

In a cover letter, a list of credits is considered helpful, though Boyers adds that most of the authors do not submit one. Editors will look at groups of stories only from writers whose work they know.

Common reasons for rejection include: "Story is familiar confessional or personal—usually domestic—trauma. No color, no particular risks taken. No sense of having been written by someone with ideas. Generally we reject standard competent writers' school pieces."

Nonfiction published in issue 12 (Winter '81–'82) included an essay on Edmund Wilson, an interview with Hilma Wolitzer, a piece subtitled "Reflections on Hegel's 'Aesthetics' and Rilke's 'Duino Elegies,' " an illustrated consideration of the art of Arshile Gorky, a consideration of Martin Scorsese and *Raging Bull*, a piece titled "Art and Politics Once More," a dialogue by Eric Bentley, poetry by John Hollander and David Wagoner, and fiction from Frederick Turner and Enid Harlow.

BENZENE

P. O. Box 383
New York, NY 10014
(212) 675-6384

SOURCE: Allan Bealy, editor

ABOUT THE JOURNAL: Triannual; no manuscripts accepted in July and August. Founded: 1980. Circulation: 1000. Distribution: subscription; bookstores regionally and in select cities. Avg. issue: 48 pp. Size: 11x17. Price: $2. Subscription: $10. Sample copy: $3.50. Back issues: available. Price: $4.

FICTION: Occupies 50% or more of pages; six to ten stories a year. Rates: copies. Rights: buys none. Reply time: usually one month. Publication time: three months. Length: no novels.

Benzene encourages "experiments in form and structure, yet work must be based on a strong understanding of the possibilities of modern literature and the history of avant-garde writing."

Most of the fiction is solicited, but unsolicited manuscripts are read and new or little-known authors are often published.

Editor Allan Bealy wants fiction that has a "compelling theme using a format that is powerful and sensible and hopefully breaks new ground in the short-story form. Traditional form is not likely to be accepted unless the writer uses it to transcend ordinary storytelling. Genre writing is read but not encouraged. . . . Ursule Molinaro is a prime example of powerful storytelling using effectively a format that is experimental and serves her 'voice' well."

Hundreds of manuscripts come in every year; maybe 5% are considered worth a second reading. Stories are read by the editor; most are returned with a handwritten form letter. Stories found interesting will lead Bealy to contact the author. He may ask to see more work, or for a revision or shortening, or he may just ask for biographical information.

Bealy does not want cover letters. He will read a group of stories from an author, but adds if the first is not good, the rest get less attention.

THE BERKELEY MONTHLY

910 Parker Street
Berkeley, CA 94710
(415) 848-7900

SOURCE: Adele Framer, editor

ABOUT THE JOURNAL: Monthly. Founded: 1968. Circulation: 75,000. Distribution: controlled circulation; delivered to selected homes. Avg. issue: 56-100 pp. Size: tabloid. Price: $1. Subscription: $10. Sample copy: $2. Back issues: available. Price: $2.

FICTION: Occupies 10% of total pages; 12-16 stories a year. Rates: $50-$150. Payment: on publication. Rights: first rights. Reply time: six to eight weeks. Publication time: two to three months. Length: short-shorts up to 2000 words; stories up to 3500 words.

The Berkeley Monthly is a controlled-circulation tabloid delivered free to upper-income homes in the Berkeley area. It publishes an eclectic range of nonfiction including a calendar of area events and consumer news. The magazine is particularly proud of its graphics and design. Regional material is favored.

Fiction is solicited from local authors as well as chosen from the 600 unsolicited pieces submitted every year. "We will print any fiction as long as it's well written, interesting, and of a length we can handle," editor Adele Framer says. She cites the work of Thomas Farber—"a fresh, clear voice who describes the nuances of relationships"—and Diane Johnson—"a master of the taut, clean, and utterly compelling."

Submissions are read by the editor or associate editor. Generally, 2% of them are found worth a second reading. Manuscripts are returned with a form letter. A personal note is included if editors wish to hear from the author again, if the story shows promise, or if it's a fine piece not right for the magazine.

Common reasons for rejection include poor technique, hackneyed plot, and maudlin intentions.

Framer adds: "Cover letters should include some biography that shows a depth of experience relevant to the story. I discount lists of publications; many are forgeries." Editors will read a group of stories.

BLACK WARRIOR REVIEW

P. O. Box 2936
University, AL 35486-2936
(205) 348-5526

SOURCE: Dev Hathaway, editor

ABOUT THE JOURNAL: Biannual; fall and spring. Submission deadlines: October 1 for fall; February 1 for spring. Founded: 1974. Circulation: 1800. Distribution: mostly subscription. Avg. issue: 128 pp. Size: 6x9. Price: $3. Subscription: $5. Sample copy: $3. Back issues: some available. Price: $3. Affiliated with University of Alabama.

FICTION: Three to five stories per issue. Rates: two copies; $500 awarded every year for best story. Rights: none. Reply time: two weeks to two months. Publication time: one to six months. Length: no limits.

Black Warrior Review publishes fiction, poetry, and reviews. Each year it offers a $500 award to one fiction writer and one poet for outstanding work published in either the Fall or Spring issue. Winners are selected by outside judges.

Fiction in *Black Warrior* is half solicited and half chosen from the 750-1000 unsolicited manuscripts submitted annually. Editors are open to any fiction that is "literary." They do not want "cuteness, unengaging use of language, sentimentality."

Stories in the Fall 1982 issue came from Mark Costello, George Garrett, Eugene K. Garber, and Jack Matthews.

The winner of the 1981-82 award for fiction was Kurt Rheinheimer for "New Weather." The selection was made by Mark Costello.

Other writers whose work has recently appeared include Jack Butler, Charles McNair, Jr., James Tate, Brad Watson, Pamela Stewart, Eve Shelnutt, Fred Chappell, Alan Cheuse, and Philip F. O'Connor.

The fiction editor glances at all submissions. If he passes them on to his staff, two to five readers will look at them. If a story is being seriously considered, the editor reads it. Acceptance follows approval by the editor, the fiction editor, and a majority of the staff. Few rejections are accompanied by individual comments because of the volume of submissions.

Cover letters are not necessary; editors will read a group of stories "if they're interesting."

BLOODROOT

P. O. Box 891
Grand Forks, ND 58206-0891

SOURCE: Dan Eades, editor

ABOUT THE JOURNAL: Irregular; tries for two a year; address manuscripts to Joan Eades, editor. Founded: 1976. Circulation: 800. Distribution: subscription; regional newsstands and bookstores. Avg. issue: 72 pp. Size: 6x9. Price: $2. Subscription: $6 for three issues. Sample copy: $2.50. Back issues: available. Price: varies.

FICTION: Occupies two-thirds to three-quarters of total pages; 7 to 20 stories a year. Rates: copies; $5 per printed page when grants allow. Payment: on publication. Rights: all rights; reverts to author on request. Reply time: two weeks to six months. Publication time: one month. Length: no exclusive limits, but stories under 1500 words or over 5000 words have to be exceptional.

Most of *Bloodroot*'s fiction comes from the 500 unsolicited stories submitted every year. *Bloodroot* often publishes unknown or little-known writers, but is not a proving ground for the amateur.

"We believe," Dan Eades says, "writers should be 'realistic,' that is professional, in their expectations. Our average contributor has published several stories and a small-press book or two; she/he has developed a voice, a style, a certainty of craft—and our contributors must meet those standards to receive serious consideration, even if they have not published before."

Bloodroot tries to promote quality writing by women, especially from the Northern Plains. But quality is more important than sex or region, and the editors do not think of *Bloodroot* as a regional magazine.

The editors want good writing, honest writing. They are open to "an unusually wide range of styles and voices," though they do not want genre fiction. They believe there is little point in listing authors they have published. "Every good, serious writer creates a new kind of work; it is precisely this 'new kind of work' that we are looking for."

Stories are usually given a first reading within a week or two; 75% to 95% of them are immediately rejected. The rest are filed, with comments, for the second reader. After discussion, those stories both editors find weak (10% to 25%) are returned. Stories for "final consideration" are held until enough manuscripts have accumulated or a publication date has been set. A third editor reads and comments. Finally, at a series of meetings, the stories are discussed by all three editors and the final selection is made. Usually, any story not slated for publication will be returned.

For the professional writer, Dan Eades says: "You're one of the 5% to 10% whose work is read by all three of our editors, a serious writer who is a professional, or shows promise of becoming one, and you want to know the fine points. The areas most likely to be discussed in our meetings to determine which stories will be published and which will be regretfully declined usually concern: (1) the conclusion, (2) soft writing (not real mistakes, but weak spots), (3) interest (how exciting or dull the story is), (4) how promising a writer seems to be; how important publication, by us, will be for their career, and (5) the appropriateness of the story to our magazine, to the issue under consideration."

Bloodroot uses standard rejection forms. Notes of encouragement and/or criticism are written when the editors think they will be helpful. If more than one manuscript is submitted, the editors might point out areas of strength. "Serious criticism is usually reserved for serious writers. If we see a 'problem' or a set of 'problems' in an otherwise well-written work, we will outline our concerns." The editors do not want suggestions to be taken as an invitation for resubmission. If the editors want to see the piece again, or to see more work, they will say so.

The most common reason for rejection is bad writing; it could be something basic like "clumsy, unprofessional sentences." Another problem is false writing: "inaccurate rendering of characters or plot." Exposition is often a problem: "Contemporary fiction . . . does not allow much room for exposition and no room at all for clumsy exposition. . . ." Editors see too much "raw autobiography posing as fiction," and too much reportage, "telling rather than showing."

Cover letters are not necessary. But the editors want to hear if the writer reads *Bloodroot*, likes it, and why. They find that most writers do list a few of their major publications. "It is *possible* that a list of prestigious publications will make us give a story closer consideration initially; it is also possible that, when the final choice is to be made, we will favor (slightly) a writer who has no publication (especially if most of the writers in the projected issue have published extensively)."

Editors will read more than one story at a time, but warn that if the first is not very well written, the others will not be given as much time.

Dan Eades adds the following: "*Bloodroot* is a 'small-press publication.' Like many small-press magazines, our editors are not paid and work at other jobs to make a living. It is a constant struggle to find funding . . . to continue publishing. . . . We steal time from other pursuits to publish *Bloodroot* because we believe in the necessity of alternate, or small-press, publication and because we love good writing. We do not believe it is 'sentimental' or 'corny' to ask that potential contributors keep these facts . . . in mind when they communicate to us."

What the editors want is professionalism. That is return envelopes (of the right size and postage); proofread copy; submissions from writers who have looked at *Bloodroot* and honestly believe submitting will not be a waste of everybody's time.

"Writers should know that editors are idealists—they really hope that each manuscript they read will be good, publishable, perhaps even great. . . . But writers are foolish if they don't realize the problems of editors—those huge files of manuscripts, the pressures of unanswered correspondence. The awful truth is that . . . an editor only reads carefully until the editor finds a reason not to—i.e., a mistake. Therefore, we would urge prospective contributors to avoid mistakes—clumsy errors that make us stop reading carefully."

BOSTON REVIEW

10B Mount Auburn Street
Cambridge, MA 02138
(617) 492-5478

SOURCE: Ann Parson, managing editor

ABOUT THE JOURNAL: Bimonthly; address manuscripts to fiction editor. Editor: Nicholas Bromell. Founded: 1975. Circulation: 10,000-12,000. Distribution: subscription; local newsstands; national bookstores. Avg. issue: 32-44 pp. Size: 11x14. Price: $1.50. Subscription: $9. Sample copy: $2.50. Back issues: available. Price: $2.50. Formerly known as *New Boston Review*.

FICTION: Small percentage of total pages; six stories a year. Rates: up to $200 depending on author's credentials and length. Payment: on publication. Rights: first and second. Reply time: one to two months. Publication time: impossible to estimate. Length: 4000 words maximum.

Boston Review is a newsprint, tabloid-sized journal of contemporary culture. It covers literature, politics, art, history, and music, often interrelating the various disciplines. One short story every issue is usual, but managing editor Ann Parson says they are not using as much fiction as they would like. The problem is the low quality of the submissions.

Stories are both solicited and chosen from the 400 unsolicited manuscripts submitted annually. Editors are open to all styles or types of fiction. What matters is "clean prose and imagination. . . . First-rate writing ability is what we're looking for," Parson says. "That includes everything from close attention to wording—to the successful handling of imagery, metaphor, plot, characterization, etc. In short, we are looking for very good stories."

She adds that though editors read and publish stories from all over, those with a New England flavor are particularly sought.

All stories are read by a first reader, who rejects most with a standard form. If a story is promising, more work will be asked for. The best submissions (5% to 10%) are given to editors to read. At least two editors must approve before acceptance. Editors also write encouraging notes, or send criticism, if they think it will be useful.

A cover letter with a list of previous publications is considered useful but not necessary. Editors will read a group of stories.

Boston Review would like to see more quality work by new or little-known writers.

CALLIOPE

Creative Writing Program
Roger Williams College
Bristol, RI 02809
(401) 255-2185

SOURCE: Martha Christina, editor

ABOUT THE JOURNAL: Biannual (December and May); no manuscripts accepted April through August. Founded: 1977. Circulation: 300. Distribution: subscription; regional bookstores. Avg. issue: 40-50 pp. Size: 5½x8½. Price: $1. Subscription: $1.50. Sample copy: $1. Back issues: available except for vol. 1, no. 1 and vol. 2, no. 2. Price: $1. Affiliated with Roger Williams College.

FICTION: Occupies one-third of total pages; four to eight stories a year. Rates: two copies. Rights: copyright reverts to author. Reply time: up to three months. Publication time: six to eight weeks. Length: up to 12 pages (about 3000 words).

"*Calliope* is an eclectic collection of poetry and short fiction with occasional interviews and reviews of other little magazines," editor Martha Christina says.

The four to eight stories published annually are most likely to come from unsolicited submissions. The magazine often publishes the work of little-known or new writers; in fact, the editor prefers not to receive a cover letter, especially one listing previous credits as "though earlier publications justify another, automatically."

"We look for material that is rich in concrete detail," Christina says. "Fiction should show a good sense of pace, characterization, and dialogue if appropriate. We like innovative work, but not sloppy self-indulgence. In addition, a sense of intelligence, wit, sarcasm (if applicable), sensitivity to language and tone. . . . We like to include innovative and traditional work in each issue."

Writers published include Mark Costello, Raymond Carver, Tillie Olsen, William Ferguson, Donald Barthelme, and Richard Grayson.

Between 50 and 100 manuscripts are submitted annually. In a good year, 10-12 of them will be worth considering. Christina is the first reader; to be published the story must be approved by the majority of the staff (varies in size from 7 to 13).

All manuscripts are returned with a personal note, though Christina adds that those "patently bad" get a standard, though handwritten, note. She writes back with sometimes very specific comments if a story shows overall strength but weakness in one area. Sometimes she asks to see another story. Editors will not read more than one story submitted at a time.

Listed as common reasons for rejection are a sloppily typed manuscript (Christina adds that she realizes this has nothing to do with content, but that it does seem to reflect the author's seriousness); gross grammatical errors; extensive summation (what Christina calls the "and then . . . " syndrome); and gratuitous violence, sex, or profanity that is not an integral part of the story.

Finally, Christina suggests, "Authors who have been rejected twice should try elsewhere."

CENTRAL PARK

Box 1446
New York, NY 10023
(212) 362-9151

SOURCE: Stephen-Paul Martin, coeditor

ABOUT THE JOURNAL: Bi- or triannual; send manuscripts to Stephen-Paul Martin, Richard Royal, coeditors. Founded: 1979. Circulation: 500. Distribution: subscription; bookstores. Avg. issue: 80 pp. Size: 7x8½. Price: $3. Subscription: $8. Sample copy: $2.50. Back issues: available. Price: $2.50.

FICTION: Occupies 35% of total pages; nine stories a year. Rates: one copy. Rights: first publication rights. Reply time: six weeks. Publication time: three months. Length: 1 to 25 typed pages.

Central Park is subtitled "A journal of the arts and social theory." Coeditor Stephen-Paul Martin says, "We believe in a synthesis of progressive political concerns and radical aesthetic approaches. . . . We are looking for work that will state forcefully an involvement with some issue of importance to more than just the writer. Some of our editors are focused on issues like disarmament, the reforming of a viable progressive political position in the United States, experimental prose and music, etc."

Most of the up to nine stories published every year come from the approximately 25 unsolicited submissions (editors would like to see this figure rise). Almost all the writers published are little-known.

In fiction, " . . . we would like to see either an exploration of some urgent social issue (as in the work of Richard Wright) or an experimental approach to basic issues of time and perception (as in Robbe-Grillet, Borges, etc.). We like language that is both hard-hitting and suggestively poetic. And if a work is based on traditional assumptions behind the short-story form, it should nonetheless give off the resonance of an extended metaphor. . . .

"We are especially fond of the work of J. A. Crawford, whose prose is straightforward and suggestive at the same time, and who is able to work in both narrative and experimental modes with equal power. He is able to use narrative techniques to explore sociopolitical issues, and able to use experimental techniques to penetrate the depths of a metaphor. These two approaches—the narrative/political and the experimental/metaphoric—define our basic interest. In either case, the work should have the condensed power of a well-written poem."

Stories are read by one of the co-editors or an associate editor. If there is interest (about 40% of the time), the story is circulated among all five staff members. Three editors have to approve a story before publication.

There is no standard rejection form. "Rejection letters are very personal, specific, and encouraging," Martin says. Criticism will be offered if editors see an area open to specific improvement. If there are only minor problems with a story, a revision will be requested.

"The absence in a story of any resonance beyond a merely personal conflict or resolution is the most common reason for rejection," Martin says. "Since we also are looking for precise and even poetic use of language in our fiction, its absence will also lead to lack of interest."

Editors encourage the inclusion of a brief list of credits in a cover letter, but add that credits do not influence acceptance. They also want the kind of brief biography included in a contributor's notes section. Editors will read more than one story at a time only if the pieces are under five pages.

THE CHARITON REVIEW

Northeast Missouri State University
Kirksville, MO 63501-0828
(816) 785-4499

SOURCE: Jim Barnes, editor

ABOUT THE JOURNAL: Biannual (spring and fall). Founded: 1975. Circulation: 650. Distribution: mainly subscription; a few national bookstores. Avg. issue: 100-112 pp. Size: 6x9. Price: $2. Subscription: $4. Sample copy: $2. Back issues: available. Price: from $50 (for rare first issue) to $2.

FICTION: Occupies 50% of total pages; four to eight stories a year. Rates: $5 per magazine page plus one copy. Payment: on publication. Rights: first North American serial. Reply time: one week to a month. Publication time: two to six months. Length: no limits.

"*The Chariton Review* has consistently published fine fiction and will continue to do so as long as I am editor," Jim Barnes says. "It is the aim of *Chariton* to provide an outlet for the best in contemporary world fiction, especially the short story. The competition is fierce. I would advise only writers with good stories to submit their work."

The review publishes fiction, poetry (particular interest in translations), and reviews. The fiction is generally chosen from unsolicited submissions. Between 200 and 300 manuscripts are submitted annually, and Barnes estimates that maybe 40% of them are good enough for more than a first reading. Little-known writers are very often published.

Chariton is open to all types of stories—traditional, experimental, genre, and so on. "We are committed to publishing the best, whatever it may be," Barnes says.

Writers published include Gordon Weaver, William Kittridge, Steve Heller, Winston Weathers, Elizabeth Moore, Mariann Novak, and Brian Bedard.

"I admire the work of these writers," Barnes says, "because they are expert in the art *and* craft of fiction. They know that good fiction must involve conflict, that good fiction does not rely on chance or coincidence, that good fiction must be an exercise in artistic unity, whether the piece be experimental or traditional."

No cover letter is necessary. All manuscripts are read by the editor and the associate fiction editor. The editor has the final word on acceptance.

There is a standard rejection form for stories clearly unacceptable. Criticism or encouragement is added whenever editors like a story but cannot use it. They have, in a few instances, liked a story enough to accept it on condition that the author make some revisons.

The editors will read up to two or three stories at a time.

Listed as reasons for immediate rejection: "Sloppy writing: no concept of character, of conflict, of style, of what good fiction is, was, and will be."

CHELSEA

Box 5880
Grand Central Station
New York, NY 10163
(212) 988-2276

SOURCE: Sonia Raiziss, editor

ABOUT THE JOURNAL: Annual. Founded: 1958. Circulation: 1000. Distribution: subscription; newsstands; bookstores. Avg. issue: 175-235 pp. Size: 6x9. Price: $4.50. Subscription: $8 for two issues. Back issues: from $3 to $15 for rare numbers.

FICTION: Publishes up to six stories a year. Rates: copies. Rights: copyright reverts to author. Reply time: one to three months. Publication time: can be over a year. Length: 25 typed pages maximum.

  Chelsea describes itself as an eclectic magazine with flexible attitudes. Its general approach is multimedia and experimental. Issues can include fiction, poetry, articles, interviews, criticism, plays, drawings, photos, architectural designs, and musical scores. There is a strong emphasis on translations. Issues are often built around a theme—*Chelsea* 38 included a collection of stories and poems about animals; *Chelsea* 39 was an "Ambimedia Issue": a sampling of work in a second medium by artists, writers, and composers. There have also been sociopolitical issues.

  Fiction is generally not solicited, and the amount published often depends on the quality of what comes in and how it holds up against the poetry, art, and essays that are also submitted. There is no firm rule as to the number of stories published per issue.

  The criterion, editor Sonia Raiziss says, is excellence—"the best quality in whatever discipline we are covering."

  In all disciplines, there is a decided slant toward the avant-garde, the experimental, the oblique approach.

  Chelsea has published well-known names and many newcomers. No. 40 (1981) included short stories by François Camoin, Elizabeth Inness-Brown, and David Evanier, the three finalists in the 1981 Associated Writing Programs Award Series for Short Fiction. The contest was judged by Stanley Elkin, but *Chelsea* editors made their own choices as to which examples of the finalists' work were published. Other short stories in that issue were by Betsy Adams, James Spencer, and Robert Pope.

Raiziss estimates she receives 5 to 15 submissions a week, most of which she describes as "inept, unprofessional, and not worth reading through. There is a great deal of repetition in plot and much badly done experimental prose.

"Otherwise, the work is often too slick, merely competent, mediocre, or routinely well-made. It doesn't take off in unexpected directions."

Raiziss estimates that three or four pieces a month are seriously read. She passes the best submissions to other editors. All work is chosen by consensus.

Editors use printed rejection forms and on acceptance correspond with authors. They may ask for slight changes in stories. If because of lack of room or the limitations imposed by a theme issue they cannot use a fine story, they will explain and suggest the writer resubmit in the future.

Raiziss prefers that writers not send more than one story at a time. She also does not want long, rambling cover letters: "One sign of the nonprofessional."

CHICAGO REVIEW

Box C
University of Chicago
Chicago, IL 60637
(312) 753-3571

SOURCE: Anne Orens, co-fiction editor

ABOUT THE JOURNAL: Quarterly; send manuscripts to Jan Deckenbach, Anne Orens, fiction editors. Founded: 1947. Circulation: 1700. Distribution: subscription; newsstands; bookstores. Avg. issue: 160 pp. Size: 6x9. Price: $3. Subscription: $12. Back issues: available. Price: $3. Subsidized by the University of Chicago.

FICTION: Five to eight stories an issue. Rates: one copy and a subscription. Rights: copyright reverts on request. Reply time: three to five months. Publication time: six months. Length: generally nothing over 25 typed pages unless it is exceptional.

Chicago Review is one of the best-known journals publishing experimental prose. "The fiction staff aims to publish 'innovative fiction' . . . fiction that is not straightforward narrative but attempts to do something new with language or structure."

Published writers include John Mella, Gilbert Sorrentino, Jerome Klinkowitz, Ronald Sukenick, Beth Tashery Shannon, and Jonathan Baumbach.

Editors make an effort to find stories from unpublished writers. Most of the magazine's fiction is chosen from the approximately 1200 unsolicited manuscripts submitted annually. Though fiction coeditor Anne Orens adds that only around 5% of them are generally found worth more than a single reading.

Vol. 33, no. 2 (1982) was titled: "A Special Section on {In/Re} novative Fiction, part I." Contributions came from George Chambers, Raymond Federman, Steve Katz, Ronald Sukenick, Beth Tashery Shannon, and Richard Flint, as well as a first translation of a piece by Samuel Beckett. Other pieces were John Mella's "On Innovative Writing," Brian Stonehill's "On Harry Matthews," and John Morse's "On Italo Calvino."

In the introduction, special section editor Sarah E. Lauzen wrote: "In Part I and II of the Special Section of the *Chicago Review* devoted to In/Re novative Fiction, we offer you at least 31 provocative additions to the house of fiction. Here is a collection of images, illusions, imitations to which you can regulate at will the degree of your intimacy. These are linguistic concentrates (versus the Tang of mainstream fiction)."

Every story submitted is read by a member of the fiction staff. The vast majority are sent back with a standard rejection slip. Promising stories are read by the entire fiction staff—each editor attaches written comments before the considered piece goes to the general editor. Written comments are sent to authors only if the editors would like to see more work.

Editors do not pay attention to lists of credits. They will read a group of stories.

Chicago Review also publishes poetry, art, essays, reviews, and criticism.

CIMARRON REVIEW

208 LSE
Oklahoma State University
Stillwater, OK 74077
(405) 624-6573

SOURCE: Jeanne Adams Wray, managing editor

ABOUT THE JOURNAL: Quarterly (Jan., Apr., July, Oct.). Founded: 1967. Circulation: 500. Distribution: subscription; selected bookstores nationally. Avg. issue: 64 pp. Size: 6x9. Price: $2.50. Subscription: $10. Sample copy: free. Back issues: most available. Price: $2. Review is a subunit of the Dean's Office, College of Arts and Sciences, OSU.

FICTION: Occupies about 50% of total pages; 12 to 16 stories a year. Rates: copies (but when CCLM grant in effect, some cash payment). Payment: on publication. Rights: all rights (a university requirement). Reply time: two to three weeks. Publication time: six to nine months. Length: tends to reject stories longer than 20 typed pages, but flexible.

Cimarron Review publishes fiction, poetry, essays, and art with the emphasis on fiction and poetry. "Since we don't solicit manuscripts," managing editor Jeanne Adams Wray says, "our editorial mix varies. Contemporary fiction and issues interest us. Adolescent recollections do not. We have on occasion assayed 'theme' issues—but that's rare. What we look for is uniqueness of subject, character, and writing style."

Most of the published fiction comes from a group of writers who have published in *Cimarron* over the past ten years, but some also comes from the 400-500 unsolicited submissions received annually.

"*Cimarron Review* has no preconceived notions about genre or format. We encourage experimental prose, whatever that is! We look for a story that 'works' within the constraints the author sets up. Given an author's concept, we seek to discover whether he develops the concept with integrity, grace, and style."

Published writers include Lester Goldberg, Robert Taylor, Jr., and Ellen Votaw Miller. Wray says: "These writers have distinct 'voices' when they write. They have mastered their craft. Their stories have substance, evocativeness, grace, and integrity." She adds, "These are empty words. . . . A good writer has his own style."

First readers pass promising stories (one-eighth of submissions) to second readers (faculty members of Oklahoma State University). If two readers judge a story promising, it is read by the managing editor and chief editor, who make the final decision. Four people must approve a story before publication.

Manuscripts are rejected by a word-processor-produced letter that is semipersonalized by the addition of the author's name, the title, and the genre. Editors rarely critique a piece or encourage a writer whose story has been rejected. Occasionally, editors will ask for minor revisions or further work.

Cover letters are unnecessary; previous credits are not considered important. Editors prefer one story at a time and certainly not more than two.

COLUMBIA: A MAGAZINE OF POETRY AND PROSE

404 Dodge Hall
Columbia University
New York, NY 10027
(212) 280-4391

SOURCE: Kirsten Dehner, editor

ABOUT THE PUBLICATION: Annual; no manuscripts accepted March 1 through September 1. Address stories to the Fiction Editor. Founded: 1977. Circulation: 500. Distribution: subscriptions and local bookstores. Avg. issue: 150 pp. Size: 5¼x8¼. Price: $3. Subscription: $3. Back issues: available. Price: $3. Affiliated with Columbia University Master of Fine Arts Writing Program.

FICTION: Occupies 50% of total pages; around eight stories a year. Rates: copies plus $100 award for best piece. Payment: on publication. Rights: first publication. Reply time: two weeks; several months if story is being considered. Publication time: two to three months. Length: 5000-word limit; exceptions made if story is very good.

Columbia's editors both solicit stories and choose work from the 100-150 unsolicited manuscripts submitted annually. Each year, the Carlos Fuentes Fiction Award and the Stanley Kunitz Poetry Award are given for the best story and poem published in the year's issue. In 1982, the winner for fiction was Pamela Erbe for "I'm Waiting for the Man in the Moon." In 1981, it was Raymond Carver for "The Bath."

Editor Kirsten Dehner says, "We just try to print the most interesting work we can. . . . We are interested in any kind of fiction as long as it has what we think is a unique vitality, whether it be the prose or the story form, or idea. We treat each piece individually and have no rules other than what comes from our own instincts."

Fiction in the 1982 issue came from Pamela Erbe, Jiri Sykora, Madison Smartt Bell, James C. Schaap, Michael Krekorian, Robert R. Hellings, C. Jane Warren, and Peter Krussi. The 1981 issue included Debra Lintz, Greg Leichner, Raymond Carver, George Chambers, Enid Harlow, Robert Whitaker, Steven Schwartz, and Gordon Lish. Almost all of these writers have been frequently published in literary magazines. Several are novelists and have published in the national magazines.

Stories are screened by the fiction editor, who presents the possibilities (not more than 2%) to the fiction board, made up of graduate writing students. The stories are rated. There is no set number of people needed to approve a story, as the board changes continually; editors make the final decisions. If editors like a story very much but think it has minor problems they will ask for a revision on spec. A standard rejection slip is used. Sometimes, if a work seems to warrant it, a letter of encouragement is sent.

Editors are not interested in cover letters. They will read a group of stories.

CONFRONTATION

English Department
Long Island University
Brooklyn, NY 11201
(212) 834-6000 ext: English Dept.

SOURCE: Dr. Martin Tucker, editor

ABOUT THE JOURNAL: Biannual; no manuscripts accepted July and August. Founded: 1968: Circulation: 2000. Distribution: subscription; bookstores nationally. Size: 6x9. Avg. issue: 160-190 pp. Price: $3. Subscription: $5. Sample copy: $1.50. Back issues: available. Price: $2. Affiliated with Long Island University.

FICTION: Publishes 20 to 24 stories a year. Rates: $20–$50. Payment: on publication. Rights: copyright reverts on request; may retain anthology rights. Reply time: six weeks. Publication time: six months. Length: rarely uses stories over 6000 words.

"*Confrontation* wishes to be eclectic," editor Martin Tucker says. "Quality of form and style is our main criterion."

Between 2000 and 2500 manuscripts are submitted annually and provide most of the fiction. Little-known and well-known authors are published side by side.

"Since our rationale is to avoid *one* set approach we look for all story forms. We do tend to be wary of publishing familiar traditional approaches.

"We've published the early work of Stephen Dixon and early prose of the poet Terry Stokes; also the first story of Walter Abish. All three are seriocomic experimental writers whose humanism is undiminished by their satire. We like irony and bite in the work we read; we also admire craft and sensibility. We've published original work by Isaac Bashevis Singer, Cynthia Ozick, Joyce Carol Oates, Paul Theroux, and Sol Yurick as well."

Summer 1981 was a story-and-poem issue. Fiction came from Thomas Fleming, Sondra Spatt Olsen, Albert Russo, F.D. Reeve, Roni Schotter, Stephen Dixon, Leslie Garrett, Linda Haverty, Nancy Potter, Elisabeth Stevens, Karen Jackel Wunsch, S.L. Adler, Christine Purkis, and Layle Silbert.

In the introduction, Tucker restates "the magazine's editorial policy, which is one of eclecticism. We have published, and intend to continue doing so, a wide range of styles, forms and content."

About 20% of the submitted manuscripts are generally found to be worth more than one reading. The fiction editor and the editor-in-chief read all stories considered for publication. Advice is sought from the editorial board and, on occasion, outside readers. At least three readers, including the fiction editor, must approve a story. The chief editor has the final say.

A standard rejection form is regularly used. Letters are often written to authors whose work is admired.

Common reasons for rejection include poor writing style, poor grasp of fiction techniques, sentimentalizing, or propagandizing.

Cover letters are considered nothing more than a courtesy that can set a pleasant mood. Editors prefer single submissions, but will read several stories.

CONJUNCTIONS

33 West 9th Street
New York, NY 10011

SOURCE: Bradford Morrow, editor

ABOUT THE JOURNAL: Biannual (spring and autumn). Founded: 1981. Circulation: 2500. Distribution: subscription; newsstands; bookstores. Avg. issue: 240 pp. Size: 6x9. Price: $7.50 paper; $22.50 cloth. Subscription: $16 paper; $45 cloth. Sample copy: $7.50 paper; $22.50 cloth. Back issues: available. Price: $7.50; first issue (312 pp.) $9.

FICTION: Occupies 30% to 40% of total pages; six to ten stories a year. Rates: copies. Rights: copyright reverts. Reply time: two weeks on clear rejections. Publication time: 6 to 18 months. Length: longest piece published was 50 pages, but shorter pieces are more usual.

Conjunctions describes itself simply as "biannual volumes of new writing." Its fiction editors are Walter Abish, Guy Davenport, and Bradford Morrow. Most of the up to ten stories it publishes every year are either solicited or come with recommendations from other authors. Unknown or little-known writers are only occasionally published.

Contributors have included Walter Abish, Guy Davenport, Gilbert Sorrentino, Coleman Dowell, Frederick Busch, James Purdy, and William Gass.

Unsolicited manuscripts are read. Of the 150-250 annually submitted, a fairly small percentage are found worth consideration. Morrow says he is looking for "voice, direction, language, form, technique. Prose fiction should be as finished, perfect, polished as poetry."

One or more of the editors reads each submission. There is no hard and fast system for handling stories. "Contributing editors can be at any moment all over the world. So much depends on general circumstances as to who reads what and how much." Rejections are usually made with a standard form. If there is time or circumstances warrant it, editors will write a personal note.

Morrow adds that 90% of the rejections are due to "inferior technique, bad writing, or wholly conventional work."

Cover letters are only of interest if the author has a personal recommendation. Morrow will not look at more than one story at time.

COTTONWOOD REVIEW

Box J Kansas Union
Lawrence, KS 66045
(913) 846-4520

SOURCE: Erleen J. Christensen, editor

ABOUT THE JOURNAL: Triannual; address manuscripts to Erleen J. Christensen or Sharon Ord Warner, assistant editor. Founded: 1965. Circulation: 500. Distribution: subscription; regional bookstores. Avg. issue: 100-150 pp. Size: 6x9. Price: $3.50. Subscription: $9. Sample copy: $2. Back issues: available. Price: $2 for year-old issues; cover price for special issues. Receives partial support from the Graduate Student Council and the English Department at University of Kansas.

FICTION: Occupies 30% of total pages; three stories per issue; yearly special issue may feature fiction or poetry exclusively. Rates: two copies. Rights: copyright reverts. Reply time: two to three months. Publication time: four to five months. Length: tries to be flexible, but often finds below 2000 words not developed enough to suit needs and over 10,000 not practical.

Cottonwood Review is a Kansas-based magazine that is proud of its roots, but not confined by them. About 200 short stories are submitted every year—more when a special fiction issue is announced. Most of the nine or so stories published annually are chosen from unsolicited submissions—from "writers who are just beginning to establish their reputations."

"Our editors are primarily people who write," editor Erleen Christensen says. "We look for work with sophistication and control in the use of language, and we value consistency in story line, sound resolution, and careful character development. We want stories that will be enjoyable to a discerning and well-educated audience and shy away from both predictable genre fiction and stories which are merely experiment for experiment's sake.

"We are very much aware of traditional story form. The experimental fiction which we consider successful and are likely to accept plays with traditional form in ways which delight or surprise a reader while acknowledging the expectations which traditional form gives rise to. Since our readers are not specialists hooked on some particular genre, the genre fiction we publish has met our general standards about language, character development, and consistency of story line; it has proved itself as short fiction, not as a special genre of short fiction.

"Robert Day, whose best-known novel (*The Last Cattle Drive*, Putnam, 1977) was made into a movie, has published both short stories and his short novel, *In My Stead*, with *Cottonwood*. We especially value Day's work for its tight story line, quick and perceptive characterizations, and its dry humor. Another author who exemplifies the kind of work *Cottonwood* likes to print is Tom Averill, who also treats Midwestern characters with deftness and skill. A work by Edwin Moses (*One Smart Kid*, Macmillan, 1982) which appeared in our *19 Stories* illustrates the sort of experimental fiction we are most likely to be receptive to.

"We strongly urge those interested in submitting fiction . . . to examine our anthology of contemporary fiction by Kansas authors (*19 Stories*, 1982; Cottonwood Review Press). This collection will give a clearer idea of what we print than any marketing guide is able to." (The Cottonwood Review Press, edited by Denise Low, prints exclusively regional material.)

Editors prefer to see only one manuscript at a time. Stories are screened by the assistant editor. Those that merit another reading (about 50%) are commented on by the five-member fiction staff. It usually takes recommendations from four readers for a story to be accepted. The procedure for special issues is determined by the editor-in-charge.

If stories are found promising, marred only by clearly defined problems, they may be sent back for revision. No standard rejection forms are used. "We endeavor to give as much encouragement as possible to people who have promise as writers but have not as yet submitted stories suitable for publication." The assistant editor usually writes at least a few comments on all rejections.

Editors appreciate a cover letter that indicates the writer has read *Cottonwood* and knows what it stands for.

CROTON REVIEW

P. O. Box 277
Croton on Hudson, NY 10520
(914) 271-3144

SOURCE: Ruth Lisa Schechter, editor

ABOUT THE JOURNAL: Annual; no manuscripts accepted June, July, August. Founded: 1978. Circulation: 2000. Distribution: subscription; bookstore. Avg. issue: 16 pp. Size: tabloid. Price: $2. Subscription: $6. Sample copy: $2.20. Back issues: available. Price: $1.70. *Croton Review* is the magazine of the Croton Council on the Arts, a nonprofit organization stimulating interest in the arts as a means of improving the quality of life in the community.

FICTION: Four to six stories annually. Rates: copies; pays up to $25 when grant money is available. Payment: on publication. Rights: author retains rights. Reply time: about two months. Length: wants short-shorts up to 16 pages.

Croton Review is a literary tabloid; its fiction is chosen from 400 unsolicited manuscripts submitted annually. It is interested in short-shorts. Many first published pieces from writers and poets have appeared in its pages. Its editorial mix is eclectic. Editor Ruth Lisa Schechter says, "We hope for diverse and imaginative prose. Stories with quality and substance. We like to see use of contemporary themes. We prefer experimental writing that has something to say and isn't pretentious, out of syntax, and muddled."

Writers published include David Evanier, Al Gillespie, Carol Emschwiller, Vanessa Ochs, T. Alan Broughton, Deena Linett, and Linda Lerner.

Stories are read by members of the editorial board, who add comments for the senior editors. Only a small percentage of the manuscripts are seriously considered for publication. A standard rejection form is used. If a story is admired but does not fit into the "overview for a particular issue," a note is added suggesting the writer try again.

Editors have no interest in cover letters or previous credits; they will not read group submissions.

Schechter says, *"The Croton Review* is a quality literary and art publication that accepts work from the local area of Westchester County and elsewhere . . . from known and unknown writers. The editorial board (volunteers) are known and new writers, most with published books and some published in literary magazines.

"*Croton Review* is supported by grants as well as subscribers and libraries. It has won awards from the Council for the Arts in Westchester, Inc., the Coordinating Council on Literary Magazines, and, in 1982, the National Endowment for the Arts.

Issue no. 5, 1982, included a first published story by Vanessa L. Ochs, a story by Daisy Aldan, and a short prose piece by Ramona Weeks.

CUTBANK

English Department
University of Montana
Missoula, MT 59812

SOURCE: Bob Ross, coeditor

ABOUT THE JOURNAL: Biannual. Founded: 1973. Circulation: 800. Distribution: subscriptions; regional bookstores. Avg. issue: 112 pp. Size: 5x7. Price: $3. Subscription: $5. Sample copy: $3. Back issues: some available. Price: $2.50–$3. Affiliated with the Univ. of Montana; funded by the Associated Students of the Univ. of Montana.

FICTION: Occupies 25% of total pages; five to eight stories a year. Rates: two copies. Rights: copyrighted. Reply time: two to six weeks. Publication time: three to five months. Length: no limits.

CutBank primarily publishes fiction and poetry; editors "hope to see stories that are very well written, that contain real thought that is unobscured by dullness, and that do not assault us with obvious truths." Experimental and traditional forms are looked at impartially, coeditor Bob Ross adds.

Most of the five to eight stories published every year are chosen from 150 to 200 unsolicited submissions. One or two stories will be solicited. Writers published include James Welch, John Haines, Barry Lopez, Rick DeMarinis, James Crumley, Raymond Carver, David Quammen, Tess Gallagher, Patricia Mac-Innes, and Madeline DeFrees. Little-known and new writers are often published.

Every story is read by the magazine's three editors in turn. Those with three "no" comments are returned by the last reader. The remainder (approximately 15%) are discussed at a weekly conference. Acceptance means all three editors have approved a story; Ross adds that approval does not always mean enthusiasm.

A standard rejection form is used, but comments are frequently added ("hardly ever with the intent of being discouraging"). When a piece is admired, but thought unsuitable, editors will ask for more work. Ross adds that most of the pieces accepted are sent back for revision.

Common reasons for rejection: "1. dialect; hackneyed use of the language; 2. violence that is excessive (it doesn't take much) 3. material that is insulting to any age, sex, ethnic or religious group; 4. material that betrays immaturity by its language or subject matter; 5. rampaging 'ism'; A social or political agenda that is apparent on the first page is too apparent; 6. cuteness."

Editors will read groups of stories. There is no requirement for a cover letter, but they are read. Ross says, "I think we would prefer that writers of cover letters not strive to be amusing; they will be so unintentionally often enough."

Ross also adds that they would like to see more work from women. In the past, *CutBank* had leaned toward publishing work by male writers and now the editors find the number of submissions from women to be smaller than they would like.

CutBank also receives a lot of Western (cowboy) stories; these are generally sent back "fairly rapidly."

CutBank 18 (Spring/Summer '82) included fiction from Greg Michalson, Barry Kitterman, Nixa Scell, and Joan Colby.

DARK HORSE

P. O. Box 9
Somerville, MA 02143
(617) 776-8012

SOURCE: Seth Steinzor, editor

ABOUT THE JOURNAL: Triannual. Founded: 1974. Circulation:
600-700. Distribution: subscription; local newsstands and bookstores. Avg. issue: 24 pp. Size: tabloid. Price: $1.50. Subscrip-
tion: $6 for 4 issues. Sample copy: $2. Back issues: available.
Price: $2.

FICTION: Occupies 30% of total pages; two to three stories an
issue. Rates: two copies. Rights: first North American serial; one-
time anthology. Reply time: three months. Publication time: up
to six months. Length: no limits.

Dark Horse is a literary newspaper with a particular commitment to publishing new and emerging writers. Besides fiction, it
publishes reviews, essays, and announcements of interest to the
literary community. It uses its large-size pages to advantage in
reproductions of art and photos.

Fiction is chosen from the 300-400 unsolicited stories submitted annually. Editor Saul Steinzor says, "We favor emotionally
intense, honestly expressed, well-crafted stories, poems, and essays on nonliterary subjects. We espouse no political or social
point of view, save that racist or sexist material will be looked at
especially critically. We try to avoid being partisans of any literary theory or mode. We try to be open to everything. Traditional
forms were experimental once; experimental forms are only
worth reading if the experiment succeeds."

Fiction editors can change from issue to issue (announcements
are made an issue in advance). The Spring 1982 issue fiction
editor was John Hogden. Stories were by Joan Campbell, Jan
Solet (work-in-progress), and C. Kassel. The Summer '81 fiction
editor was Patricia Wild; story from Michelle Dionetti. The Win-
ter/Spring 1981 fiction editor was Mopsy Strange Kennedy. Fiction was by Harold J. Jewell and Nancy Slonim Aronie (the latter
a first published piece).

The fiction editor reads all submissions. Probably 15% will get
more than one reading. The managing editor has the final say on
publication.

There is no standard rejection form, the type of response is left to the discretion of the editorial staff. But Steinzor adds that specific comments or requests for revision are infrequent. Editors do not accept pieces contingent on revision or generally ask for rewrites. Only if a piece is found promising will criticism and/or encouragement be offered.

A list of previous credits makes no difference in how a story is handled; editors do want a brief biographical note for the Contributors' Notes section. They will read a group of stories.

EPOCH

251 Goldwin Smith Hall
Cornell University
Ithaca, NY 14853
(607) 256-3385

SOURCE: C. S. Giscombe, managing editor

ABOUT THE JOURNAL: Triannual. Founded: 1947. Circulation:
800. Distribution: subscription; selected bookstores. Avg. issue:
75 pp. Size: 6x9. Price: $2.50. Subscription: $6.50. Sample copy:
$2.50. Back issues: available. Price: $2.50 and up. Published by
Cornell University.

FICTION: Occupies 60% to 70% of total pages; 16 stories in 1982.
Rates: copies. Rights: first North American serial. Reply time:
two months. Publication time: two to six months. Length: no
limits.

Epoch has a rotating editorship policy for fiction and poetry
that opens the magazine to a particularly wide range of types
and styles. The guest fiction editor of each issue is free to solicit
work and is expected to read unsolicited submissions, determin-
ing the tone of the issue. At the same time, the managing editor
and two senior editors who are permanently on staff give the
magazine "some degree of issue-to-issue continuity." As is explained in magazine's "Guidlines for Issue Editors": "*Epoch* has
traditions, tendencies, and prejudices and these are sometimes
taken into consideration in the process of putting an issue together."

Managing editor C. S. Giscombe says, "We're interested in a
lot of different kinds of fiction and have no one school to promote
and exclusively publish. We are not committed to anything except excellent writing."

Some of the well-known contributors to the magazine include
William Kennedy, Alice Adams, R.V. Cassill, Bobbie Ann
Mason, Austin Wright, Jerry Bumpus, and B.H. Friedman. The
Spring 1982 issue included stories from Eric Wilson, R.D. Skill-
ings, Allen Woodman, and Fred Haefele and a "first" story from
Richard Davenport. The issue's guest editor of fiction was Ed-
ward Hower.

Most of the fiction is chosen from the over 400 unsolicited
manuscripts submitted each year. Every story is read by at least

two staff members. If both agree that it is unacceptable, it will be rejected. If one of the editors likes a story, it will be read and given written comments by most of the staff and probably will be discussed at a fiction meeting.

If editors think a story is almost good enough to publish, they will accept it if the author is willing to make specific changes. Occasionally, a staff member might suggest general revision and resubmission on spec.

Editors are encouraged to write to authors with criticism and/or encouragement. "We don't, of course, respond personally to each manuscript, nor do we have this as a goal," Giscombe adds. "There are some writers who we simply do not wish to encourage."

Most stories are rejected because the editors find them "badly written, sentimental, silly, easily moralistic, predictable, etc.," but "some stories are obviously rejected even though they're intelligent and ambitious and use language well. These are returned (*usually* with notes) for a variety of reasons, including (in no particular order) poor endings, unevenness of tone, and the story simply not going far enough into what it started."

There is no particular information editors are looking for in cover letters, though Giscombe adds that he is "curious about what information people choose to give out about themselves." Lists of credits do not change the way a story is handled but are found interesting. Sometimes editors will look up previous work in an effort to better see what an author might be attempting. Editors will read a group of stories.

Giscombe adds that they would like to be receiving quality work from members of racial and ethnic minorities and that while fiction is *Epoch*'s main prose concern, they are also interested in a variety of forms of nonfiction prose.

EUREKA REVIEW

90 Harrison Avenue
New Canaan, CT 06840
(203) 544-9190

SOURCE: Roger Memmott, editor

ABOUT THE JOURNAL: Annual (irregularly). Founded: 1975. Circulation: 1000. Avg. issue: 112 pp. Size: 5½x8½. Price: $2. Subscription: $7 for four issues. Back issues: available. Price: $2.

FICTION: Primarily devoted to fiction; 10-16 stories a year. Rates: two or three copies. Rights: copyright reverts on request. Reply time: one to six weeks. Length: above 7500 words may run into problems of space.

Each issue of *Eureka Review* opens with a printed "Manifesto": "*Eureka Review* is published by Orion Press, an independent organization devoted to furthering the literary arts. The magazine welcomes fiction primarily, some poetry, artwork, photographs, articles, and reviews. It is receptive to both established as well as previously unpublished and relatively unknown writers of worth.

"*Eureka* is eclectic. There are few taboos regarding length, style, and subject matter. . . . Material must be well written, honest, and 'literarily sound,' whether conventional or avant garde. Literature at its best achieves a balance of content and form."

Editor Roger Memmott adds that the 10-16 stories published every year are mostly chosen from the 300-400 unsolicited manuscripts submitted. He adds that only 10%-15% of them tend to be worth any consideration.

The Winter 1980-81 edition included a first published story from Margaret Risk. Other contributors included Steve Stern, Lee K. Abbott, Tom Friedman, Marcia Tager, Alfred Schwaid, Janice Eidus, Roger Ladd Memmott, Ernest J. Finney, Alvin Greenberg, Anthony E. Stockanes, and Tom Whalen, all writers who have published in top-quality literary magazines.

Memmott says that common reasons for rejection range from an inability to tell a story to bad prose. He is looking for "style, form, and the unpredictable. Perhaps as Emily Dickinson said— [fiction] should make the top of my head come off or make me so cold no fire can ever warm me."

FICTION

c/o Department of English
The City College of New York
138th Street and Convent Avenue
New York, NY 10031
(212) 690-6694

SOURCE: Mark Mirsky, editor

ABOUT THE JOURNAL: Annual; no submissions during summer.
Founded: 1972. Circulation: 1000-3000. Distribution: subscription; bookstores. Avg. issue: 200-220 pp. Size: 9x6. Price: $5.
Subscription: $5. Back issues: available. Price: $4.

FICTION: Entirely devoted to short stories and novel excerpts;
approximately 20 a year. Rates: copies. Rights: copyright reverts
on request. Reply time: three months for rejection. Publication
time: next issue. Length: no limits.

Most of the stories published in *Fiction* are solicited (though
often from little-known writers). One to two unsolicited stories
are generally published per issue.

"Unsolicited stories get a lot of attention," editor Mark Mirsky
says. "We don't want to be an authoritating ground. The challenge is to take the known and the unknown and let the one
introduce the other."

Fiction is interested in exploring narrative forms. Its first dedication is to "experimental fiction." "We don't like the predictable," Mirsky says, "and language is important to us. We are
looking for a sense of surprise and of being able to lose yourself
in a story.

"But we are not committed to experimental fiction to the exclusion of anything else and we want to see anything that is well
done."

Well-known writers published in *Fiction* include Donald Barthelme, Italo Calvino, Ronald Sukenick, Ann Beattie, Manuel
Puig, and Max Frisch. Lesser-known writers, some of whose
work was pulled from the unsolicited pile, include Cori Jones,
Ivy Goodman, Stephanie C. Gunn, and Sharyn Jeanne Skeeter.

An estimated 1000 stories are submitted annually. All of them
are read, though few are found worth considering. First readers
pass possibilities to the two associate editors. They pass roughly
100 stories a year on to Mirsky, who makes the final decisions.

Any story with a cover letter listing credits in other journals or top magazines is read by Mirsky. Encouraging letters are sent back instead of standard rejection notes if a story is found promising.

Fiction occasionally does theme issues. Vol. 6, no. 1 (1978) was devoted to contemporary German fiction. Vol. 6, no. 3 (1981) featured ten Cuban writers.

Fiction was originally published quarterly. Increased mailing costs are responsible for the cutback to one issue a year.

GARGOYLE

P. O. Box 3567
Washington, DC 20007
(202) 333-1544

SOURCE: Richard Myers Peabody, Jr., editor/publisher

ABOUT THE JOURNAL: Bi- or triannual. Founded: 1976. Circulation: 1000 copies printed. Distribution: subscription; bookstores in Baltimore, Washington, Richmond area as well as scattered outlets in California, New York, Massachusetts, Texas, and Arizona and in several cities abroad. Avg. issue: from 100 pp. (8½x11) to 464 pp. (4¼x7). Size: changes constantly. Price: $4. Double issues: more. Sample copy: $4. Back issues: available. Price: inquire.

FICTION: At least 18 stories every year, but not in every issue; it is important to check editorial plans. Rates: one copy; half off on additional copies. Rights: copyright reverts on publication. Reply time: tries for within a month. Publication time: usually three to six months; often as long as ten. Length: generally 2-10 typed pages; has published longer stories as individual books; longer work featured in some issues and novel excerpts welcome.

Gargoyle is a magazine of fiction, poetry, interviews, graphics, and reviews. Its editor, Richard Peabody, is a strong advocate of the vitality and importance of small presses.

"In the 1980s, I sense a move back toward fiction," he says. "Most of the poets I know are writing novels. The poetry market seems glutted. We've emphasized fiction over poetry recently because most of the short fiction we receive has the dynamics and language poetry should have. William Goyen's writing is a fine example (his *House of Breath*) of language doing in prose what good poetry should do. More and more this explosive writing comes packaged as a prose poem, fragment, or parable. Now it's not uncommon to find novellas or novels with the same energy."

About 25% of *Gargoyle*'s fiction is solicited; the rest is chosen from unsolicited submissions. About 500 stories come in every year. When the 1982 fiction issue was publicized in mailings and writers' magazines, 4000 submissions came in between January

1 and June 1 (3000 of them in May). Of the 4000, 55 were seriously considered and 25 were published.

Peabody writes: "We have a very broad range of interests and a very idiosyncratic and personalized way of approaching them. We frown on new age polemics or academic vogues. We like to mix styles and regions but that certainly depends on what comes in. We do publish a lot of British and European writers. Because Washington, D.C., is a mushrooming literary community we've spent a lot of time nurturing the local crop as well. Don't make the mistake of thinking because we're in the nation's capital we publish political stories. We're very apolitical.

"We are not committed to the traditional story. We have published experimental prose. We're open-minded. But we have to *want* to publish it and that's the real deciding factor. We're more concerned with *how* writers say what they say, than in *what* they say. If you think Judith Krantz and John Jakes are the cutting edge then *Gargoyle* is not for you. This doesn't mean we're anti-plot, or anti-linear. We have no objection to genre fiction per se, though what we see is usually not very interesting. My own definition of a work of art is that repetition does not diminish the work, or the pleasure I receive from it. . . . We are attracted to vitality, contemporary subject matter, verbal tension and all things new. . . . We're very interested in young and forgotten writers. Writers born from 1950 on get close attention."

Peabody reads everything that comes in. If he finds a story interesting he gives it to another editor for comments. If the second reader also likes the story, it is put aside for a week, then read again. The editors decide quickly and "trust gut reactions. Normally you can tell a story's wrong for the magazine after reading a couple of paragraphs."

No standard rejection forms are used. The editors always try to give some encouragement. It might take the form of a gentle suggestion that the writer buy a dictionary or the name of a more open market. If editors want a story with minor flaws they will point them out and it is up to the author to decide if he wants to make these changes. Peabody adds that he will listen to an author's argument as to why a story should not be changed. "In the end, if we want a story bad enough, we don't care how it's spaced, whether or not the copy is spotless, or anything else. We have often done heavy editing work on longer manuscripts with the author's assistance and approval."

Peabody adds, "The majority of people submitting work to the magazine have never seen a copy (let alone read one) and if they had would never have wasted their time. . . . I'd say that cleans out about 60% of the submissions we receive. I then read for flow and often reject stories because the writer seems unconcerned with the language, or because the writing is stilted. . . . We stress that writers read their work aloud. If it embarrasses the writer when heard it also embarrasses us. We avoid the same old stories. We want the new image, the exciting juxtaposition. We always want to be surprised. . . . "

Peabody is willing to read several stories submitted together. When he likes something about a writer's work, he will often ask for a group of stories. "This is not a guarantee of publication," he says, "but it does give us a better feel for what an author is attempting and might mean acceptance somewhere down the line."

Peabody adds that cover letters make no difference; work stands or falls on its own. It is important to check on *Gargoyle*'s editorial plans; manuscripts have been rejected only because no fiction was needed at the time.

THE GEORGIA REVIEW

University of Georgia
Athens, GA 30602
(404) 542-3481

SOURCE: Stanley W. Lindberg, editor

ABOUT THE JOURNAL: Quarterly; does not consider manuscripts in June, July, August. Founded: 1947. Circulation: 4400. Distribution: subscription; newsstands; bookstores. Avg. issue: 240 pp. Size: 6¾x10. Price: $4. Subscription: $9. Sample copy: $3. Back issues: write for list. Price $3. Affiliated with University of Georgia.

FICTION: Occupies 15% to 20% of total pages; eight to ten stories a year. Rates: $10 a printed page; one year complimentary subscription; contributor's copy; reduced charge on extra copies. Payment: on publication. Rights: first North American serial; publication copyrighted. Reply time: two months. Publication time: 6 to 12 months. Length: "set by the quality of the work . . . a novella would have to distinguish itself mightily to earn its pages, but it would not be declined unread soley because of its length."

Well-known and widely circulated, *The Georgia Review* chooses 75% of its short stories from the approximately 1200 unsolicited manuscripts submitted annually.

Unknown or little-known writers are often published. In the last five years, 25 short-story writers and poets were published for the first time. Editor Stanley Lindberg adds that in every case the work merited publication; no separate standards were applied.

The Georgia Review tries "to present a blend of interdisciplinary essays and book reviews, together with the best in contemporary fiction and poetry. Most issues contain some graphics; some issues have interviews and occasionally correspondence, drama, or other fine writing that doesn't fit neatly into any genre is published. National and international in scope (although aware of its regional roots), *The Georgia Review* is eclectic in its pursuit of excellent writing. . . . Authors range from Nobel Laureates and Pulitzer Prize winners to the as-yet-unknown."

"What we hope to see," Lindberg says, "is writing that is better than any we've ever seen before; writing that forces us to accept it despite the intimidating backlog awaiting publication; writing that invites and sustains subsequent readings."

During the past five years writers appearing in *The Georgia Review* have included Harriet Simpson Arnow, Murray Baumgarten, T. Coraghessan Boyle, Robert Canzoneri, Fred Chappell, Eleanor Clark, Nicholas Delbanco, William Faulkner, Eugene K. Garber, George Garrett, Robert Gupta, James B. Hall, Barry Hannah, Jane Mayhall, James McNeice, Naomi Shihab Nye, Joyce Carol Oates, Carol Papenhausen, Phillip Parotti, Natalie L.M. Petesch, Fred Pfeil, Scott Sanders, Barry Targan, Robert Taylor, Jr., Gordon Weaver, and Eudora Welty.

Lindberg gives all manuscripts a first reading but does not necessarily read each story to its conclusion. He estimates that 15% of the unsolicited submissions are worth a second look. Stories Lindberg finds promising may be read by up to three others, but the final decision is Lindberg's and he does not always draw on other opinions.

Cover letters are read, but not considered necessary. A list of credits does not affect how a story is handled. Editors do like to have the author's assurance that the story is not being read elsewhere. Lindberg will read more than one story submitted at a time, but warns that unless there are "compelling reasons" for the multiple submissions, the practice tends to be self-defeating.

Rejection is usually by standard form—a necessity adopted due to the need to return manuscripts within a reasonable time. "Criticism and/or encouragement can be offered only if a story comes close to acceptance. . . . (Curiously, most of the writers who seem to expect detailed individualized responses as a given right are not subscribers and show no evidence of ever having looked at what we've published.)"

GRAND STREET

50 Riverside Drive
New York, NY 10024
(212) 496-6088

SOURCE: Ben Sonnenberg, editor

ABOUT THE JOURNAL: Quarterly. Founded: 1981. Circulation: 1200. Distribution: subscription; newsstands; bookstores. Size: 4½x7⅜. Avg. issue: 150 pp. Price: $4. Subscription: $16. Back issues: available. Price: $5.

FICTION: Uses two to three stories an issue. Rates: meets top magazines. Payment: between acceptance and publication. Rights: first North American serial. Reply time: rejection usually within three weeks. Publication time: tries for two to three months. Length: up to 4000 words.

Grand Street is a relatively new quarterly that has attracted a great deal of interest. It publishes short stories, poems, and essays on subjects of interest to the literate, educated reader.

"A principal goal of *Grand Street*," editor Ben Sonnenberg says, "is to bring little-known writers of unquestionable distinction together with others who are very well known in a magazine for nonspecialized, so-called common readers."

Fiction in the magazine is usually solicited. Sonnenberg looks at, but does not necessarily read, unsolicited submissions. Approximately 65-70 come in every week. In the first four issues, three of those were published. Sonnenberg has written to encourage writers who have sent in material he thought was promising.

He is somewhat hesitant about encouraging writers to send in stories. When *Grand Street* was written up in one of the writers' magazines, he was innundated with manuscripts.

"Many of them were irreproachably well-written. They were also lifeless. They had a photographic quality as if personal experience was the most important element. An actual house, a wife's real experience, with no sense of recreated life. They seemed to be written to prescription, not out of necessity and with no sense of risk."

Sonnenberg speaks of looking for work that has "a sociable quality, a civility and a forthcomingness." Writers published in *Grand Street* include Glenway Westcott, Steven Millhauser,

Alice Munro, Laura (Riding) Jackson, Charlotte Holmes, Daniel Menaker, Joseph McElroy, Penelope Gilliatt, and Perdita Schaffner.

Essays have included "Henry Miller," by Czeslaw Milosz; "Spying in Spain and Elsewhere," by Claud Cockburn; "Edmund Wilson in Middle Age," by Leon Edel; "Life in a Sect," by Irving Howe; "An American Psychiatrist," by Steven Marcus; "Allen Tate and John Peale Bishop," by Andrew Lytle.

Poetry contributors have included Djuna Barnes, Ted Hughes, W.S. Merwin, Kenneth Koch, Peter Green translations of Ovid, and Amy Clampitt.

Grand Street is one of the only quarterlies that matches the top newsstand/consumer magazines in payment. This may make the journal more desirable, but it does not make it more accessible.

HANGING LOOSE

231 Wyckoff Street
Brooklyn, NY 11217
(212) 643-9559

SOURCE: Robert Hershon, coeditor

ABOUT THE JOURNAL: Quarterly; address manuscripts to the editors. Founded: 1966. Circulation: 1500. Distribution: national. Avg. issue: 72-80 pp. Size: 8½x7. Price: $2. Subscription: $5.50. Sample copy: $2.75. Back issues: available. Price: varies.

FICTION: No more than two stories per issue, sometimes none. Rates: copies and small cash payment. Payment: on acceptance. Rights: first serial. Reply time: two to three months. Publication time: six to nine months. Length: reasonable short-story length.

"Anyone interested in having stories published in *Hanging Loose* should have the common sense to read it first," coeditor Robert Hershon says. The magazine publishes fiction (including a lot of short prose pieces), mostly chosen from unsolicited submissions, and poetry. It regularly includes a selection of writing by poets of high school age.

Hershon says he want to see "fresh, original, energetic, surprising, honest writing. What would anyone hope to see?" What he does not want is "dishonest writing, inept writing, cliché-ridden writing, boring writing, stupid writing, sneery writing, etc."

Published prose writers include Donna Brook, Chuck Wachtel, and Cathy Cockrell.

The magazine has four editors; if a piece is admired by one editor, it is read by the other three. Writers are encouraged if the editors think there is a real chance they may eventually publish his/her work. "Criticism is given as the impulse hits, but remember that a magazine is not a school and editorial time is limited."

Hershon adds that he finds most cover letters "idiotic" and would prefer to have time to react to one story before seeing any others.

THE HUDSON REVIEW

684 Park Avenue
New York, NY 10021
(212) 650-0020

SOURCE: Richard Smith, managing editor

ABOUT THE JOURNAL: Quarterly; no manuscripts accepted June through September. Founded: 1948. Circulation: 3500. Distribution: subscription; newsstands; bookstores. Avg. issue: 160 pp. Size: 4½x7½. Price: $4. Subscription: $14. Sample copy: $4. Back issues: some available.

FICTION: One long or two shorter stories per issue. Rates: 2½¢ per word. Payment: on publication. Rights: first rights; nonexclusive reprint rights. Reply time: one to three months for immediate rejection. Publication time: may be over a year. Length: 10,000 words maximum.

The Hudson Review is one of the best-known quarterlies. It considers a wide range of cultural and social topics in a rigorous and thought-provoking way. The review has no narrow academic or political aims; its only commitment is to excellence. Fiction is one part of an editorial mix that includes essays, poetry, book reviews, and "chronicles" covering current developments in music, dance, art, film, and theater.

All fiction published in *The Hudson Review* is unsolicited. It is very often by little-known or unpublished writers. Still, the editors were hesitant about a listing in this book. "We do not want to see floods of stories," managing editor Richard Smith says. "The quality of most submissions is not high."

Approximately 40 stories are received each week. Smith is the first reader. If he admires a story it is given to other editors for additional readings. Acceptance means as many as five people have read and admired a piece. Smith estimates that in any given week, four stories at most are worth a second reading.

"The only criterion for fiction is quality," Smith says. "We have not recently published a lot of 'experimental' fiction, but I read what comes in with an open mind. It is often neither competent nor interesting. We do want stories to be interesting. There should be a reason to read them. There are so many structural devices available to an author to pull a reader into a story. If the writer is skilled enough to succeed using only a few of them, such as the evocation of a mood or description of a setting, well and good. But this means that even more rides at stake on the sheer quality of the prose.

"We also use satire. For instance, a series of imaginary letters between William Carlos Williams and Wallace Stevens on the subject of red wheelbarrows."

Cover letters do not influence the handling of stories. Standard rejection forms are regularly used. Smith might ask a writer to send more work or he might make concrete suggestions about a piece if the story is found promising. Rewrites are rarely requested, but the possibility of a rewrite and resubmission on spec may be suggested.

There are qualities common to rejected manuscripts. There is the competently written story containing no original ideas or interesting use of language. "Almost any story that begins with someone waking up in bed is bound to be dull," Smith says. "If a writer has nothing to say, there is little point in his writing."

Common also is the chronicle of the dissolution of a marriage or relationship in which the events are well related but no insight is provided as to why things happened the way they did or what it all means.

"Stories have come in out of the blue and been published," Smith adds. "One writer was rejected several times, but encouraged to try again and we finally did buy something. It is very gratifying when that happens."

Writers published include Richard Hoffman, Fred Licht, John O'Brien, and Joseph Epstein.

INTRO

Associated Writing Programs
Old Dominion University
Norfolk, VA 23508
(804) 440-3840

SOURCE: Kate McCune, assistant director

ABOUT THE JOURNAL: Annual; manuscripts read only during September and October; *open only to students in an Associated Writing Program*; address story to the Editor. Founded: 1969. Circulation: 2000. Distribution: subscription; newsstand; bookstores. Avg. issue: 265 pp. Size: 6x9. Price: $7.95. Sample copy: $7.95. Back issues: available. Price: $4. Affiliated with Associated Writing Programs.

FICTION: Occupies 50% of total pages; 15 stories a year. Rates: copies. Rights: none. Reply time: three months. Publication time: four months. Length: no limits.

Intro is the magazine of the Associated Writing Programs (a nonprofit national organization of writers and writing programs supported by the National Endowment for the Arts; write to AWP for program dates and locations). Students of an AWP associated course (or June graduates) can submit one story or novel excerpt, up to four poems, or one play. Work must be previously unpublished. Writers can submit in more than one genre but must include a separate $1 reading fee for each category. Editors also want a cover letter with the name of the school attended, graduation date, teachers' names, and a brief biographical note.

Intro has two editors, who change yearly. Editorial perspective shifts with editors, as does the amount of correspondence with authors. A standard rejection form is regularly used.

Some 200 stories are submitted every year. Assistant director Kate McCune says that 20% of them are generally found worth more than one reading. *Intro* has become well known as a showcase for promising writers.

THE IOWA REVIEW

308 EPB
Iowa City, IA 52242
(319) 353-6048

SOURCE: staff member

ABOUT THE JOURNAL: Quarterly; no manuscripts over the summer; address stories to Fiction Editor. Founded: 1970. Circulation: 1000. Distribution: subscription; regional newsstands. Avg. issue: 220 pp.; double issues. Size: 6x9. Price: $4. Subscription: $12.

FICTION: Occupies one-third to one-fourth of total pages; 12-16 stories a year. Rates: $10 a printed page. Payment: on publication. Rights: first North American serial. Reply time: one to four months. Publication time: up to a year. Length: no limits; has published novellas.

The Iowa Review is a literary quarterly sponsored and published by the School of Letters and the Graduate College of the University of Iowa. Most of its fiction is chosen from the 2000 unsolicited stories submitted annually. "We're led by what we find," according to the editors. "We find, at different times, different kinds of good stories." Little-known writers are frequently published.

In vol. 12, no. 4 (Fall/Winter '82), fiction came from William Baer, Hugo de Hasenberg, Lillian Jen, and David Louie. Claude Richard, professor of American Literature at the University of Montpelier, France, was interviewed, and his essay "Destin, Design, Dasein: Lacan, Derrida and 'The Purloined Letter' " was published. Also other essays (including "More Phlegmiana," "several sets of missing pages from Grayson d'Auly's massive Phlegmiana," provided by Alexander S. Gourlay, Acting Director of the Phlegm Archives), poetry, small-press reviews.

Vol. 12, no. 2/3 (Spring/Summer '81): "Extended Outlook: The Iowa Review Collection of Contemporary Writing by Women." Contributors included Marge Piercy, Laura Riding, Grace Paley, Margaret Atwood, Becky Birtha, Jane Cooper, and Madeline DeFrees.

The Spring/Summer 1980 issue included fiction from Anne

Halley, Katherine D. Haman, David Hughes, Michael Kerkorian, Robert Taylor, Jr., Alexander Theroux, and Douglas Unger.

Cover letters are not necessary; groups of stories will be accepted, but editors warn that they will read one, *then* decide whether to read the others.

KANSAS QUARTERLY

Department of English
Kansas State University
Manhattan, KS 66506
(913) 532-6716

SOURCE: staff member

ABOUT THE JOURNAL: Quarterly. Editors: Harold Schneider, Ben Nyberg, W.R. Moses. Founded: 1968 as *Kansas Quarterly*; published intermittently since 1872 as *Kansas Magazine*. Circulation: about 1200. Avg. issue: 128-224 pp. Size: 6x9. Price: $3. Subscription: $10. Sample copy: $3. Back issues: available. Price: $3.

FICTION: Occupies 40% to 50% of total pages; about 30 stories a year. Rates: two copies; chance at yearly awards up to $300. Rights: first rights; will release if and when republication is scheduled. Reply time: two to six months. Publication time: at least 18 months. Length: 250 to 10,000 words (2-45 pages).

Kansas Quarterly describes itself in its masthead as "a periodical focusing on but not restricted to the culture, history, lifestyle, art and writing of Mid-America." It has a very strong focus on fiction, but also does special issues on literary criticism, art, and history. It publishes unknown and little-known, as well as very well-known, writers. "We look for good material, from whatever source."

Editors do not solicit fiction; everything is chosen from the approximately 1000 unsolicited manuscripts received annually. Nearly all these manuscripts are described as "professionally able"; 15% to 20% of them are generally found to be good enough for more than a first reading.

The editors "seek a variety of forms, and types of fiction. We avoid any special viewpoint that is narrow or restrictive, though of course we personally as editors have such views. . . . We are interested in good, serious fiction, whether traditional or experimental. We do not take genre fiction, ordinarily, unless it goes beyond the genre."

Manuscripts are read by one of the three editors who handle fiction. "We do use rejection forms, frequently adding personal notes of criticism or explanation; at times even writing full-page letters for stories that come close. Occasionally we suggest that changes be made and a story returned. We prefer that all three editors approve a story, but occasionally we take stories if only two editors like it and the other editor accedes. We emphasize and work hard to maintain a sense of personal relationship with all authors who submit, unless their work seems to us not to merit either encouragement or submission to other sources."

For the last ten years, *Kansas Quarterly*, with the aid of the Kansas Arts Commission, has been able to give awards for the best fiction and poetry published in the magazine. Winners are chosen by a distinguished roster of judges that has included William Inge, William Gass, John Cheever, David Madden, John Gardner, Anne Tyler, Ken Boyle, George Garrett, and Natalie L. M. Petesch. The intent of the awards is to "give some recompense to all recipients and in some instances to bring new but deserving writers to national attention." The prizes are $300 for first place, $200 for second place, and $100 for honorable mentions. Several other stories will be cited as deserving notice. (There is another set of awards limited to Kansas writers.)

In 1981-82, first prize was awarded to Jack Matthews' "Quest for an Unnamed Place" (Summer/Fall '81); second prize was awarded to Joe David Bellamy's "The Weeds of North Carolina" (Winter '82). Honorable mentions went to Myron Taube's "Sarai" (Summer/Fall '81) and Carl Adler's "The Visitation" (Winter '82).

In a statement published in the Winter 1982 *Kansas Quarterly*, Natalie L. M. Petesch (1981-82 judge) wrote about why she chose the winning stories: "First Prize goes to Jack Matthews' 'Quest for an Unnamed Place' for his daring probe of our unnameable and ineffable longing for what has gone forever. His dialogue constructs a trellis skillfully laid over with garlands of language. Through the latticework of the dialogue the reader is allowed to glimpse, like sunlight irradiating the rose bower, a long marriage still full of compassion, tenderness and love, fiercely protecting itself against the erosions of time: an exquisitely rendered story of the yearning for our lost innocence and the days of our youth, with a gently heroic ending that is unforced and honest.

"Second Prize goes to Joe David Bellamy's 'The Weeds of North Carolina,' a story which deals with profoundly ethical subjects with the deftness and verbal precision of a scientist and, at the same time, with the whimsical good nature of a moralist who has no absolute answers: a well-orchestrated, daring and sustained performance."

The editors do have a suggestion for writers trying to place their work: "Writers should *read* the magazines they consider sending to—in the library or by sending for a copy. If they like the fiction, *then* they should submit theirs."

Some writers who have published in *Kansas Quarterly*: Susan Fromberg Schaeffer, Joyce Carol Oates, H.E. Francis, Nancy Potter, Rolaine Hockstein, L.J. Schneiderman, and Annabel Thomas.

THE KENYON REVIEW

Kenyon College
Gambier, OH 43022
(614) 417-3339

SOURCE: Frederick Turner, editor

ABOUT THE JOURNAL: Quarterly; no manuscripts accepted June, July, August. Founded: 1978. Circulation: 8000. Distribution: subscription; newsstands; bookstores. Avg. issue: 128 pp. Size: 7x10. Price: $5. Subscription: $15. Sample copy: $5. Back issues: available. Price: $5.50-$6.50.

FICTION: About 25% of total pages; approximately ten stories a year. Rates: $10 a printed page. Payment: on publication. Rights: first serial rights; anthology rights with financial terms to be negotiated. Reply time: approximately three months. Publication time: 9 to 18 months. Length: upper limit of 30 pages that is occasionally ignored.

The Kenyon Review is among the best-known and most widely circulated literary magazines. Saul Bellow and Joyce Carol Oates are advisory editors; George Steiner is the European editor. The magazine's commitment is to literary excellence.

Each issue can include between one and four short stories; half will come from contacts with writers, half from unsolicited submissions; 2000 unsolicited stories are submitted every year. Editor Frederick Turner estimates that 8% of these are good enough for more than a first reading and about one-third of that number (about 50 manuscripts) are seriously considered for publication.

The Kenyon Review describes itself in the masthead as "an international journal of literature, culture, arts and ideas." Turner describes the editorial mix as 25% fiction, 25% poetry, 25% criticism, and 25% general essays and articles.

The journal is "suspicious of conventional left-wing and right-wing attitudes; 'upbeat' on human culture and society in general, and America in particular; very hospitable to cultural and religious diversity; interested in science and philosophy."

On the subject of fiction: "We look for an original combination of powerful and elegant writing, vivid detail and observation, striking narrative or linguistic technique, profound psychology and philosophy, and—in the subtlest sense—a constructive and humane morality. This last is *not* a code-word for a particular religious or ideological viewpoint, nor are we squeamish about 'bad language' if appropriate. Good genre fiction, especially science fiction, is welcome. Experimental prose is welcome only if the experiment is a success."

Published writers include Woody Allen, William Gass, Ursula K. LeGuin, Joyce Carol Oates, E.L. Doctorow, Julio Cortázar, Robert Hemenway, Lynda Saxon, Janet Lindquist Black, Eugene Garber, Susan Engberg, Amy Herrick, and T.E. Holt.

Stories are initially looked at by "screening" readers from the Kenyon College literary faculty. Most are rejected using one of two standard forms. The first is a straight rejection; the second invites the writer to send more work. Those stories held after the first reading (approximately 160 out of 2000) are given to an editorial advisory committee of three. They make comments and recommendations before passing the story to the editor who makes the final decision. Occasionally, outside advisory editors are also consulted.

Any story seriously considered and still rejected will be returned with a letter of criticism, encouragement, and explanation.

THE LITERARY REVIEW

285 Madison Avenue
Madison, NJ 07940
(201) 377-4050

SOURCE: Martin Green, editor

ABOUT THE JOURNAL: Quarterly. Founded: 1957. Circulation: 1000. Distribution: subscription mainly; some bookstore sales. Avg. issue: 152 pp. Size: 6x9. Price: $3.50. Subscription: $9. Sample copy: $3.50. Back issues: available. Price: varies. Affiliated with Fairleigh Dickinson University.

FICTION: Approximately 15 stories a year; fiction is not necessarily published in every issue. Rates: copies. Rights: first. Reply time: three months. Publication time: six months to a year. Length: no limits.

Editor-in-chief Martin Green says of *The Literary Review*: "We are a traditonal university-based magazine devoted to good writing and *Literature*. We publish essays, reviews, poetry, translations, fiction.

"We are open to traditional and experimental forms. What we look for is imagination, skill, and craft. Genre fiction occasionally appeals to us but we haven't usually found the genre submissions successful because they lack freshness or stylistic polish."

Published writers include James Ferry (included in *Best American Stories 1982*, ed. John Gardner), Eve Shelnutt, Jay Neugeboren, Janet Lindquist Black, Steven Dixon, Phil Greene, Lester Goldberg, and Gordon Lish.

Around 15 stories are published annually. Stories are generally chosen from the 800-1000 unsolicited manuscripts submitted every year.

Manuscripts are initially read by the chief editor or one of two other editors. Stories found worth a second reading (less than 5%) are circulated for comments. At least two of three readers must agree to a story's inclusion before acceptance, though even that is not a guarantee.

Any editor may reject a story after an initial screening. Most are returned with a form rejection. Authors of material that seems particularly promising get some comment and encouragement, though this does not always result in better treatment on the next submission.

Revisions may be suggested if the perceived problem seems easily fixed and, of course, if the author agrees with the editor's critique.

Common reasons for fast rejection include: "trite pieces; familiar themes and situations; insufficiently developed plots and characters; poor style; incoherent structure (without a clear purpose for incoherence); patently autobiographical work; overly moralizing tales; no redeeming literary value; pointless violence or sexism or other prejudices."

Editors will read more than one submission from a writer "as long as they're not burdensome." Green adds: "A list of previous publications is informative but not essential. Occasionally it works against authors when material submitted doesn't live up to expectations generated by a long list of credentials. We actually prefer not to know much about previous publications. Obviously familiar names are their own best credentials. For unknown writers, it makes little difference if they've had little magazine exposure."

THE LITTLE MAGAZINE

Box 78
Pleasantville, NY 10570

SOURCE: David G. Hartwell, editor

ABOUT THE JOURNAL: Occasional. Founded: 1965. Circulation: 1000. Distribution: subscription; bookstores. Avg. issue: 112 pp. Size: 5½x8½. Price: $4.75. Back issues: available.

FICTION: Varies from none to half of total pages per issue. Rates: copies. Rights: first North American serial. Reply time: two weeks to eight months. Publication time: varies widely. Length: under 10,000 words.

The Little Magazine has been in publication for 17 years. It was originally a quarterly; mailing and printing costs have made it an occasional magazine. But editors still plan to publish four numbers per volume. The "Frontmatter" section in vol. 13, nos. 3 and 4 reports that vol. 13, nos. 1-2 sold out, "and the future, if not really bright, is still there. We have plans and hopes."

The editors also say they will not be open for submissions until a new schedule is set; check with the magazine.

The Little Magazine concentrates on fiction and poetry—the ratio between them changing issue by issue. In volume 13, nos. 3-4 (Winter '82-83) fiction contributors were Jean McGarry, David Ives, Rudy Rucker, R. Bartkowech, Lesley Krueger.

When The Little Magazine was founded, editor David Hartwell says, the idea was to come out with a publication that would not support any special groups of writers or poets, any locales, or any style, but would be a general national and international literary magazine with the best poetry and fiction the editors could find.

Hartwell says that philosophy has essentially not changed. By definition it is a literary magazine and is looking for fiction of some literary ambition. A straightforward narrative in journalistic prose—maybe a good commercial piece—is not appropriate. But at the same time editors try to stay away from obscurity. They are open to any kind of fiction—experimental, science fiction, mystery—as long as it's excellently done. The magazine's only goal is to provide a place where "good fiction" can get published.

Because of its recent publishing history, it is hard to estimate how many manuscripts come in. But when publication was more regular, the magazine received between 60 and 100 unsolicited stories a week; 10% or less were of any real quality.

It takes two editors to reject a story; if one editor likes a piece, everyone on staff reads it. Standard rejection forms are used and rewrites are asked for only on accepted pieces.

LOOK QUICK

P. O. Box 222
Pueblo, CO 81002

SOURCE: Joel Scherzer, coeditor

ABOUT THE JOURNAL: Annual or biannual; address manuscripts to Joel Scherzer or Robbie Rubinstein. Founded: 1975. Circulation: 200. Avg. issue: up to 32 pp. Size: 8½x5½. Distribution: mostly subscription. Price: 75¢. Subscription: $2.50. Sample copy: $1. Back issues: available. Price: $1.

FICTION: Occupies 10% of total pages; at most one story per issue. Rates: copies. Rights: first periodical. Reply time: up to four months. Publication time: up to a year. Length: not over 750 words.

Look Quick finds its fiction through unsolicited submissions, but uses at most one story per issue. Because the magazine generally runs about 32 pages, there is a 750 word maximum limit on story length.

"We favor brief, tightly written vignettes," coeditor Joel Scherzer says. "Most of the stories we've published have been first-person narratives. We are also looking for short detective stories. . . . We lean toward stories with urban themes.

"We'd like to see imaginative fiction with realistic dialogue. We're open to experimental writing, although we don't publish much of it. We're not committed to traditional forms. Genre fiction is fine, especially mystery."

Among previously published writers, "Charles Bukowski tells a good tale, packed with dialogue, eroticism, and humor. William Burroughs' cut-up technique, in our opinion, is the best approach to experimental writing.

"Many writers are oblivious to the size and format of our publication. A 25-page story would fill an entire issue. Most stories we read don't have enough dialogue. A good story should grab the reader's attention in the first paragraph; very few achieve this."

Scherzer suggests that authors "edit and rewrite until they can't eliminate another word. Try to get at least some dialogue on every manuscript page. There's no better source of material than your own experience—expand upon unusual incidents from your past. Keep those paragraphs short. Make sure you land on your feet; too many stories run out of steam."

Look Quick's editors say cover letters are unnecessary and they will read a group of stories.

Approximately 50 stories are submitted every year. Generally, 10% of them are found worth reading more than once. Both editors must approve before acceptance. There is no standard rejection form. The editors will critique a story if the author requests it.

MAENAD

84 Main Street #7
P. O. Box 738
Gloucester, ME 01930
(617) 283-7401 or 0828

SOURCE: Paula Estey, publisher

ABOUT THE JOURNAL: Quarterly. Address manuscripts to editorial staff. Founded: 1980. Circulation: 2000. Distribution: subscription; bookstores. Avg. issue: 120 pp. Size: 7x8½. Price: $4. Subscription: $16. Sample copy: $3. Back issues: available. Price: $2.50.

FICTION: Occupies one-third of pages; 12 stories per year. Rates: copies. Rights: none. Reply time: three months. Publication time: two months. Length: 15 typed pages maximum, although there have been exceptions.

Maenad is "a women's literary journal." It is looking for work that is "innovative, creative, provocative in stimulating women's growth." It is open to feminist writing in all forms and genres of fiction, in fact and theory articles, in biography, history, and so on. Published writers include Gabrielle Burton, Marge Piercy, Grace Shinell, S. Diane Bogus, Susan Weinburg, Barbara Wilson, Katharyn Machan Aal, and Kristen Andersen.

Nonfiction found in *Maenad* has included "Mary Rowlandson's Narrative: A Puritan Best-Seller": an article about a 1682 book that was the first best-seller written by a woman. Other essays have considered women in publishing, the writing of Shirley Jackson, the work of Radclyffe Hall, and the changing heroine in fiction.

Two hundred unsolicited stories are submitted every year; 15% are found to be worth more than one reading. There are three people on staff and all read each manuscript. Editors hope to reach agreement on what will be published, but *sometimes* a story will be published without mutual agreement.

Standard rejection forms are not used. Editors regularly comment on manuscripts. "Many authors have appreciated our comments," publisher Paula Estey says. "Many have objected strenuously. Therefore, we do prefer when authors specifically ask us to be free with our criticisms."

A cover letter should briefly explain what type of submission is enclosed; editors want a brief biography of the writer. They do not want more than one story at a time unless the stories are related.

MAGICAL BLEND

Box 11303
San Francisco, CA 94101
(415) 282-9338

SOURCE: Lisa Shulman, literary editor

ABOUT THE JOURNAL: Triannual or quarterly. Founded: 1979. Circulation: 5000. Distribution: subscription; bookstores; newsstands. Avg. issue: 64-80 pp. Size: 8½x11. Price: $3. Subscription: $10. Sample copy: $3. Back issues: available. Price: $5.

FICTION: Occupies 10% of pages; three to five stories an issue. Rates: five copies. Rights: first North American serial. Reply time: three months. Publication time: three to six months. Length: 500 to 3000 words.

Magical Blend "prints only material with a positive, uplifting approach or message. We like science/speculative fiction, fantasy, fairy tales, experimental work; but it must not be negative, dark, horrifying, violent, or sexist. Much material with a spiritual, mystical, magical slant is used. We believe in people and magic," literary editor Lisa Shulman says.

Magical Blend publishes newcomers all the time; its fiction (only about 10% of its pages) is chosen from the 150-200 unsolicited manuscripts submitted annually. Shulman adds that too many of the stories are from writers who have not looked at the magazine and are sending conventional science fiction or horror pieces.

Shulman says, "I want to see quality writing, new ideas, interesting style and form. No cute, trite, overworked stuff. Be original, be daring. Experimental to classical folk tale are all fine if appropriate and well written."

Published writers include Jerry Snider ("Saying Goodbye to Marie"; no. 3, Oct. '81), S. A. Smith ("The Magician's Daughter"; no. 5, Mar. '82), and Carolyn White ("Michael Henley and the Sea"; no. 8, Mar. '83).

Shulman likes to receive a short cover letter and to know about previous credits; she adds these don't affect decisions.

She reads, or at least begins to read, all stories. The obvious rejections are returned with a standard form, often with a small note of criticism or suggestion. Possibilities (an estimated 5% to

10%) are read by three to five others on staff. Again, rejections are returned with a standard form and often a comment. Stories are usually accepted by majority consensus. Those that show promise, or that are good but too long, will be sent back with a request for revision.

Shulman would prefer receiving one story at a time, but will read more.

THE MASSACHUSETTS REVIEW

Memorial Hall
University of Massachusetts
Amherst, MA 01003
(413) 545-2689

SOURCE: Carol Fetler, secretary

ABOUT THE JOURNAL: Quarterly; no manuscripts considered June through October. Address stories to the fiction editors. Editors: John Hicks, Mary Heath, Fred Robinson. Founded: 1959. Circulation: 2000. Distribution: subscription; bookstores; newsstands; international. Avg. issue: 180-190 pp. Size: 6x9. Price $4. Subscription: $12. Sample copy: $4.50. Back issues: available. Price: $4.50; rare issues more. Published independently with the support and cooperation of Amherst, Hampshire, Mount Holyoke, and Smith College and the University of Massachusetts.

FICTION: Occupies 25% to 30% of total pages; two to three stories an issue. Rates: $50 per story. Payment: on publication. Rights: copyright reverts. Reply time: two months. Publication time: can go over a year. Length: 18 to 25 typed pages maximum.

The Massachusetts Review is one of the better-known literary journals. All of its fiction is chosen from the close to 2000 unsolicited manuscripts submitted every year, and editors are always on the lookout for new writers.

The review is a journal of the arts, letters, and public affairs. The effort is to produce a reader for an audience interested in a wide variety of subjects. "We use more fiction and poetry than some more academic magazines and tend to take chances on what we choose," Carol Fetler says.

The review is open to all kinds of fiction (excluding genre fiction) and prides itself on its catholicity. Issues are usually eclectic—though there have been theme issues. Vol. XXII, no. 4 was devoted to comedy with fiction contributions from Robert Coover, John Hawkes, Lawrence Raab, Ladislav Jerga, Clarence Major, and Barbara Reisner; other published writers include Kenneth Lash, Sydney Harth, Peter La Salle, K.L. Gewertz, and Lissa McLaughlin.

Editors are looking for stories that are original and vivid in voice and that will speak to the reader. *MR* fiction has consistently been awarded prizes in the annual anthologies.

First readers look at all submissions. Of the 40 stories received every week, maybe five will be passed on to the fiction editors. Impressive stories are discussed during editorial conferences and chosen by consensus.

There is a form rejection letter. More personalized responses depend on which editor is interested in a story. Some of the editors write back often, others never do. Rewrites, on spec, might be asked for.

A cover letter as a courtesy is welcome, but Fetler adds that while the absence of a cover letter does not hurt a story, an ill-written letter does. Editors do not want to receive groups of stories.

MICHIGAN QUARTERLY REVIEW

3032 Rackham Building
University of Michigan
Ann Arbor, MI 48109
(313) 764-9265

SOURCE: Laurence Goldstein, editor

ABOUT THE JOURNAL: Quarterly. Founded: 1962. Circulation: 1700. Distribution: subscription; newsstands in New York and locally. Avg. issue: 160 pp. Size: 6x9. Price: $3.50. Subscription: $13. Sample copy: $2. Back issues: available. Price: usually $2. Affiliated with University of Michigan.

FICTION: Occupies 15% to 20% of total pages; eight stories a year. Rates: about $8 to $10 a printed page plus a free subscription. Payment: on acceptance. Rights: first publication. Reply time: four to six weeks; two months in summer. Publication time: six months to a year. Length: up to about 8000 words.

Michigan Quarterly Review "is an academic journal," editor Laurence Goldstein says, "so we prefer stories of some sophistication and genuine originality. Our stories are read by people who read a great deal of first-rate fiction. Except for special issues (one per year) on a prescribed topic, we do not choose on the basis of subject matter or political viewpoint or social vision. We like to publish Michigan writers, but ultimately the best work that comes into the office is what's printed."

Most of the fiction is chosen from the 1500-2000 unsolicited stories submitted annually. Occasionally a story is solicited. Goldstein estimates that one out of 30 submissions is worth more than one reading.

"It's impossible to say what we want until we see it, since we don't market stories for a particular audience whose every need we know. We publish short and long stories, on the poor and the rich, in traditional and experimental prose, realistic and surrealistic, foreign and native. The underlying similarity is an *intelligence* in the writing and crafting that results from a deep understanding in the possibilities of fictional forms.

"We look for well-plotted stories, and for fiction with an original use of the language. Slice-of-life stories, scenes, sketches, 'yarns'—this kind of thing is not for us. Again, our audience expects sophisticated writing, usually with a capacious vocabulary, wit, insight, serious purpose, or subtle humor. We have no use for stories with lots of explicit sexual material, or an ax to grind, or abundant time to waste (stories of more than 35 pages are returned without being read). Stories written to be 'marketed'—formula stories that simply redo familiar plots—don't interest us."

MQR has published fiction by well-known writers such as Paul Bowles, Arthur Koestler, Max Apple, and Joyce Carol Oates. But little-known or unpublished writers also appear. Charles Baxter's story from MQR was chosen for *Best American Short Stories 1982*; a first published story by Lyn Coffin was in *Best American 1979*.

Of these two stories, Goldstein says, "These are intricately plotted, with each episode advancing understanding of the characters; both have excellent suspense, and best of all, the use of the language is entirely fresh, imaginative not just utilitarian. There is pleasure in reading the sentences apart from plot interest."

Submissions are read by either a staff member or the editor, depending on season and workload. Most manuscripts are rejected immediately. Those being considered are read by one or two more staff members (volunteers from the University of Michigan English Department faculty), who make comments. The editor rereads, considers the comments, and makes daily decisions on whether to return a story or keep it for further rereading and, perhaps, possible acceptance. Acceptance means three staff members and the editor want the piece.

Revisions are rarely asked for. Editors have found that half the time the story comes back in worse shape. A standard rejection form is used in most cases; notes of encouragement are sometimes sent.

Goldstein adds: "The first rule for a young writer, as always, is *know the magazine*. It's a waste of everyone's time and effort if a formula story about fishing or sexual escapades or melodrama in a small town or children-as-cute-beings is sent to an academic-based journal that publishes mainly essays and reviews on significant cultural subjects. Because we publish so little fiction we are highly selective; this is not a local publication. Though our circulation is small, it is sophisticated and intolerant of lazy writing or casual yarn spinning.

"Every journal wants to publish undiscovered writers; that is one of its chief functions as a journal. Despite all the rejections we send out, we still anticipate with considerable excitement each day's mail, and hope for that occasional story that will command national and international attention and respect by its compelling craft."

Editors like to see a list of previous publications and rarely read more than two stories submitted at one time.

THE MINNESOTA REVIEW

Department of English
Oregon State University
Corvallis, OR 97331
(503) 754-3244

SOURCE: Michael Sprinker, coeditor

ABOUT THE JOURNAL: Biannual; address stories to Fred Pfeil, fiction editor. Founded: 1961. Circulation: 1000. Distribution: subscriptions; bookstores; newsstands; nationally. Avg. issue: 160 pp. Size: 5½x8. Price: $4. Subscription: $8. Sample copy: $4. Back issues: available. Price: $4. Editors all teach at Oregon State University.

FICTION: Occupies one-third to one-quarter of pages; four to seven stories a year. Rates: three copies. Rights: copyright reverts. Reply time: tries for 90 days. Publication time: 6 to 15 months. Length: no formal limits, but it is difficult to publish anything over 50 typed pages.

the minnestoa review is subtitled "a journal of committed writing." It encourages submissions that are political in nature with special interest in socialist, feminist, and Marxist work.

"We publish a wide range of fiction in terms of technique," coeditor Michael Sprinker says. "We wish, in general, to publish political writing of various stamps, but especially leftist and progressive, since there are very few outlets for this kind of writing in the United States."

Published writers include Harold Jaffe, Joe Ashby Porter, Patrick Beal, and Lorna Tracy.

"All these writers," Sprinker says, "are working critically with the social environment and are experimenting with various fictional styles and modes to achieve the critical production at which they aim."

Stories are chosen from the approximately 200 unsolicited manuscripts submitted annually. The review is particularly "interested in encouraging the publication of unknown writers whom we feel are undeservedly neglected."

Every submission is read at least twice, by each of the two fiction editors. Other editors may read a piece when there is any question as to its appropriateness.

Stories that do not merit more than a cursory reading (approximately two-thirds) are rejected with a standard form. Comments or advice are added only when the story is considered good but not right for the magazine or the story shows promise.

Cover letters are neither needed nor considered important. Editors will read more than one story submitted at a time, but are very unlikely to take more than one for publication.

MISSISSIPPI REVIEW

Southern Station
Box 5144
Hattiesburg, MS 39406-5144
(601) 266-4321

SOURCE: Rie Fortenberry, managing editor

ABOUT THE JOURNAL: Biannual; no stories accepted in June, July, or August. Send manuscripts to Frederick Barthelme, editor. Founded: 1974. Circulation: 1500. Distribution: subscription; newsstands; bookstores. Avg. issue: 140 pp.; some double issues. Size: 6x9. Price: $4.50; $5.50 for a double issue. Subscription: $8. Sample copy: $4.50. Back issues: available. Price: $4.50. Affiliated with Center for Writers, University of Southern Mississippi.

FICTION: Occupies 75% of pages; 12-15 stories an issue. Rates: copies. Rights: first North American serial. Reply time: two to three months. Publication time: six months. Length: no limits.

Mississippi Review is a well-known journal primarily devoted to short fiction. It regularly mixes known and unknown authors and chooses most of its work from the 1200-1500 unsolicited manuscripts submitted annually. Managing editor Rie Fortenberry estimates that 10% of those manuscripts are worth more than a first reading.

MR 30 (Winter/Spring '82) opens with an excerpt from the novel *Virginie: Her Two lives*, by John Hawkes. Stories are from J.F. Sellers, David Diefendorf, Judy Lopatin, Jonathan Baumbach, Jonathan Brent, Bruce Kleinman, and Alvin Greenberg, and a first fiction publication from poet Michael Cadnum.

MR 27 (Winter, '81) opens with "Rovera and Angisele," a romance by nineteenth-century French poet Albert Samain. Other authors are Doug Crowell, Mary Robison, Richard Burgin, Vern Rutsala, Richard Kostelanetz, Edward Zorensky and a first published piece by Sandra J. Kolankiewicz.

Fortenberry says that a cover letter listing credits is found helpful and editors will read a group of stories.

MISSISSIPPI VALLEY REVIEW

Department of English
Western Illinois University
Macomb, IL 61445
(309) 298-1514 or 1103

SOURCE: Forrest Robinson, editor

ABOUT THE JOURNAL: Biannual (Fall/Winter; Spring/Summer); no manuscripts accepted in June and July. Address stories to Loren Logsdon, fiction editor. Founded: 1971. Circulation: 450. Distribution: subscription. Avg. issue: 64 pp. Size: 6x9. Price: $2 (vol. 13 $3). Subscription: $4. Sample copy: $2 plus postage. Back issues: available. Price: $2 plus postage. Funded by Western Illinois University.

FICTION: Occupies approximately 60% of pages; six stories a year. Rates: two copies of issue carrying story plus copy of next two issues. Rights: none. Reply time: about three months. Publication time: six months to a year. Length: ideal length 10-20 typewritten pages; the longer the story the better it has to be to win acceptance.

"*Mississippi Valley Review* has an eclectic editorial philosophy. We accept, in other words, the best we can find. If we have an editorial bias, it is towards a more traditional story form; however, we are open to—and have published—experimental work."

Over half the review's pages are generally devoted to fiction. Most of it is chosen from the 300 to 400 unsolicited stories submitted annually. Published pieces usually are from experienced writers, though unknown or little-known writers are sometimes published.

"I wish that more writers would regard their craft and art," editor Forrest Robinson says, "instead of just 'making it' as writers, merely sending out their work as fast as they produce it in a 'shotgun' effort to 'hit' somewhere.

"Our best fiction is written by those who have read and loved the great tradition of storytelling. Our fast rejections go to those who evidence no awareness of the basic ingredients of sound characterization and careful regard for language."

Published writers include Jack Matthews, Laurence Lieberman, Lucien Stryk, Joan Colby, Ralph Mills, Jr., and Lester Goldberg.

Submitted stories are distributed to readers (mostly faculty members at Western Illinois University). Any story that passes the initial screening is looked at by at least two more readers before being discussed as a possibility for publication. The fiction editor and the editor make the final decisions. Robinson estimates that one-third of the stories are worth more than one reading.

A standard rejection form is used in most cases. Only in rare circumstances will an editor comment or request that a writer submit more work. Editors are very concerned not to mislead writers; when they do write back, the words are meant to count. Revision is suggested only when publication is being seriously considered, and even then the writer is warned that rejection is still a possibility.

Cover letters make no difference and are not necessary. Editors prefer one story at a time.

NEW ENGLAND REVIEW AND BREAD LOAF QUARTERLY

Box 170
Hanover, NH 03755
(603) 795-4027

SOURCE: Sydney Lea, editor

ABOUT THE JOURNAL: Quarterly; no manuscripts accepted June through August. Founded: 1977. Circulation: 2000. Distribution: subscriptions; bookstores; national. Avg. issue: 160 pp. Size: 6x9. Price: $4. Subscription: $12. Sample copy: $4. Back issues: available. Price: $4 to $8. Affiliated with Bread Loaf Writers' Conference.

FICTION: Occupies 50% of total pages; 8 to 16 stories a year. Rates: money and copies. Payment: on publication. Rights: first serial. Reply time: six weeks. Publication time: a year maximum (although can be longer when a story is exceptionally long or when a story is being held to coincide with book publication). Length: rarely accepts over 30 pages.

The New England Review and Bread Loaf Quarterly (formerly known as *The New England Review*) publishes fiction, poetry, book reviews, and essays. Half of its pages are usually for fiction —most of it chosen from the 1000 unsolicited manuscripts submitted annually. Editors make an effort to give some kind of personal response on all or almost all rejections (though editor Sydney Lea adds that as volume increases it is becoming harder to do).

"Our inclination," Lea says, "is to fiction with allegiances to narrative. We rarely publish 'experimental' fiction."

Rejected is "inept writing . . . or writing which is competent, controlled, and not very interesting."

Well-known writers whose work has appeared in the review include Joyce Carol Oates, Raymond Carver, Ann Beattie, Gordon Weaver, and Richard Selzer.

Vol. IV, no. 4 (Summer '82) included fiction by Charles Brownson, Robert Phillips, Charles Baxter, and Daniel Curley. Also published was "Reflections on Recent Prose," by J. D. O'Hara.

Stories are screened by the managing editor, who passes the possibilities (and work from previous contributors) to Lea. An estimated 20%–30% are worth a second reading. Though there is a standard rejection form, editors do try to make at least some brief comment on each piece. If a story just fails of being taken, Lea encourages the author to submit more work. He rarely asks for revision and resubmission unless he can be very specific.

Editors have no interest in cover letters and will not read more than one story at a time, unless they are short.

NEW LETTERS

5346 Charlotte
Kansas City, MO 64110
(816) 276-1168

SOURCE: Marilyn Cannaday, editorial assistant

ABOUT THE JOURNAL: Quarterly; sometimes restricts summer submissions. Address stories to David Ray, editor. Founded: 1934; since 1972 as *New Letters*. Circulation: 2500. Distribution: subscription; bookstores; international. Avg. issue: 128 pp. Size: 6x9. Price: $3. Subscription: $10. Sample copy price: $3. Back issues: available. Price: $5. Affiliated with University of Missouri—Kansas City.

FICTION: Occupies 20% to 25% of total pages; 10 to 12 stories a year. Rates: $5 to $25 plus two copies. Payment: on publication. Rights: first serial. Reply time: six weeks to two months. Publication time: six months to a year. Length: no limits.

Most of the fiction in *New Letters* is chosen from the work of previously published contributors. Unknown or little-known writers are not often published.

The 1200-1300 unsolicited stories submitted every year are read, but editorial assistant Marilyn Cannaday says that only a small percentage of them are found good enough for more than one reading.

Cannaday says the editors are looking for "originality, dramatic verve. We are not locked into specific expectations, but we give no points for gimmickry, including the 'experimental,' often a cover for those who have nothing to say."

Published writers include Esther Broner, Natalie Petesch, Daniel Curley, and Robert Day. They write stories "that grab our interest and keep us turning the page."

When stories are received, a comment sheet is attached. Several readers—volunteers, students and staff—screen the manuscripts and write short comments. If several readers comment positively the story is brought to the editor's attention. He makes selections from the recommended manuscripts as time permits and has the final say on publication. A standard rejection form is used. The editor might make comments on a piece or ask for revisions. "Comments and encouragement are kept to a minimum because of the constant deluge of poor-quality manuscripts."

Inept or unoriginal writing is, of course, the main problem. There are too many "tired stories about academics, painters, sex-crazed adolescents, midlife-crisis executives and suicidal housewives."

"We are particularly put off," Cannaday says, "by writing that shows no awareness of our tradition; often this work is misdirected in terms of market."

Cannaday adds: "In an age in which all contests for publishing work require an entry fee and most publishing houses refuse even to read manuscripts not submitted by agents, and given the immense burden placed upon us by great amounts of unsolicited material and by the necessity to assure the magazine's survival, we feel it is perfectly fair to require that a subscription order accompany an unsolicited manuscript. It is inappropriate for writers to submit to a magazine they have not really studied, and which they have no interest in helping survive."

Cover letters should list publications only if significant; otherwise, mention types of publications. Editors prefer one submission at a time.

THE NEW RENAISSANCE

9 Heath Road
Arlington, MA 02174

SOURCE: Louise T. Reynolds, editor

ABOUT THE JOURNAL: Biannual (spring and fall); no manuscripts read in July and August or December 10 to January 14. Address stories to Louise Reynolds or Harry Jackel. Founded: 1968. Circulation: 1500. Distribution: subscription, regional bookstores and newsstands. Avg. issue: 104-120 pp. Size: 6x9. Price: $4.25. Subscription: $8.50. Sample copy: $4.25. Back issues: available. Price: fiction issues: no. 7 for $2.10; no. 9 for $2.90; no. 11 for $3.20; no. 13 for $3.75.

FICTION: Occupies about 30% of total pages; six to ten stories a year. Rates: money (around $18.50, depending on length) plus one copy. Payment: on publication. Rights: all rights. Reply time: usually 5 to 7 months, but can be as long as 11 months. Publication time: one to two years. Length: 3 to 35 pages.

the new renaissance is an international magazine, "catholic" and "eclectic" in its editorial mix. It generally publishes at least two and as many as four unknown or little-known writers an issue along with one or two well-established authors.

Most of the fiction comes from the unsolicited submissions: 350-450 a year. About 20% to 30% of these are generally found worth more than one reading. Three to four of them will actually be accepted for publication; another three to five will come close.

"This means a lot of writers are submitting to the wrong market," editor Louise Reynolds says, "to a magazine they have never seen and might not like if they did."

Too many writers "see that you will read unsolicited manuscripts and that you pay and they send off their work before carefully examining (perusing) a couple of issues.

"We would never publish heavily plotted or formula fiction or propaganda fiction or popular once-over-lightly 'light' fiction, but we receive these, especially after a listing in a writers' market guide. Beyond that, tyro writers—and lately, many established writers as well—do not respect or trust their readers, so they will 'explain' a story rather than let it develop. Other writers are very self-consciously 'literary,' pretentious and portentous, and are anxious to let the reader know how erudite they are; we are not in the market for these works.

"What we look for at *tnr* is excellence and honesty. We want writers who have something to say (i.e., personal vision), who can say it with some degree of style or grace, and, above all, who can speak in a personal voice. We want to see well-crafted stories by writers who respect and know the language and who know why the precise word is the right word; generally, we want three-dimensional characters and/or a unique, highly personal view of an age-old situation.

"We like the traditional short story and we welcome experimental fiction; we publish fiction that is in the literary mainstream and fiction that is outside the literary mainstream because we judge on the individual work itself.

"We would not absolutely rule out genre fiction—we have published some gothic manuscripts—but we are not the best marketplace for this type of story; however, if it's well done, it could stand a chance here.

"We especially liked Madeleine Costigan's story "Summer People," Sheila S. Thompson's "The Seeker," and Gordon Weaver's "Elements of the 10th Mountain Infantry Reconnoiter"—all in issue no. 7.

"We especially liked E.J. Neely's "Onward to Tellehavee" in no. 8. Also G.P. Vimal's "The Other Face," Michael Fedo's "Before His Time," Carlos Jordan's "Just One G-Shot"—all in no. 10—and Gary Karasik's "The Tower" and Estelle Gilson's "The Baby's Room" in no. 13.

"These are all stories with personal visions; they all yield different meanings with levels of reading. But we are not interested in derivative fiction or fiction that is simply similar to that of our strong fiction issues."

All manuscripts are read by a staff editor. Generally, only one editor has to like a piece for it to be accepted. Standard rejection forms are used for stories found really unsuitable or badly written. Otherwise, a brief letter explaining the rejection or, perhaps, mentioning strong points will be enclosed. Letters of serious criticism and encouragement are sent only when either the story or the writer is considered to be a good possibility for the magazine.

"We ask all writers who submit to *tnr*, " Reynolds says, "to buy a copy of a strong fiction issue. . . . We have a wide variety of styles of writing in *tnr*—but our philosophy is not that of 'anything goes.' We publish work, styles, and statements that are in contradiction to each other, but our background is that of the classicist and we are looking for material that can be read and reread throughout the decade and generation. We are not in the market for stories of the moment, that reflect our time and place only; we are looking for a more universal statement than that.

"We also like writers who actually like reading; many do not and they have a very scanty background in literature."

Cover letters are considered neither necessary nor important. Editors will accept only one story at a time for pieces over ten pages, two stories of nine pages of less, and three stories of four pages or less.

NIMROD

Arts and Humanities Council of Tulsa
2210 South Main
Tulsa, OK 74114
(918) 583-1587

SOURCE: Francine Ringold, editor

ABOUT THE JOURNAL: Biannual; send manuscripts to Francine Ringold or Geraldine McLoud, fiction editor. Founded: 1956. Circulation: 1000. Distribution: subscriptions; bookstores. Avg. issue: 124 pp. Size: 6x9. Price: $5.50. Subscription: $10. Sample copy: $4.50. Back issues: available. Published by Arts and Humanities Council of Tulsa.

FICTION: Occupies 50% of total pages; six stories a year. Rates: $5 a page when money is available or three copies. Payment: on publication. Rights: copyright reverts. Reply time: at least two months. Publication time: six months to a year. Length: no set limits; prefers nothing over 40 typed pages.

Nimrod devotes 50% of its pages to the short story. It publishes mostly little-known or unknown writers, and its editors make an effort to send helpful responses to writers whose work they cannot use. A yearly fiction contest offers a first prize of $500 and a second prize of $250. Most of *Nimrod*'s fiction is chosen from the 1000 or more unsolicited stories submitted annually.

"We constantly insist," editor Francine Ringold says, "that literature is intricately tied to life. We are looking for 'style,' for writing that stands up and walks off the page, that has the earmark of vivid personality.

"We don't want a formula story, but we do insist that something grab our attention in the first paragraph, certainly by the end of the first page. Usually this amounts to style—language, color, surprise. We are not interested in an explosion on the first page or anywhere in the story for that matter, just a hand that reaches out from the page and grabs the readers and says—stay for a while, we have something to give you."

Ringold suggests that the best way to comprehend what *Nimrod* wants is to read a few issues. She cites several examples: "In our . . . Awards IV issue, I particularly admire "Ishmael Green Author," by Fredric Koeppel . . . its unusual combination of humor, literary sophistication, and mystery. The story keeps you reading without sacrificing character or style to plot.

"In Awards III, 1981, let me mention Ruth Jespersen's "Two Girls: A Chromatic Fantasy and Fugue," which makes use of a complex structure, in a subtle and unobtrusive fashion. At the same time, the story is inviting on a literal level; a distinctive voice announces its opening and remains tight and brisk though-out. It begins: 'One of the forms depression takes with me is shopping. I bought a silk shirt today, and a novel by a radical feminist, and a tape of Margo Mirowsky playing some Chopin nocturnes.' Any story with that opening lures me to read further. There is obviously a complex narrator who is experiencing emo-tions we all feel, but, at the same time, is aware of the ridiculous, and willing to laugh at herself.

"A quite different story in that issue is the first prize winner: 'The Salisbury Court Reporter,' by Jane Vandenburgh. It is tender, direct, yet has an edge of brilliance. A taut structure keeps genuine sentiment from slipping over into sentimentality. Once again, let me quote from the first lines of the story: 'Nine-teen years ago this month my father stepped forward, fell six stories and disappeared. After that my mother finished going crazy. She bought a new house with a bomb shelter. . . . ' "

Every story is checked in and a card of receipt sent to the author; if no word has come within two months, writers should get in touch. Each story is read by at least two people. Editors like to have three approvals before acceptance, but final judg-ment rests with the editor.

There is a standard rejection for what the editors call the "dead possums." At least 90 manuscripts a year receive a more encouraging letter of rejection with comments when appropriate and when editors have the time.

Revisions are asked for only when the work seems very prom-ising and the direction of the revision very clear.

Cover letters should be short and simple; editors try not to read lists of credits before making decisions. They will read more than one story submitted at a time, but would prefer a single piece with a note indicating there is more to be read.

Nimrod publishes special theme issues—announcements ap-pear in the writers' magazines. Some recent examples have been women in literature, Indians, Latin American voices, and Arabic literature.

The magazine runs an annual prize competition. Ringold suggests that it might be worthwhile to submit all stories to the prize competition; runners-up are often published and the writer will have a chance at the cash award. For prize rules, write to *Nimrod*.

THE NORTH AMERICAN REVIEW

University of Northern Iowa
Cedar Falls, IA 50614
(319) 273-2681, 266-8487

SOURCE: Robley Wilson, Jr., editor

ABOUT THE JOURNAL: Quarterly; no manuscripts accepted April through September. Address stories to Fiction Editor. Founded: 1815. Circulation: 4200. Distribution: subscription; newsstand; international. Avg. issue: 72 pp. Size: 8⅛x10⅞. Price: $2.50. Subscription: $9. Sample copy: $1.50. Back issues: available. Price: write for list. Affiliated with University of Northern Iowa.

FICTION: Occupies about 50% of total pages; 35 to 40 stories a year. Rates: $10 a published page and two copies. Payment: on publication. Rights: first North American serial and anthology rights. Reply time: one to three months. Publication time: 6 to 12 months. Length: no limits but longer pieces are sometimes harder to place.

Well-known and widely circulated, *The North American Review* chooses all stories from the over 5000 unsolicited manuscripts submitted every year.

Editor Robley Wilson, Jr., reads all submissions. He also has the final say on content. He estimates that maybe 4% of the stories are worth more than an initial reading. The only criterion is quality, and editors try to be catholic in their selections.

Over half the chosen stories are written by little-known or new writers. Wilson says, "I don't pay much attention to names when I read. When we won the National Magazine Award for Fiction in 1981, it was with three stories, two by unknowns (one of them publishing for the first time) and one by a well-known novelist/reporter" (Mar. '82; June '82; June '81; all included "first" published stories).

Wilson does not care for cover letters unless the author is being recommended. Even then, the letter is not necessary; the story has to stand on its own.

Wilson will read more than one story submitted at a time but expects the author to make the selection of work worth reading.

Standard rejection forms are used, and Wilson rarely writes

more than "sorry" on the form. A common reason for rejection is "amateurism." Wilson adds that competence not allied with imagination also leads to rejection.

His advice to writers: Read the magazine.

NORTHWEST REVIEW

369 P.L.C.
University of Oregon
Eugene, OR 97403
(503) 686-3957

SOURCE: Deb Casey, fiction editor

ABOUT THE JOURNAL: Triannual. Founded: 1957. Circulation: 1300. Avg. issue: 175 pp. Size: 6x9. Price: $3. Subscription: $8. Sample copy: $2.50. Back issues: available. Price: $3.

FICTION: Occupies 35% to 50% of total pages; 12-15 stories a year. Rates: three free copies, reduced price on further copies. Rights: first North American serial. Reply time: up to eight weeks; longer if story is being considered. Publication time: three to nine months. Length: no formal limits; stories over 25 pages can run into problems with space.

Northwest Review is committed to "quality prose in any form" as long as it has "energy and heart." Most of the up to 15 stories published annually are chosen from 1200 unsolicited submissions. "It is one of our intentions to publish unknown or little-known writers," fiction editor Deb Casey says, "and each issue includes several."

No type of fiction is automatically excluded. The intent is to achieve an eclectic mix. Recently published stories include: "Lovers of Today," by Maria Flook; "Grim Want and Misery," by Robert Taylor, Jr.; "Serious Fontaine," by Paulé Bartón; "Theft," by Joyce Carol Oates; "The Missionary Has Some Thoughts," by John O'Brien; "First Wife," by Andrea Carlisle; and "Mr. and Mrs. Hairful," by Kevin McIlvay.

"Whether we're looking at a sound and resonant piece like Oates' or a rhythmic and energized, jolting piece like Maria Flook's "Lovers of Today," we want to see some risks being taken, the unexpected met head-on. We admire ambition and need to feel an integrity within the piece."

At *Northwest Review* there are standard rejection forms, but correspondence is central to the editing process. If a story is good or a writer shows talent, a personal letter will be sent encouraging revision and resubmission, or asking to see other work. Accepted pieces are frequently the consequence of a correspondence spanning months or even years. The fiction staff is composed of the fiction editor and five assistant editors. Once a writer enters into correspondence with an editor, his or her work is always handled by that person.

One of the members of the fiction staff is the first reader. If he or she sees merit, is interested, or perhaps feels it would be more to another editor's taste, the story is passed on. Casey estimates that 30%-40% of the manuscripts are given more than one reading. An effort is made to make sure that every story is read by "the person likely to be its best defender."

Stories considered good by several editors, or stories of high interest to any single staff member, are read and commented on by the entire staff and discussed at a weekly meeting. Several readings and discussions usually precede acceptance; generally, majority opinion holds.

Reasons for rejection by the first reader include "unresolved or contrived plot; unearned developments; unmotivated characters; poor writing (bad sentences and paragraphs); stories that are flat, didactic, too told."

Further along in the consideration process, rejection follows "workshop prose, derivative writing; stories that are too slick, too easy, not new, or skillful but lacking heart—'so-what?' writing."

Editors like to receive a brief cover letter including basic biographical notes. Casey encourages the listing of credits, because they might gain a poor story a second reading and a fuller response. But, she adds, all stories, credits or not, are considered seriously.

Editors will read a group of stories; Casey recommends sending one or two. Three will be read but only if they are very short.

THE OHIO JOURNAL

Ohio State University
Department of English
164 West 17th Street
Columbus, OH 43201
(614) 422-2242

SOURCE: Martha S. Hendricks, managing editor

ABOUT THE JOURNAL: Biannual; no manuscripts accepted June through August; address stories to William Allen, editor. Founded: 1972. Circulation: 1000. Distribution: subscriptions; regional bookstores; newsstands. Avg. issue: 40 pp. Size: 8½x11. Price: $2. Sample copy: $2. Back issues: available. Price: $1.50. Affiliated with Ohio State University, College of Humanities and Ohio Arts Council.

FICTION: Occupies 45% of total pages; six to eight stories a year. Rates: three copies. Rights: first North American serial. Reply time: four weeks. Publication time: six months. Length: no limits.

About 50% of the stories in *The Ohio Journal* (subtitled "a journal of literature and visual arts") are by writers being published for the first time. Stories are chosen both from the 400 yearly unsolicited submissions and from work that comes in with recommendations.

There is an emphasis on Ohio authors, but policy is to publish the best work available.

"We tend to publish more traditional stories than anything else," managing editor Martha Hendricks says, "but that is because the writing quality is higher in those works than in any other type."

Published writers include Mary Robinson, Joyce Reisner Kornblatt, Robert Canzoneri, and Nolan Porterfield.

"Each of these writers has a highly developed, unique style which is consistent, yet at the same time is fluid enough to embrace a variety of subject matter," Hendricks says.

The managing editor, often aided by the staff, is the first reader. Editor William Allen makes the final decision. Hendricks says that 4% of the submissions are generally found worth more than a single reading.

Editors are not interested in cover letters. They will read a group of stories.

THE PARIS REVIEW

541 East 72nd Street
New York, NY 10021
(212) 539-7085

SOURCE: Mona Simpson, associate editor

ABOUT THE JOURNAL: Quarterly; address stories to Fiction Editor or George Plimpton. Founded: 1953. Circulation: 6500. Distribution: subscription; newsstands; bookstores. Avg. issue: 250 pp. Size: 8½x5¼. Price: $4. Subscription: $16. Sample copy: $4. Back issues: available. Price: varies.

FICTION: Four to six stories an issue. Rates: prefers not to specifiy, but described as higher than most literary magazines; pays according to length. Payment: on publication. Rights: first North American serial. Reply time: trying for six weeks; can go longer. Publication time: varies from next issue to over a year. Length: no formal limits but does not encourage novella length.

The Paris Review is a very well-known quarterly with a wide circulation. Most of its fiction comes from agents' submissions and regular writers who range from the very famous to the little-known. Editors do try to continually publish work from new writers.

Material is often taken from the slush pile—"first" published stories as well as work from lesser-known but published writers. Associate editor Mona Simpson points out that the slush pile runs to 20,000 submissions a year.

Besides fiction, *The Paris Review* publishes poetry, art, reminiscences, notebooks, memoirs, and correspondence. Probably its most famous feature is its series of interviews with writers on the craft of writing (these have been collected and published in paperback by Penguin Books). Among those interviewed have been E.M. Forster, François Mauriac, Thornton Wilder, William Faulkner, Frank O'Connor, Robert Frost, Ezra Pound, Boris Pasternak, T.S. Eliot, Ernest Hemingway, William Carlos Williams, Saul Bellow, Norman Mailer, Isak Dinesen, and Eudora Welty.

Simpson calls the review's fiction "eclectic." She says, "We are looking for the best-quality work we can find; simply the best four stories available in the period before publication."

Editors are active in keeping up with what other magazines are publishing. If they see a piece they admire, they will ask the author to submit work. In fact, they have compiled a long list of interesting writers who might be potential contributors.

Issue no. 86 (Winter '82) included an excerpt from a work in progress by Norman Mailer, stories from Michael Cunningham, Lamar Herrin, Craig Nova, and Barbara Milton (her first published story appeared in *Paris Review*), and a first published story from Jay McInerney. Issue no. 85 included fiction from Mary Alice Ayers, T. Coraghessan Boyle, R. Michael Benson, and Allan Gurganis. No. 83 (Spring '82) included fiction from Andrei Codrescu, Norman Kotker, and Robert Shacochis and a first published story by Susan Welch. No. 82 had fiction from Julio Cortázar, James Fetler, Jamaica Kincaid, Gordon Lish, Ray Russell, Joy Williams and a first published story by R. D. Pohl.

The assistant editors read all submitted stories. They use two standard rejection forms. The first is intended to discourage; the second is slightly encouraging. If the editors are very impressed with a piece but do not take it, they will write and say so, probably asking to see more work.

Stories of interest are given to the associate or managing editor to read. Final decisions are made after discussion between those two editors and fiction editor George Plimpton.

Simpson says that the editors like to see a list of credits with a story or to know if it would be the writer's first published piece.

PARTISAN REVIEW

128 Bay State Road
Boston, MA 02215
(617) 353-4260

SOURCE: William Phillips, editor

ABOUT THE JOURNAL: Quarterly. Founded: 1934. Circulation: 8000. Distribution: subscription; newsstands; bookstores. Avg. issue: 164 pp. Size: 4¼x7. Price: $3.50. Subscription price: $12.50. Back issues: available. Price: $3.50.

FICTION: One or two stories an issue. Rates: $100–$300. Payment: on publication. Rights: first North American serial. Reply time: two months. Length: any reasonable length.

Partisan Review is among the best-known and most widely circulated quarterlies. Fiction is both solicited and chosen from the approximately 1500 unsolicited stories submitted annually, of which something like 50 a year are found worth a second reading.

Editor William Phillips says simply that he wants quality not banality and that he is pleased to find new writers.

Authors published include Stephen O'Connor, Michael Malone, John Shea, Carolyn Kraus, Beatrice Tauss, Italo Calvino, Jerry Bumpus, Joyce Carol Oates, and Arno Schmidt.

Phillips does not encourage submissions from people who have not read the magazine, a situation that he finds unacceptable. He believes that writers working on the level that *Partisan Review* publishes read extensively and know which magazines, journals, or reviews would be the proper place for their work.

Submissions are screened by first readers. The possibilities are passed to editors. If a story is seriously considered it might be rejected with a personal letter asking to see more work, though not with specific criticisms.

PLOUGHSHARES

Box 529
Cambridge, MA 02139
(617) 926-9875

SOURCE: DeWitt Henry, editor

ABOUT THE JOURNAL: Quarterly. Editor: Peter O'Malley—policy of revolving editorship. Founded: 1971. Circulation: 3400. Distribution: subscriptions; newsstands; bookstores. Avg. issue: 200-300 pp. Size: 8½x5½. Price: $4.95 (more for double issues). Subscription: $14. Back issues: available.

FICTION: Roughly 20 stories a year, but does not use fiction in every issue; check editorial schedule. Rates: $5 per page up to $50 maximum for story (hoping to go to $100 in future). Payment: on publication: Rights: copyright reverts on request. Reply time: three months minimum; faster for rejection. Publication time: depends on issue deadlines. Length: wants short-story length.

   Ploughshares is among the best-known, most widely respected literary journals. Though it publishes essays, interviews, etc., its major commitments are to fiction (about 20 or more stories a year) and poetry. *Ploughshares* considers discovering new writers and publishing little-known writers an important part of its job. Everything submitted is read carefully and with hope. Because of its policy of revolving editorship, there is allowance for a wide range of styles, tastes, and approaches.

   At the same time, *Ploughshares'* prestige and level of submissions effectively bar it to all but the most talented writers.

   Close to 2000 short stories are submitted for each issue using fiction. First readers, who are non-staff volunteers, cut the number to 500. (Anything from a known writer or one with a list of good credits automatically makes the first cut.) Editor DeWitt Henry further reduces the number of manuscripts to about 50. Finally, the guest editor will choose maybe ten manuscripts for publication. The rest of the fiction will be solicited.

   Out of 2000 stories, 300 to 400 are usually very good, Henry says. The rest range from showing some talent to no talent at all. "In the end," he continues, "an issue can hope for three or four stories that are superb; the rest will be the best of what was offered.

   "We try, without forcing it, to have one-third of the magazine discoveries; one-third, the editor's peers; one-third, the editor's heroes. This reflects the values of the magazine. Its object is to discover, to show the work of writers in mid-career, and to print what everyone is reaching toward.

"About 50% to 75% of the unsolicited manuscripts are from people who have read a writers' guide but have not read *Ploughshares*. These pieces are not only not good, they are also innappropriate. This self-delusion is costing writers money and is an empty exercise.

"*Ploughshares* is meant to be a continuing forum about good writing. The object is to create a literary community at a time of diverse directions. Literature is a form of argument. It ought to be talked about as a community, without pot-shotting. *Ploughshares* also wants to deconventionalize its readers. To expose people to a range of possibilities they might not normally see."

Issues are structured with a sense of counterpoint and balance. If one issue is on formal poetry, the next could be a woman-writers issue.

Because there are theme issues, research has to precede submission. In every masthead, *Ploughshares* lists editorial plans for four issues ahead—for instance, an all-poetry issue and the name of an editor, to be followed by a Southern-writing issue and the name of an editor. There might be no point in submitting a story at all for the next several months. (Manuscripts are returned unread if it is too long before the next fiction issue.)

Generally, the goal is to do one fiction, one poetry, and one double-mixed issue every year.

Revolving, or guest, editorships, are a way to explore differences in taste while maintaining consistency of standards.

Guest editors for fiction have included James Randall, Tim O'Brien, Rosellen Brown, Dan Wakefield, Jayne Ann Phillips, Jay Neugeboren, Henry Bromell, Donald Hall, Raymond Carver, and DeWitt Henry.

The actual choosing of stories is based on a complex editorial process. An issue could include many different types of fiction chosen only by merit. Or it could have a clear-cut theme with stories chosen to fit. More often, the theme is not clear-cut; it is, instead, a matter of tone and style. "Issues create their own limits," Henry says. "Unless variety is the point, you want some kind of coherence. This organic sense of coherence controls the editing process."

After all the considering and weeding out, an editor will still have too many stories for the pages allotted. "Distinctions of merit at this level are so slight," Henry continues, "that other reasons to choose and reject become important." This is when the collage quality of an issue comes to the fore. It is no longer only what is good, but also what stories work with other stories.

There is no kind of fiction that is automatically excluded. It is true, however, that *Ploughshares* has an interest in realistic or moral fiction (as in John Gardner's definition). At the time *Ploughshares* was founded, many of the literary magazines were focusing on experimental prose. Some of the major critics were equating straightforward fiction with creative bankruptcy. *Ploughshares* was intended to redress that imbalance.

Writers published include Andre Dubus, Richard Yates, James Alan McPherson, Rosellen Brown, Seymour Epstein, Alice Munro, John Williams, Raymond Carver, Tim O'Brien, Jay Neugeboren, Ronald Sukenick, Maxine Kumin, and John Hawkes.

Rejection is most often by standard form. First readers are free to write back to a rejected writer. Henry often writes to say he liked and admired a story and to suggest another market.

PRAIRIE SCHOONER

201 Andrews Hall
University of Nebraska
Lincoln, NE 68588
(402) 472-1800

SOURCE: Hilda Raz, associate editor

ABOUT THE PUBLICATION: Quarterly; address manuscripts to the editor. Founded: 1926. Circulation: 2000. Distribution: subscription, newsstands. Avg. issue: 96 pp. Size: 6x9. Price: $3.25. Subscription: $11. Sample copy: $1. Back issues: available. Price: $2.50. Affiliated with Department of English, University of Nebraska and the University of Nebraska Press.

FICTION: Occupies 35% to 50% of total pages; 12 stories a year. Rates: copies and prizes. Payment: on publication. Rights: ask for copyright. Reply time: two to three months. Publication time: a year or less. Length: no limits.

Prairie Schooner is a well-known literary magazine, particularly noted for its fiction. It also publishes poetry and reviews with occasional interviews and essays. Most of its fiction is chosen from the 2500 unsolicited manuscripts submitted annually.

Prairie Schooner regularly publishes very well-known authors and lesser-known writers, most of whose work has appeared in small-press magazines.

The Spring 1982 issue was a "Focus on Translations: A Gathering of Work in Translation, Writings from Italy, Finland, Germany, Spain, Greece, Japan and Portugal."

Writers who have appeared in *Prairie Schooner* include Joyce Carol Oates, Tom Disch, David Milofsky, Susan Fromberg Schaeffer, Catherine Petroski, and Ellen Gilchrist.

Stories may be read by the editorial assistants, the associate editors, the editor, or volunteers—members of the Department of English, University of Nebraska–Lincoln. According to associate editor Hilda Raz, 5% of the submitted manuscripts are found worth more than one reading. Final decisions on publication are made by the editor, who consults with the associate editors. Editors "rarely, if ever, ask for revision or provide criticism. Our staff is small, the volume of submissions great."

The magazine has two standard rejection forms. One encourages a writer to continue to submit his work; the other only says "Thanks, but no."

Cover letters listing credits make no difference in the handling of a story. Editors will not read more than two or three stories at a time.

PRIMAVERA

University of Chicago
1212 East 59th Street
Chicago, IL 60637

SOURCE: Karen Peterson, editorial staff

ABOUT THE JOURNAL: Irregular; approximately every 1½ years. Address stories to the Editorial Board. Founded: 1975. Circulation: 1000. Distribution: mostly subscription; regional bookstores. Avg. issue: 100 pp. Size: 8½x11. Price: $5. Sample copy: $3.90. Back issues: available. Price: $3.90. Loose affiliation with University of Chicago.

FICTION: Occupies about 40% of total pages; five to eight stories an issue. Rate: two copies. Rights: first publication. Reply time: one week to six months. Publication time: up to two years. Length: no more than 40 pages; prefers less.

Primavera is interested in publishing work that reflects a variety of women's experiences. Its staff members are women with a feminist orientation, but the magazine's main concerns are literary, not political.

Primavera is published irregularly (averages out to once every year and a half) and regularly devotes 40% of its pages to fiction. Editors are particularly looking for the chance to publish unknown writers and take pains to provide feedback to authors.

All of the fiction is chosen from the approximately 250 unsolicited manuscripts submitted every year. Editor Karen Peterson estimates that "maybe a third" of those are good enough to be read more than once.

"Originality and reflection of women's experiences are the most important criteria. Right now there is an editorial preference for the traditional short-story form, though occasionally experimental prose appeals to us. We haven't found any acceptable genre fiction yet, but we're willing to consider it."

An author Peterson names as exemplifying what *Primavera* wants is Marian K. Blanton: "Original and vivid treatments of important subjects: breast cancer, relationships, awareness of self."

Cover letters on submitted stories are sometimes found interesting, but never necessary. Once a story comes in, anyone on staff might be the first reader. Ideally, more than one reader will look at a story before it is rejected, but if there is a backlog, and the story is clearly inappropriate, the first reader will reject. A decided majority of the staff must approve an acceptance; the number of staff members fluctuates considerably from year to year.

Peterson offered the following list of common reasons for rejection: "Ungrammatical, trite, sentimental, preachy, 'cutesy' stories; unconvincing characterization, incredible dialogue, trick endings, poorly structured, self-obsessive pieces that are often just uninteresting." *Primavera* does have a standard rejection form, though editors try to include comments if they feel they might be helpful and particularly if the author asks for them.

Most accepted stories go through revision, some of them several times. Peterson says, "These writers generally express appreciation for the editorial dialogue."

Editors will read more than one story submitted at a time, but sometimes do it resentfully.

PULP

720 Greenwich Street
New York, NY 10014
(212) 989-0190

SOURCE: Dr. Howard Sage, editor/publisher

ABOUT THE JOURNAL: Biannual (January, August). Founded: 1974. Circulation: 2000. Distribution: subscription; bookstores. Avg. issue: 12-16 pp. Size: tabloid. Price: 50¢. Subscription: $2. Sample copy: $1. Back issues: available. Price: $1.

FICTION: Occupies 40% of total pages; two to four stories a year. Rates: copies. Rights: first North American serial. Reply time: month (but may be longer). Publication time: no more than five months. Length: no limits.

Pulp is a newsprint tabloid that publishes fiction (uses a lot of short prose pieces), poetry, art, and interviews, and other nonfiction forms. Original translations of poetry are particularly important.

Editor Howard Sage says he is open to "all good writing with perhaps a slight bias toward the experimental."

Vol. 8, no. 1 (1982) included a novel excerpt by Rona Spalten and a short story by Juan Ritty, and also a conversation with Marge Piercy. Vo. 7, no. 2 (1981) included three short prose pieces by Kathleen Spivack.

Most of *Pulp*'s fiction is chosen from the 100-150 unsolicited manuscripts submitted annually. Sage reads all manuscripts, finding 10% of them worth a second look. He uses a standard rejection form, but will write to suggest and encourage if a story shows promise (and, he adds, if he has time). He does not ask for major revisions ("Most revisions are worse than the original") and asks for minor changes only if he intends to accept the story.

A common problem with many of the submissions is lack of craft: "People writing not fiction, but thinly concealed autobiography."

He does not want to see cover letters; only the work is important. He will read more than one story at a time.

QUARTERLY WEST

317 Olpin Union
University of Utah
Salt Lake City, UT 84112
(801) 581-3938

SOURCE: Robert Shapard, coeditor

ABOUT THE JOURNAL: Biannual; hoping for triannual starting in 1984-85. Address manuscripts to Robert Shapard or Pete Hager, fiction editor. Founded: 1975. Circulation: 1000. Distribution: subscriptions; bookstores; newsstands. Avg. issue: 140 pp. Size: 6x9. Price: $3.50. Subscription: $6.50. Sample copy: $3.50. Back issues: available. Price $2, except for some rare early issues. Published out of University of Utah; staffed primarily by people in the university's creative writing Ph.D. program.

FICTION: Occupies two-fifths to one-half of total pages; 8 to 12 stories a year. Rates: $40 to $75, plus copies. Payment: on publication. Rights: first North American serial. Reply time: two to eight weeks depending on interest; slower in summer. Publication time: usually accepts only work needed for next issue. Length: no formal limits, but tends to favor medium-to-shorter-length stories because of space limitations; does publish novel excerpts.

Unsolicited submissions at *Quarterly West* have reached nearly 1000 a year. "Generally the quality of submissions is high," coeditor Robert Shapard says, "more uniformly so than some longer established magazines I know or have worked with. Maybe half are worth a second look."

Occasionally stories are solicited, but most are chosen from the unsolicited submissions. Contributors are usually writers little known by the general public (though Shapard adds that a few are beginning to reach a wider audience).

Shapard describes *Quarterly West* as "generally in the literary mainstream," though "on the lookout for the new, the experimental." Shapard likes to see "attention to language, a sharp style that makes us sit up and read. Or a compelling voice. Unusual or freshly treated situations. (Not necessarily an overtly sophisticated style, of course.) We tend to want stories that are affecting, meaningful, insightful—a tall order since these things are impossible to define—in a traditional story form. We are open to experimental prose, or fiction which directly or indirectly comments on itself or language. In principle, anyway, we're open to anything, though we especially shy away from genre stuff, erotica, etc., unless it's really something unusual, and of literary quality."

Writers published in *Quarterly West* include Eve Shelnutt ("Nobody like her. Difficult, but worth it. Unusual point of view, technique, mastery of language"), Gordon Weaver ("Humor, poignancy, usually —not always—traditional stuff, but a master at it. Characters always interesting"), Robert Taylor, Jr. ("Stories traditional enough, but distinctive style. Usually historical or period pieces"), Fred Chappell ("Does all kinds of stories—sci-fi, historical—one we published was traditional mainstream. A fine poet, Chappell's prose has an elegant simplicity that's a joy for a fiction writer to read").

Others published have included Raymond Carver, T.R. Hummer, Stephen Dixon, and Lynne Barrett.

Editors prefer not to see more than two stories at a time unless they are short-shorts. Shapard says that editors pay differing amount of attention to cover letters; in any case, letters should be brief. The highlights of a writing career are preferred over a list of every credit. All stories are read seriously. Editors like to discover new writers, and are pleased when they are the first to publish someone with talent. There is no strict hierarchy of readers. Everyone on the staff reads manuscripts. A definite no from the first reader generally leads to rejection, but close to half the stories submitted are given a second reading, while one-fourth of all submitted stories are put into a "hold pile" and considered for possible acceptance as need arises.

Rewrites on spec are sometimes requested. Stories are usually rejected with a standard form, but Shapard says he and other staff members often add comments: "We do write criticism—constructive, we hope—fairly often and enjoy doing so, though we're getting less and less time for it and our remarks are getting briefer. We think writers, especially unestablished ones, don't get enough feedback, and we like to encourage them—though it is discouraging to have to keep rejecting them because of the amount of material we get."

Most rejections are due to poor writing: clichés, verbosity, uninteresting dialogue, and so on. Too-familiar situations also put the editors off (the story that starts with the morning alarm clock, for example). Shapard says, "Structurally, traditional mainstream stories most often fall short in depth of or deftness of characterization. The writer apparently feels more—pro or con—for the character than the reader does. It's not coming across on the page. And generally, if you think of sentimentality very broadly as emotion elicited from the reader that's n t grounded in the story—even, say, cynical sophistication—then we get a fair amount of sentimental fiction."

Quarterly West occasionally does a "special issue," and occasionally there are contests, with cash prizes. The last was a nationwide novella competition supported by a grant from the NEA.

Shapard adds a final note to say that editors, everywhere, do make mistakes and reject stories that should have been published. "If the story's good," he says, "it'll get taken sooner or later—as established writers well know."

SALMAGUNDI

Skidmore College
Saratoga Springs, NY 12866
(518) 584-5000

SOURCE: Peggy Boyers, executive editor

ABOUT THE JOURNAL: Quarterly; address manuscripts to Robert Boyers, editor-in-chief, or Peggy Boyers. Founded: 1975. Circulation: 5000-8000. Distribution: subscriptions; newsstands; bookstores. Avg. issue: 178 pp. Size: 4½x7½. Price: $4. Subscription: $9. Sample copy: $4. Back issues: available. Price: varies. Affiliated with Skidmore College.

FICTION: About four stories a year; some issues have no fiction. Rates: five copies. Rights: one-time use. Reply time: as long as six months. Publication time: can be as long as two years. Length: no limits.

Salmagundi is "a quarterly of the humanities and social sciences." It publishes an average of four stories a year. Executive editor Peggy Boyers says about half the published fiction consists of translations. The rest of the stories are chosen from the approximately 300 unsolicited stories sent in every year.

Salmagundi often considers large social questions and issues. The Fall/Winter 1982 issue was titled "Homosexuality: Sacrilege, Vision, Politics." Edited by Robert Boyers and George Steiner, it included essays, memoirs, letters, and an interview. The 15th-anniversay issue (Fall '80 Winter '81) was titled "Art and Intellect in America," with contributions from Susan Sontag, George Steiner, John Lukacs, Martin Pops, and Leslie Fiedler. It included two stories from Jorge Luis Borges.

The Spring 1982 issue included fiction by Peter Schneeman and Layle Silbert. Other writers published have included William H. Gass, Cynthia Ozick, and Varlam Shalamov.

Robert and Peggy Boyers read all manuscripts. Stories are then also read by a number of other staff members including Barry Targan. In general, form rejection letters are used. Comments or explanations are sent only when editors come close to accepting a story.

Cover letters are not necessary. Editors prefer one story at a time.

THE SEWANEE REVIEW

University of the South
Sewanee, TN 37375
(615) 598-5931, ext. 245/246

SOURCE: George Core, editor
        Mary Lucia Cornelius, managing editor

ABOUT THE JOURNAL: Quarterly; address manuscripts to George Core. Founded: 1892. Circulation: 3200. Distribution: subscription; newsstands; bookstores. Avg. issue: 192 pp. Size 6x9. Price: $4. Subscription: $12. Sample copy: $4.75. Back issues: available. Price: $5.75. Published and subsidized by the University of the South.

FICTION: Occupies 15% of total pages; four to eight stories per year. Rates: money and two copies. Payment: on publication. Rights: first serial; handles reprint permissions. Reply time: two weeks to two months. Publication time: 3 to 18 months. Length: 7500 words is the usual limit; though longer stories have been published, the occurence is rare.

The Sewanee Review is a very well-known and widely circulated journal. The magazine is primarily literary and critical; fiction accounts for a relatively low percentage of editorial space. Some stories are chosen from the unsolicited submissions (1080 in 1982), but many of them are from literary agents or past contributors. Editors estimate that .5% of the submissions are accepted; about 4% are "arresting enough to warrant further consideration."

The editors add that they "have always decided about work on the basis of merit—not who wrote it. In the past ten years we have published at least three first stories. Even regular contributors of fiction have much more material rejected by us than accepted."

Exemplary published writers include "William Hoffman, Stephen Minot, Andre Dubus, Susan Engberg, Gloria Norris, and Eugene K. Garber."

"The work by these writers is admirable because it demonstrates a joining of high literary intelligence, imagination, and substance with a style that is appropriate for the mode and occasion," Core says.

Submitted stories "must be fiction, not reminiscences or autobiography; they should not involve popular forms such as science fiction; they should not deal with trivial or light subjects.

"The most important movement in the story is the opening; the conclusion is nearly as important. The story must have a beginning, middle, and end; it must have a narrative dimension and contain a plot; the economy should be severe and the exposition held to a minimum. Usually the point of view should not shift.

"If the writer who is interested in submitting something to the *Sewanee Review* will read three or four stories published here since 1973, he or she will immediately infer what kind of fiction the editor seeks."

The editors add: "We don't want prose-poetry or experimental prose in the usual sense. In general, the stories published here would be considered traditional in form, but a fair number of them would not be.

"The two dullest subjects in fiction just now involve the life of the writer, especially the writer in the academy, and the last days of a sick and dying old person who is a terminal case in every sense.

"We are looking for fiction that tells a story and has a plot (a complication, a rising action, denouement); if this is what you mean by traditional fiction, I plead guilty to looking for it. In general our fiction tends to be realistic, but on one occasion we published a ghost story and other stories have contained elements of fantasy and the fantastic, of allegory, and of naturalism."

A single editor is generally the only reader, though he sometimes asks the opinions of one or two additional readers. Acceptance or rejection is entirely the editor's decision. There is a standard rejection form, but comments on stories are frequently returned regardless of whether the editor wants to see more work from the writer. Core asks about a dozen authors each year to revise and resubmit a story.

As far as rejection is concerned, the editors say, "Many authors spend more time writing than reading, a bad habit that results in their sending work to the wrong forums. They should acquaint themselves with a magazine before sending submissions. (For instance, we don't publish translations, but we get dozens a year.) Besides unsuitability, most rejected material has one thing in common: It is badly written, ranging from mediocre to wretched in style. Often the stories are wildly improbable, with no hint of plot. However, many rejections are caused by the simple lack of space."

Editors like to see a succinct cover letter with the author's qualifications, especially major publications. They don't want form letters with lengthy lists of publications or letters with long explanations or defenses of the work. Editors will read only one story at a time and want at least a month between submissions.

SHENANDOAH

P.O. Box 722
Lexington, VA 24450
(703) 463-9111 ext. 283

SOURCE: James Boatwright, editior

ABOUT THE JOURNAL: Quarterly. Founded: 1950. Circulation: 1000. Distribution: subscriptions; bookstores; international. Avg. issue: 100 pp. Size: 6x9. Price: $2.50. Subscription: $8. Sample copy: $2.50. Back issues: available. Price: $4. Subsidized by Washington and Lee University.

FICTION: Occupies 45% of total pages: about 16 stories a year. Rates: money and copies. Payment: on publication. Rights: first North American serial. Reply time: two months. Length: no limits.

Shenandoah is a well-known literary magazine with a particularly fine reputation for fiction and for publishing more fiction and poetry than criticism, interviews, or essays.

Most of the fiction is chosen from the approximately 300 unsolicited stories submitted every year. Editor James Boatwright reads all of them and says that 10% are interesting enough to be read more than once. He adds that *Shenandoah* is more committed to traditional short-story forms than to the experimental. He suggests that a writer study the magazine carefully and see if the stories in it are the kinds that he admires and emulates. Stories are most often rejected simply because they are not of professional caliber.

Writers recently published include Jane Barnes, Jerry Bumpus, Carolyn Chute, James McCourt, Michael Martone, Heather Ross Miller, Leslie Norris, Jean Ross, Alma Stone, Jonathan Strong, Diane Vreuls, David Wagoner, and Patricia Zelver.

Shenandoah does use a standard rejection form. An editor will offer criticism or ask for minor revisions only if it is likely the story will be published.

THE SOUTHERN REVIEW

43 Allen Hall
Louisiana State University
Baton Rouge, LA 70803
(504) 388-5108

SOURCE: Lewis P. Simpson, editor

ABOUT THE JOURNAL: Quarterly; address manuscripts to "The Editor." Founded: new series since 1965; original series published from 1935 to 1942. Circulation: 2900. Distribution: subscription; bookstores. Avg. issue: 240 pp. Size: 6x10. Price: $2.50. Subscription: $9. Sample copy: $2.50. Back issues: available. Price: $2.50. Affiliated with Louisiana State University.

FICTION: Occupies about 25% of total pages; approximately 12 stories a year. Rates: honorarioum plus two copies. Payment: on publication. Rights: first American serial. Reply time: approximately two months. Publication: approximately one to two years. Length: prefers stories under 6000 words.

The Southern Review is among the best-known and most highly regarded literary journals. It publishes fiction, poetry, critical essays, and book reviews and places "some emphasis on the Southern scene."

Stories are generally chosen from the 3000-4000 annually submitted unsolicited manuscripts, of which 10% are generally found worth more than one reading.

Editors prefer traditional modes; genre fiction may be acceptable but is not emphasized.

Published writers include Joyce Carol Oates, Rosanne Coggeshall, Kent Nelson, Louis D. Rubin, Jr., Anne Tyler, David Madden, Leigh Allison, and Robb Forman Dew.

Submitted stories are read by the editors. A standard rejection form is used in most cases. Occasionally an author may be given some criticism, but revisions are asked for only when a manuscript has been accepted.

Editors sometimes find a brief statement of previous publications helpful. They will read a group of stories submitted together, but would prefer not to.

STORIES

14 Beacon Street
Boston, MA 02108

SOURCE: Amy R. Kaufman, editor

ABOUT THE JOURNAL: Bimonthly. Founded: 1982. Circulation: no
figures available yet. Distribution: subscription; newsstands;
bookstores. Avg. issue: 70 pp. Size: 7x10. Price: $4. Subscrip-
tion: $20. Sample copy: $4. Back issues: available. Price: $4.

FICTION: Publishes fiction only; approximately 24 stories a year.
Rates: $150 minimum; often goes considerably higher depend-
ing on length and other factors. Payment: $100 on acceptance;
balance on publication. Rights: first North American serial.
Reply time: eight to ten weeks. Publication time: two weeks.
Simultaneous submissions: will read but must be informed that
story has been sent elsewhere. Length: 14,000 words maximum.
  Stories is a bimonthly short-story magazine designed to encourage the writing of a particular kind of story—described most
accurately by the term "affective fiction"—for which the editors
believe there is a demand.
  "Simplicity is achieved after a struggle and universality is possible only to a degree," acknowledges editor Amy Kaufman, "but
we feel that these are the qualities most likely to evoke a reader's
sympathy and concern. Timelessness is another ideal we pursue
by avoiding language and subjects that are fashionable."
  At present, *Stories* (a relatively new publication) is receiving
around 3500 unsolicited manuscripts annually. Occasionally a
piece is solicited, but the magazine does not plan to go after
work by well-known writers or to cultivate a group of regular
contributors. It is hoped that the unsolicited submissions will be
the major source of material.
  Kaufman is first reader and chooses what will be published.
Two consulting editors might be applied to for opinions.
  Kaufman has found herself working closely with authors both
on spec and with a commitment to buy. "We get a lot of material," she says, "in which the potential might be there, but the
story has not been worked on enough."
  Rejection is always by personal letter, though the pressure of
time and the number of submissions are making the letters in-

creasingly brief. The extent of criticism in a letter also depends on whether the author has asked for comments.

"It may be helpful for the writer to consider," Kaufman says, "that transparent literary devices and overworked topics are easily recognized by literary magazine editors, who rarely find imaginative and sophisticated work. I would rather see the influence of a great writer on an aspiring writer than the attempts of an aspiring writer to reinvent the wheel."

Genre fiction—science fiction, fantasy, adventure, romance, sports stories—is usually rejected.

All Kaufman wants to see in a cover letter is name, address, telephone, and date. Groups of stories will be read.

STORYQUARTERLY

P. O. Box 1416
Northbrook, IL 60062
(312) 272-9418

SOURCE: Janine Warsaw, coeditor

ABOUT THE JOURNAL: Irregular; no manuscripts accepted December, July, and August. Address stories to *StoryQuarterly*. Founded: 1974. Circulation: 1000. Distribution: subscription; newsstands; bookstores. Avg. issue: 100 pp. Size: 5½x8½. Price: $3. Subscription: $10 for 4 issues. Sample copy: $3. Back issues: some available. Price : $3.

FICTION: Occupies 90% of pages: about ten stories an issue. Rates: copies or small gratuity. Payment: on acceptance. Rights: copyright reverts. Reply time: one to six months. Publication time: three to six months. Length: no limits.

StoryQuarterly is a "magazine of the short story," publishing approximately ten stories a year. Most of the fiction is chosen from unsolicited submissions. However, *StoryQuarterly* is one of the better-known literary magazines and the unsolicited submissions run close to 2000 annually, many from well-known writers.

Little-known or new writers are often published, but coeditor Janine Warsaw adds that only about 2% of the slush pile is normally found to be worth more than an initial reading.

StoryQuarterly is open to all forms of fiction if "they are well written and contain the elements of a short story," Warsaw says.

Writers who have published in *StoryQuarterly* include Grace Paley, Steve Dixon, Frederick Busch, Robley Wilson, Jr., Jack Matthews, Ann Beattie, John Bennett, Norbert Blei, Maria Thomas, and Henry Roth.

"Their stories are unique and show three-dimensional characters who try to cope with life. They bring something different and important to the reader to think about and though they do not always solve their problems, we are left with an understanding of why . . . or why not."

Manuscripts submitted by writers published in the magazine before, or by very well-known writers, go directly to the editors. Everything else is read by a staff of first readers who pass on the promising pieces. Each of these must be read by three editors, who discuss and eventually vote on the stories being considered for publication. A majority vote determines acceptance or rejection.

Cover letters are not considered necessary. Editors prefer not to receive more than one story at a time from a writer and will not *read* a story that comes without SASE.

A poor story is rejected with a standard form. A better story is returned with a note of encouragement asking the writer to submit again. An established or previously published writer will receive a more personal letter. Editors do not give in-depth critiques on stories. At the most a suggestion may be made.

Some of the common reasons for rejection were listed as "a poorly written piece, a story that is not unique or important, nor literary; too, too long, too trendy; too self-indulgent, too wordy."

THE TEXAS REVIEW

Office of the Division
English, Foreign Language and Journalism
Sam Houston State University
Huntsville, TX 77341
(713) 294-1435, 295-1402

SOURCE: Phillip Parotti, fiction editor

ABOUT THE JOURNAL: Biannual. Founded: 1976. Circulation: 750-1000. Distribution: subscription. Avg. issue: 120-160 pp. Size: 6x9. Price: $2. Sample copy: $2. Back issues: available. Price: $1.50. Affiliated with the English Program, Sam Houston State University.

FICTION: Occupies 30% to 40% of total pages; four to eight stories a year. Rates: two copies and a year's subscription. Rights: first publication. Reply time: two to three months. Publication time: six months to a year. Length: no limit; but most accepted manuscripts are between 10 and 20 typed pages (2000-5000 words).

The Texas Review publishes fiction, poetry, photography, interviews, reviews, and essays on literary and cultural subjects. Almost all the stories are chosen from the approximately 400 unsolicited manuscripts submitted annually. Fiction editor Phillip Parotti estimates that 5% of those—20 manuscripts—are good enough for more than one reading and are the source for the up to eight stories published each year.

"We do not want to bore our readers," Parotti says. "Judging from the manuscripts I read for the magazine the Horatian dichotomy has fallen out of balance among aspiring writers; that is, they too often seek to *instruct* without remembering to *delight* while they are doing it.

"We are, in fact, very interested in the traditional story form and in serious fiction, but I define a serious writer as one who takes a professional attitude toward his work; a writer may take as professional an attitude toward comedy as anything else, and from time to time, I am tempted to wonder whether or not all of the comic writers have disappeared into the film industry. We also read and publish experimental prose."

Writers who have appeared in the review include R.E. Smith, George Garrett, Steve Heller, Margaret Kingery, Don Meredith,

Richard Costa, Larry Sams, Walter McDonald, Bill Toole, and Dorothy Stanfill.

All submitted manuscripts are read by the fiction editor, who has final say. In most cases, rejected stories are returned with a printed form. If Parotti likes an author's work he might ask to see more. "I avoid criticism of individual stories for two reasons: (1) we hope to receive finished, polished stories from authors (mechanics and style are the writer's problems, not ours; if we don't like the punctuation or style, we reject rather than rewrite); (2) time is short; the editors of *The Texas Review* are all college teachers carrying twelve-hour teaching loads; editing is a collateral, not a primary duty."

Among reasons for rejection are graphic sex and foul language. All pulp Westerns, romances, and true confessions are also rejected. (Historical fiction has been published; science fiction will be read.) Another problem is professional writing from authors who cannot plot; editors "want something to happen in the material we publish." On the other hand, storytelling without quality writing is no more acceptable.

Editors do not want to see more than one story at a time. Lengthy cover letters including press clippings and pages of bibliography are useless; stories are chosen on merit. A short letter giving just enough biographical information to cover a possible contributor's note to be published if the story is taken is all that is necessary. Correct postage on a writer's return envelope is a must; " the review will not contribute a penny."

13TH MOON

Drawer F
Inwood Station
New York, NY 10034
(212) 678-1074

SOURCE: Marilyn Hacker, editor

ABOUT THE JOURNAL: Biannual; no manuscripts accepted in June, July, or August. Founded: 1973. Circulation: 3000. Distribution: subscription; newsstands; bookstores. Avg. issue: 120 pp.; double issues 200 pp. Size: 6x9½. Price: $3; $5.95 for double issues. Subscription: $11.90. Back issues: available. Price: $3 and $5.95.

FICTION: Occupies 30% of total pages; about six stories a year. Rates: copies. Rights: first North American serial. Publication time: six months. Length: 5-15 pages best; some flexibility.

13th Moon is a feminist literary magazine that publishes only work by women writers. It was founded to provide a "forum for the diversity of literature being produced by women." Its definition of feminism is inclusive: editors are interested in work from feminist, lesbian, Third World, and working-class perspective, but also in any literature that explores a woman's sensibility and point of view.

Stories are both solicited and unsolicited; editor Marilyn Hacker reports that hundreds of unsolicited submissions are received every year and that maybe one-quarter of them are worth more than a first reading. A proper feminist perspective at the expense of literary quality is not acceptable.

"Good writing, whether experimental or otherwise," Hacker says, "is the only thing to which we're committed. I'd say 'no' to genre fiction—except that some of our finest practitioners of the short story write speculative fiction/science fiction and I'd be delighted to see work of that quality."

All submissions are read by the editor. Usually, two or three other staff members will read a story before acceptance, but the final decision is hers. There is a standard rejection form. Editors will write to an author with suggestions or requests for revisions if a story is of real interest or will encourage further submissions from promising writers.

Hacker has no interest in a cover letter and prefers not to receive more than one story at a time.

Common reasons for rejection include "appalling prose; clichés; dependence on knee-jerk-feminist reader reactions; tedium and thrice-told tales; predictability."

Hacker says: "We welcome work from well-known and unknown women writers. We are especially interested in encouraging submissions of work by women of color, working-class women, and lesbians. We're also interested in encouraging submissions by women whose work has appeared in other kinds of literary journals, who haven't yet considered submitting to a feminist periodical."

Besides fiction, *13th Moon* publishes poetry, translations, art, reviews and articles. Articles have included "Natalie Barney's Parisian Salon: The Savoir Faire and Joie de Vivre of a Life of Love and Letters" by Gloria Orenstein; an article on Virginia Woolf's process as a lesbian-feminist writer, by Pamella Farley; a history of women's literary magazines and an issue on the working-class experience.

Contributors to the magazine include Joanna Russ, Bertha Harris, Shirley Anne Williams, Toni Cade Bambara, Paula Marshall, Carol Emshwiller, Alice Sheldon (a.k.a. James Tiptree, Jr.), Alice Walker, Ntozake Shange, Gloria Anzaldua, Hilary Bailey, Elizabeth Hardwick, and Djuna Barnes.

In the masthead, the magazine's title is explained: "The title derives from the lunar calendar, which has thirteen months. It commemorates the time when the moon, as mediator of our bodies' rhythms, was the symbol of spiritual transformation. It celebrates the opening of an age when we are in full control of our energies."

THE THREEPENNY REVIEW

P. O. Box 9131
Berkeley, CA 94709
(415) 849-4545

SOURCE: Wendy Lesser, editor and publisher

ABOUT THE JOURNAL: Quarterly. Founded: 1980. Circulation: 10,000 (3000 paid; 7000 controlled). Distribution: subscriptions; and bookstores. Avg. issue: 28 pp. Size: tabloid. Price: $2. Subscription: $6. Sample copy: $3. Back issues: available. Price $3-$8.

FICTION: Occupies 10% of total pages; four to eight stories a year. Rates: copies and five gift subscriptions. Rights: first serial, reverting to author; review must be acknowledged in reprints. Reply time: two weeks to two months, depending on time of year. Publication time: three to nine months. Length: 5000 words maximum.

A lively newsprint tabloid, *The Threepenny Review* uses one or two stories an issue. "We are slightly 'left,' but I doubt this shows in our fiction," editor Wendy Lesser says. "It's more evident in our articles. We also publish poetry, essays, theater/film/book/art/musc reviews, and other writing."

Most *Threepenny* fiction is solicited. Once a year, or less, something sent in unasked-for is bought. Lesser adds that she wishes they were getting better stories through the mail; she would like to be able to use more unsolicited fiction.

Of the 250 unsolicited stories annually submitted maybe 5%, or 10 to 15 stories a year, are found to be worth more than a first reading.

Stories are commonly being rejected because they are "highly experimental; unjustifiably violent, racist, denigrating to men or women as a class; too cute with a tone of self-congratulation or because of cliché'd plots—such as first sexual experiences, childhood memories of family dinners, divorce or breaking-up, being a rejected writer.

"I would say we are committed to the traditonal short-story form if it includes people like Grace Paley and Paul Bowles, who are offbeat without being 'experimental.' I like stories that have emotional clout without being sentimental; that have spare as opposed to effusive language; that have at least *some* plot; that deal with serious concerns of adults, even if humorously."

Lesser reads all the unsolicited fiction and handwrites the rejection notes. She has three standard forms: we can't use this; we can't use this, but I enjoyed reading it; and we can't use this story but we'd like to see more work. When Lesser is unsure about a piece, she shows it to one of the three consulting editors (Thomas Gunn, Leonard Michaels, and Steve Wasserman) for further opinions. Lesser adds that she writes back with specific criticisms very rarely; on accepted stories, she usually asks for minor revisions. "Writers have told me that my rejection notes are among the least painful they get; but that probably says more about other magazines than about us."

Lesser does like to see a cover letter listing credits; she also appreciates hearing that the writer reads the magazine and is familiar with its tastes. She prefers that writers do not send in more than one story at a time.

The Threepenny Review often publishes lesser-known writers; Lesser adds that two of them, Elizabeth Tallent and Kate Wheeler, had their stories reprinted in *Pushcart* and *O. Henry* editions.

Writers published include Paul Bowles, John L'Heureux, Mary Ward Brown, Grace Paley, Millicent Dillo, Nella Bielsk, Robert Walser, and Evan Connell.

TRIQUARTERLY

1735 Benson Avenue
Northwestern University
Evanston, IL 60201
(312) 492-7614

SOURCE: Reginald Gibbons, editor

ABOUT THE JOURNAL: Triannual. Founded: 1964. Circulation: 4500. Distribution: subscription; bookstores. Avg. issue: 250-300 pp. Size: 6x9. Price: $5.95. Subscription: $14. Sample copy: $3. Back issues: available. Price: varies.

FICTION: Occupies about 80% of total pages; roughly 15 stories an issue. Rates: $15 a published page. Payment: on publication. Rights: first North American serial; reprint anthology rights. Reply time: six to eight weeks. Publication time: four months to a year. Length: no limits, but short stories preferred to novellas.

TriQuarterly is predominantly a short-fiction magazine. It is also among the best-known and best-regarded of the literary journals, with a particularly fine reputation for its fiction.

Some *TriQuarterly* fiction is solicited, much is not. Editor Reginald Gibbons says unsolicited submissions run into the "thousands" every year. He adds that "perhaps 5% to 10%" of those are good enough for more than a first reading.

"No preconceptions operate at *TriQuarterly* except the desire for distinguished, exceptional, *serious* work."

Why is the great mass of unsolicited fiction rejected after one reading? "Incompetent writing that is of neither stylistic nor imaginative distinction is the simple answer. Many stories are rejected, beyond this, because of the triviality, narrowness, or self-indulgence of their themes and occasions."

All manuscripts are read by one of the five editors who serve as first readers. Anything interesting is passed to other editors and finally to the editor-in-chief.

Manuscripts found appealing and promising, but not publishable, are returned with a note or letter from the editor or one of the assistant editors.

TriQuarterly will read groups of stories from a writer. Cover letters are considered merely a courtesy with no influence on publication. "Many are silly anyway, or pretentious," Gibbons adds.

In *TriQuarterly* no. 54 (Spring '82), Gibbons, after only a few months as editor, wrote an editorial discussing the magazine's fiction:

"If *TriQuarterly* has a recognizable identity, it arises out of its energy and its range, it seems to me. Its readers respect its devotion to short fiction . . . its seriousness (and sometimes its frivolousness), its heft, its handsomeness, and what one would have to call its tone of voice—by turns straightforward, edgy, flashy, testing, theoretical, encyclopedic, heavy, campy, once in while avant-gardish, scholarly, estoeric. . . ."

And on the writing he would like to see in *TriQuarterly*: "The most important work, the best, cannot be categorized or described in advance by anyone. But I think it will often look to the world outside the writer, to the culture swirling around his or her solitary labor. Narrow, self-regarding, clever work always has some appeal to the small reader in us, that imp of a reader who doesn't wish to be led out of himself toward others, toward the world, or even toward deeper pleasure or understanding. But there is a larger reader in us, too, who responds to work that is free of self-indulgence; that goes beyond a trivial occasion; that will break, when it needs to, all formal expectations; that has emotional and even philosophical weight; that binds us to others rather than asserting that our solitariness is an interesting state of mind. Or, when we must face our essential solitariness . . . then such work explores that state with passion as well as anger, with vision as well as accomplishment and cleverness. . . . A fundamental attitude of wonder and delight in seeing what is there—that's the mark that Conrad and Welty and Milosz and many others have found in good writing. . . . "

Writers published in *TriQuarterly* include Walter Abish, Max Apple, T.C. Boyle, Raymond Carver, Robert Coover, Julio Cortázar, Stanley Elkin, Richard Ford, Carlos Fuentes, John Gardner, García-Marquez, William Gass, William Goyen, Jim Harrison, Octavio Paz, Robert Stone, Tobias Wolff, and many others, especially many younger writers.

TQ 55 (Fall '82) welcomed several new advisory editors "with whose help the magazine will be more attentive to new writing of all kinds, from all places." Named were Terrence DesPres, Gloria Emerson, Richard Ford, George Garrett, Francine du Plessix Gray, Michael S. Harper, and Maxine Kumin.

Fiction in the issue came from Paul West, Willis Johnson,

Stephen Berg, William Goyen, David Plante, David R. Schanker, Vladimir Voinich, R.D. Skillings, Joe Taylor, Marie Luise Kaschnitz, and David Quammen.

TQ 54 included fiction from Ray Reno and Arturo Vivante, a first story from published poet Rush Rankin, and a first story from Grace Mary Garry:

TriQuarterly has also published "The Little Magazine in America: A Modern Documentary History—Essays, Memoirs, Photos, Documents" (no. 43, Fall 1978).

VIRGINIA QUARTERLY REVIEW

One West Range
Charlottesville, VA 22903
(804) 924-3124

SOURCE: Staige D. Blackford, editor

ABOUT THE JOURNAL: Quarterly (January, April, July, October).
Founded: 1925. Circulation: 4000. Distribution: mainly sub-
scription; some newsstands and bookstores. Avg. issue: 224 pp.
Size: 6x10. Price: $3. Subscription: $10. Back issues: available.
Price: $3. Affiliated with University of Virginia.

FICTION: Occupies 16% of pages: 12 stories a year. Rates: $10 per
printed page. Payment: on publication. Rights: first rights. Reply
time: three to six weeks. Publication time: one to two years.
Length: 8-25 double-spaced pages.

"The *Quarterly* describes itself," editor Staige Blackford says,
"as a national journal of literature and discussion. It does not
espouse any political or social point of view, and it does favor
regional material in the respect that many of our articles are
about the South, and many of our authors are Southern. Never-
theless, every effort is made to appeal to a national audience.

"Fiction has a high place in the *Quarterly* and always has.
The three stories we publish per issue are more than most published by our sister journals, some of which have abandoned the
short story completely. Since I feel the written word is an endan-
gered species in both fiction and nonfiction, I hope the *Quarterly* will provide some refuge for both."

Stories are chosen from approximately 1600 unsolicited submissions, annually. Blackford estimates that at best, 5% of the
stories are worth reading more than once. What he would like to
see is "a literate appealing story about realistic people."

Published authors include Ann Beattie, Ward Just, Nancy
Hale, William Hoffman, H.E. Francis, Mary Gordon, and Peter
Taylor.

Vol. 58, no. 2 (Spring '82) included fiction from Bobbie Ann
Mason and Peter Corodimas and a first published story from
Ashley Mace Havird.

Virginia Quarterly has several readers—all of whom are writers—who go through the unsolicited submissions. Acceptance
means approval by at least two people. Blackford will write to

an author if the work requires revision before acceptance or if he would like to see further work. There is a standard rejection form.

Commonly and quickly rejected are stories from "authors who obviously have no talent for fiction. Stories in which spelling, grammar, and punctuation are atrocious. Stories involving senior citizens, senility, and cancer, apparently the three favorite themes of young, aspirant writers."

Blackford finds a list of credits helpful: "Obviously a list of previous publications is going to make some impression on a reader, though sometimes one wonders whatever possessed a particular publication to publish a particular author."

Blackford will look at a group of stories, but would prefer not to be asked to do so.

THE WASHINGTON REVIEW

Box 50132
Washington, DC 20004
(202) 638-0515

SOURCE: Patricia Griffith, fiction editor

ABOUT THE JOURNAL: Six issues a year. Founded: 1975. Circulation: 10,000. Distribution: subscription and regional bookstores. Avg. issue: 36-40 pp. Size: tabloid. Price: $1.50. Subscription: $10. Sample copy: $1.50. Back issues: available. Price: $1.50.

FICTION: One or two stories per issue. Rates: honorarium and copies. Payment: on publication. Rights: first rights. Reply time: usually a month. Publication time: six months to a year. Length: 2000 words ideal; much longer will not be considered.

The Washington Review is a newsprint tabloid of arts and literature. It does not use stories that run much over 2000 words. "If you don't write literate, sophisticated fiction," fiction editor Patricia Griffith says, "don't waste your postage. We publish high literary fiction. We are always interested in experimental writing. We favor Washington-area writers but are not limited to any regions."

Published writers include Terence Winch, Ron Carter, Nancy Stockwell, and Richard Grayson.

"They write intelligent, unpredictable, very engaging and truthful fiction," Griffith says.

In the December 1982/January 1983 issue (vol. 18, no. 4) was a story by Eric John Abrahamson, a conversation with Manuel Puig, an interview with Anthony Hecht, a piece on a playwright, a selection of poetry, and reviews of art and books.

Approximately 150 unsolicited stories are submitted annually and are the major fiction source. Griffith reads all the stories and chooses what will be published. She finds maybe 5% of the submissions worth any consideration. She does use a standard rejection form, but if a writer strikes her as promising she will send a short letter making suggestions or giving a word of encouragement.

A cover letter listing credits can serve to capture Griffith's interest, but she finds that credits are often not an indication that the manuscript will be publishable. She will read a group of stories, but prefers to receive one at a time.

Additional Listings

Here are some other literary magazines worth taking a look at:

Carolina Quarterly
University of North Carolina
Chapel Hill, NC 27514

Crazy Horse
Murray State University
Murray, KY 42071

December Magazine
6232 North Hayne #1C
Chicago, IL 60659

DeKalb Literary Arts Journal
555 North Indian Creek Drive
Clarkston, GA 30021

Fiction International
St. Lawrence University
Canton, NY 13617

Helicon Nine
P. O. Box 22412
Kansas City, MO 64113

Missouri Review
University of Missouri
Columbia, MO 65211

Mss.
English Department
SUNY
Binghamton, NY 13901

New Orleans Review
P. O. Box 195
Loyola University
New Orleans, LA 70118

The Ohio Review
Ellis Hall
Ohio University
Athens, OH 45701

Quarry West
University of California
Santa Cruz, CA 95064

Some Other Magazine
47 Hazen Court
Wayne, NJ 07470

Sulfur
228-77
California Institute of
    Technology
Pasadena, CA 91225

Sun and Moon
4330 Hartwick Road
College Park, MD 20704

Unmuzzled Ox
105 Hudson Street
New York, NY 10003

The Yale Review
P. O. Box 1902A
Yale Station
New Haven, CN 06520

Appendix A: The Annual Short-Story Collections

"Read the magazine" was the one piece of advice given by almost every editor interviewed for this book. Choosing which magazines to read is the necessary preliminary to deciding where to send stories.

For the writer trying to produce quality, literate fiction, the annual short-story collections are very useful in sorting out magazines. Three major anthologies are *The Pushcart Prize: Best of the Small Presses; The Best American Short Stories; and Prize Stories: The O. Henry Awards.*

Each book presents its own selection of the best short stories from the previous year's magazines and/or literary journals. Together they provide a cross-section of "what's happening" in short fiction.

These books choose *all* their stories from previously published work, and each has its own nominating or selection process. Authors cannot submit their own work. The editors do not read unsolicited submissions, either original manuscripts or reprints.

THE PUSHCART PRIZE: BEST OF THE SMALL PRESSES

Edited by Bill Henderson
Published by the Pushcart Press
Paperback edition by Avon Books

SOURCE: Bill Henderson

The Pushcart Prize is published every summer (paperback in the following spring). In each of its editions since 1976, it has reprinted the work (fiction, poetry, and essays) of 50 to 60 authors whose prose or poetry appeared in a small press or literary magazine during the preceding year. In the last eight years, approximately 500 pieces from 250 presses have been reprinted, representing the work of over 400 authors.

Editor Bill Henderson selects the prose pieces; guest editors choose the poetry. They work from well over 4000 nominated pieces.

Nominations come from the magazines themselves and the collection's contributing editors. Henderson sends out close to 2500 nomination invitations to literary magazines all over the country and in Canada (actually, no invitation is necessary—any magazine can send in nominations). Each can nominate up to six works it has published in the preceding year by sending copies to Pushcart Press.

There are 150 contributing editors associated with the collection. Half the editors are new every year, and most are writers whose work appeared in a previous *Pushcart Prize* collection. The contributing editors can make any number of nominations and explain or lobby for them.

According to Henderson, the only criterion for selection is quality. Five of the stories may turn out to be from the same magazine. There is no fine tuning according to gender or geography. The collection is "eclectic." Henderson is looking for work that is "interesting, well-written and important." He does insist that both traditional and nontraditional short-story forms be included, and he adds that he looks out for the work of newcomers. In the average volume, two-thirds of the work will turn out to be from relatively unknown writers.

Each selection is headed not only by the name of the magazine where it appeared but also by the names of the writers and/or editors who nominated it. All the contributing editors are listed in the front of the volume. There is a further list of other outstanding fiction, nonfiction, and poetry and a list, with addresses, of all the small presses that made or received nominations.

NOTE: Authors may not nominate their own work. For more information write to Pushcart Press, P. O. Box 380, Wainscott, NY 11975.

THE BEST AMERICAN SHORT STORIES

Guest editor changes annually;
Shannon Ravenel, annual editor
Published by Houghton Mifflin

SOURCE: Shannon Ravenel

The Best American anthology has a revolving editorship. In 1982 it was John Gardner; in 1983, Anne Tyler. In 1984, it will be John Updike. Past editors have also included Stanley Elkin, Joyce Carol Oates, and Hortense Calisher.

Shannon Ravenel is the collection's regular editor. She reads approximately 1600 short stories over a year in 150 magazines and literary journals (listed in the anthology). From these, she selects 120 stories for the guest editor to read. Twenty stories will finally be included in the collection.

The only rules are that authors must be American or Canadian, that the work was written as a short story (no novel excerpts), that it was written in English, and that it was published first serially in a nationally distributed magazine or periodical.

Guest editors have a free hand. Though most do choose stories from Ravenel's selections, they have the option to include their own favorites.

The anthology is meant to be eclectic, but editors can give it a slant of their own. John Gardner, for instance, was interested in showcasing newcomers and small presses and made almost entirely his own selection.

The guest editor regularly writes an introduction to the book talking about what it contains and why. Ravenel believes that the changing point of view is one of the reasons the format is so successful.

Ravenel describes her own selection process as intuitive. She wants to fall into a story, to be captured by it. Like editors of the other collections, she does not conceive of her job as picking "the best," a task made impossible by the vagaries of personal taste. She is looking for writing that is fine, distinctive, alive.

PRIZE STORIES: THE O. HENRY AWARDS

Edited by William Abrahams
Published by Doubleday & Company

SOURCE: William Abrahams

The first collection of O. Henry Award prize stories was published in 1920, and it immediately became an annual event. Since 1967, William Abrahams has been the editor charged with the choosing of the 20 or so stories that make up the collection.

Abrahams reads approximately 100 magazines, of which half are small-press magazines (all the publications, with addresses, are listed in the book), in search of stories. The only predetermined criteria are that the authors must be American and the work written in English.

Abrahams is hesitant to call the O. Henry Award winners "the best" stories of the previous year. He considers the process of selection too idiosyncratic. Instead, he thinks of the series as presenting "stories of great distinction. Stories that have something fresh to say and say it very well."

He is particularly proud of the number of authors represented in the last 17 years who have continued to distinguish themselves with fine fiction.

Though there is no predetermined formula concerning new versus established writers in the anthology, Abrahams has found that generally at least half the stories turn out to be either firsts or from writers in the early stages of a career.

Some ten years ago, the publishers created a Special Award for Continuing Achievement, given at the discretion of the editor, to honor established writers who have made a continuing contribution to the vitality of the short-story form. The award was given for the first time in 1970 to Joyce Carol Oates; in 1976 it was given to John Updike, and in 1982 to Alice Adams.

Appendix B: Some Useful Information

Literary Organizations

Write to Poets & Writers, Inc., 201 West 54th Street, New York, NY 10019, for "12 National Groups Offering Services to Writers." $1 plus SASE.

Grants and Awards

Write to PEN American Center, 47 Fifth Avenue, New York, NY 10003, for "Grants and Awards Available to American Writers."